THE
Flexitarian
TABLE

THE
Flexitarian
TABLE

Inspired, Flexible Meals for Vegetarians,
Meat Lovers, and Everyone in Between

PETER BERLEY

WITH ZOE SINGER
PHOTOGRAPHS BY QUENTIN BACON

HOUGHTON MIFFLIN COMPANY
BOSTON · NEW YORK · 2007

For information about permission to reproduce selections from this book, write to
Permissions, Houghton Mifflin Company, 215 Park Avenue South, New York, New York 10003.

Visit our Web site: www.houghtonmifflinbooks.com.

Library of Congress Cataloging-in-Publication Data

Berley, Peter.

  The flexitarian table : inspired, flexible meals for vegetarians, meat lovers, and everyone
in between / by Peter Berley, with Zoe Singer ; photographs by Quentin Bacon.

    p. cm.

  Includes index.

  ISBN-13: 978-0-618-65865-7

  ISBN-10: 0-618-65865-3

1. Cookery. 2. Vegetarian cookery. 3. Menus. I. Singer, Zoe. II. Title.

  TX714.B3953 2007

  641.5 — dc22   2006035458

Book design by Kris Tobiassen
Photo styling and props by Michelle Ishay

Printed in the United States of America

DOC 10 9 8 7 6 5 4 3 2 1

In memory of Daniel M. Berley

Acknowledgments

First I'd like to thank my parents: my dad, for giving my mom the Baldwin baby grand that now sits in my home like a giant ebony stove, and my mother, for the music she made and the dishes she cooked.

To my teachers: the Reverend Gary Davis, Lennie Tristano, Connie Crothers, and Warne Marsh. And to my heroes: Lester Young, Charlie Parker, and J. S. Bach.

When I am burned out on cooking, I play, and when I am tired of playing, I cook. Without music, this book would not exist.

To my spirited agent, Janis Donnaud, the wise, stalwart guide who plunged decisively into the stormy seas of ideas and publishing and steered me to safety.

To Melissa Clark, who coauthored my first books and without whom I would never have had the opportunity to meet Zoe Singer.

Zoe, it has been an absolute joy tasting and writing this book with you. You understood me from the get-go and found sweet ways to express my feelings and thoughts about food, cooking, and menus when words failed me—which was most of the time.

To Rux Martin, my editor. Your belief in *The Flexitarian Table* has put wind in my sails and fire under my pots, and your fine eye for detail has made this book shine.

To Quentin Bacon, cool as a cucumber, master of light, you make me want to eat every photo. You have changed the way I see food forever.

To my radiant, extraordinary friend and designer Michelle Ishay: not only have you cheered me all the way to the finish line, you have changed the way I think about my craft.

To Kris Tobiassen, your warm, passionate, intelligent design is a dream come true.

To my new friend Jim Peterson, who should be as famous for his kind, generous spirit as for his extraordinary cookbooks. Thanks for coming through for me with your props when I was in serious weeds.

To my students at the Natural Gourmet Institute for Food and Health and the Institute of Culinary Education. To Judith Friedman and Jenny Mathau, Liz Young, and Rick Smilow, for running fine institutions that provide an extraordinary opportunity for me to share my passion for food and cooking.

To Brooke and Dan Neidich, my dream clients. Over the past seven years, my cooking has deepened and matured chez Neidich. My time in your kitchen has inspired huge chunks of this book, as I've cooked from local farms and fishermen for your wonderful family and friends. You have impeccable taste, a passion for excellence, enthusiasm to burn, and awesome digs. Thank you for kindly opening your home to our crew for the photo sessions.

To the Neidich staff, Imelda, Dulse, Menchu, and Elba, for making me feel like it's all a magic carpet ride.

To my tireless soulmate in the mad world of catering, Sista Sui Lan Chan, who has seen me through thick and thin and who lent her unwavering culinary support and sharp eye to the photo sessions.

To Paul Vandewoude and Miette Culinary Studio, for such a cozy and inspiring kitchen to cook and create in.

To the incredible folks at Houghton Mifflin, Anne Chalmers, Michaela Sullivan, Mimi Assad, and Deb DeLosa, and to Judith Sutton and Jacinta Monniere, for all your hard work.

To my daughters, Kayla Jo and Emma Jean. Kayla, thank you for graciously tackling endless mounds of pots and pans and tasting your way through the recipes. Your enthusiasm and encouragement are pure sunshine.

To Emma, your curiosity about all things food and your sensitive palate and healthy appetite make cooking a joy for me.

And to Meggan, angel, partner, love of my life.

Contents

Introduction:
What's a Flexitarian? 1

About the Ingredients 5

Cooking with the Seasons 13

SPRING 16

SUMMER 96

FALL 168

WINTER 250

Index 331

What's a Flexitarian?

Since I'm the former chef of the all-vegan Angelica Kitchen in New York City and teach vegetarian cooking classes, it sometimes surprises people to learn that I eat not only fish but also poultry and meat. Mind you, I'm not a passionate carnivore: my diet is primarily plant-based, but it does include some fish and meat, preferably sustainably caught or raised. Aside from a few months during my teens, I've never been a strict vegetarian. My way of eating is becoming so common that a new word has even been coined for it: "flexitarian," a union of the words "flexible" and "vegetarian."

While my wife, Meggan, and I are flexitarians, my older daughter, Kayla, is a strict vegetarian. Almost from the moment of her birth, though, my younger daughter, Emma, was constitutionally different from her sister. Kayla always insisted on vegetables, but Emma wanted chicken, fish, or meat too. In a lot of households, the majority of the family eats meat while one vegetarian member subsists on side dishes or else requires entirely separate, "special" meals that are hard on the cook. Putting together a meal that our whole family could enjoy together was important to me, so I felt determined to cook delicious, wholesome meals that could accommodate Kayla and Emma's different food preferences.

I began building meals that were flexible enough to suit all of us, improvising as I went along. I'd serve a quick seared tuna as an optional add-on to a salad, along with hard-cooked eggs and beans, or I'd crumble some bacon so that anyone who wanted some could sprinkle it over their greens. Gradually I devised other meals that were slightly more elaborate, without requiring much more work in the kitchen. I discovered that I could often use meat and vegetable proteins interchangeably to create two dishes similar in flavor, texture, shape, and color. Many of the recipes in this book, such as Crispy Pressed Chicken/Tofu with Garlic and Mint and Portobello Mushrooms/Steak with Bread Crumb Salsa, come out of the years when the girls were growing up.

Through decades of cooking as a personal chef and caterer, I've honed my approach while creating everything from lavish dinners celebrating meat, wine, cheese, and pastry to everyday meals for families with eating habits even more divergent and varied than my own family's. This book is a culmination of my thirty-year experience.

The menus that follow are not strictly one thing (vegetarian) or the other (meat-based). Some of them reflect get-dinner-on-the-table nights, like White Beans/Shrimp with Brown Butter, served over Soft Polenta. Others are slow vegetarian food made to be supremely satisfying to everyone.

Many of the recipes are "convertible," so you can prepare a vegetarian and a meat version simultaneously without going to extra trouble—you just separate the ingredients into two bowls or pots before you incorporate the protein. Typically they make two to three servings each, so you end up with a meal for four to six. Not everybody feeds two vegetarians and two meat eaters at each meal, of course, but when some diners are flexible eaters and only one or two are vegetarians, most people are happiest if they can try both options, reserving a little more of the meatless dish for the vegetarian contingent. This way of cooking is very conducive to sharing. And if everyone has the same leanings and wants to eat, say, all chicken, all beef, or all tofu, you can easily convert the recipes to a single option by doubling the meat or the vegetarian version.

I've arranged the menus by season to reflect the pleasures of eating produce when it's at its best and prepared by methods suited to the time of year. Eating with the seasons and relying on what grows, swims, and grazes within a 500-mile radius (the standard definition of "local") requires determination, passion, and—let's be realistic—compromise. Even those of us who have the resources and desire to support local farmers are likely to rely on a great deal of conventionally grown food that has been trucked long distances. But adding seasonal foods to your shopping basket is a way to lessen your dependence on fossil fuel and to support small farmers. It's also a great way to get the most flavor from your cooking without resorting to complex sauces and fancy techniques.

All the recipes in this book stand on their own, and I hope you'll use them outside of the menus as well, preparing them individually and mixing and matching as you see fit. If you're planning in advance, you might choose to shop for a whole menu, but on a night when you have come home with some especially bright, tight-headed broccoli or when there's not much in the house except a can of beans and a handful of tomatoes, check the index to find a recipe to use what you've got.

This book is all about inclusion: including people who eat in different ways, including different ingredients, and including great taste and good nutrition in every menu. It's about relationships and respecting the different needs of everyone who comes to the table and making them all feel welcomed and richly provided for, however they choose to eat. Whether you're tentative in the kitchen and need to rely on the explanations of techniques that I include in my recipes, or you cook a lot and are interested in new ideas and new combinations, whether you're cooking for vegetarians or for meat eaters, or for both, I hope this book will encourage you to be open to food and expect a cuisine that offers health and pleasure in equal measures.

About the Ingredients

The choice of foods available to us today is enormous, and considerations in choosing them range from quality and price to personal and environmental health to the fate of the small farmer. In navigating the options, I believe in seeking sustainability—that is, a way of eating that can be sustained physically and financially and with our natural resources.

Does this mean I always choose organic? No, in fact, I often prefer local foods, which I know are fresh and in season, even if they are not organic. Small, independent farmers generally take better care of their land than huge agribusinesses, which, while they may have organic certification, are likely to deplete the soil by not rotating crops or letting land lie fallow, and to rely more on fossil fuels and energy-draining refrigeration to store and ship their products. In the case of fish, local is not possible in a great deal of this country. Instead, I recommend seeking out sustainably caught wild fish.

For most of us, it's nearly impossible to eat completely locally, but it is possible to become a conscious shopper, to learn what options are available and make deliberate choices. In doing so, you will regain a sense of control over how you eat, participate in leaving the world a better place, and become sensitized to the connection between food and the environment. To find sources of local foods in your area, check out www.localharvest.org.

Poultry

An organic label on poultry indicates that the bird had access to the outdoors, wasn't treated with antibiotics, and was fed a vegetarian diet. Although "free-range" and "cage-free" birds are a step up from those crowded into the tiny cages of factory farms, they may not actually have spent time outdoors.

Pasture-raised birds truly taste better. Additionally, birds that have been humanely raised are better for you, with higher nutrient levels and more omega-3 fatty acids than their factory-raised counterparts. Conformity is an issue for mass-market nonorganic farmers, who want to raise chickens that all look and taste the same—every perfect three-pound package of them. But head to your local farmers' market or a nearby farm, and you'll find birds of slightly different sizes that have been raised in the light of day, with room outside to scratch for food. You can buy tender young chickens for roasting and frying or tougher, larger ones for stews and soups.

A bonus of purchasing chicken outside of a supermarket is that you can often buy the whole bird, including the glorious feet. Because of the high concentration of gelatin, chicken feet make the most flavorful stock. One of my earliest kitchen memories is of watching my Bubbi Esther make stock for her chicken soup. Seeing the feet and claws poking up from the giant cauldron of simmering stock always gave me a thrill, and they never deterred me from slurping up the rich, golden broth she served with tiny homemade egg noodles and a sprinkling of dill.

Heritage chickens and turkeys are the equivalent of heirloom vegetable varieties—breeds that have been all but abandoned in favor of mass production. They are being revived by committed farmers who are likely to have gone the extra mile in terms of how they raise the birds, and they are an opportunity to taste what folks are talking about when they lament, "They don't make 'em like they used to." Many heritage breeders accept orders and ship poultry, especially holiday turkeys (check out www.heritagefoodsusa.com for one source).

Meat

I prepare red meat simply, relying on its inherent taste and quality for the flavor of the finished dish. I favor lamb that has been finished on grass, and grass-fed beef. My recipes are geared toward these slightly leaner meats, which require gentler treatment, and usually a shorter cooking time, than their fattier, grain-fed counterparts. Ruminants (animals that chew their cud) are unable to process the large amounts of grain they are fed in feedlots without chemical supplements and antibiotics, whereas grass-fed or pasture-raised animals are allowed to roam and graze and eat a diet that they are able to digest naturally.

Grass-fed animals can be fed entirely on grass or sent to a feedlot to fatten on grain before slaughter. Grass-fed meat has ivory-colored fat and usually contains higher levels of health-supporting omega-3 fatty acids. Grain gives meat a higher fat content, more of which is saturated fat, and makes the fat whiter, a look that consumers have become used to. In contrast to the assembly-line slabs of plastic-wrapped meat on little trays in supermarkets, grass-fed meat is a variable, natural food. The animals eat what grows in their pastures from season to season, and so they too are a seasonal product, varying in flavor (and price) throughout the year. Some farms simply do a better job of handling their animals, from breeding to pasture to market, so there's a lot of variability in the grass-fed steak you can buy. Try different farms to see what's best in your area.

I love natural center-cut, uncured (nitrite-free) smoked bacon, which I use as a flavoring agent, crumbling it over greens and salads and straining the fat to use for searing scallops and the like.

Fish and Seafood

Similar types of fish and seafood can be used interchangeably in these recipes depending on what's freshest, and I usually indicate a range of choices that are appropriate. You can find out how to avoid fish that are overfished and endangered by consulting a listing of sustainable fish, such as the one at www.audubon.org.

I prefer line-caught wild fish. The long lines and nets of the huge trawlers flatten the ocean floor and catch many other sea creatures in addition to the intended ones. Wild fish are a more sustainable option than farmed fish, both because fish farms pollute the water if in the ocean and can pollute the land if they're inland, and because farmed fish live in overcrowded conditions and must be treated with antibiotics. Furthermore, many farmed fish are higher in mercury and lower in healthful omega-3 fatty acids than their wild counterparts. And their flavor definitely doesn't compare to the complex taste that wild fish develop as they swim great distances through cold waters.

Most good fishmongers are passionate about their product and happy to share, so the more you ask questions and the more informed you are, the more they'll respect your interest and go out of their way to help you.

When possible, I buy whole fish and have them filleted by the fishmonger, rather than choosing fillets or steaks of large game fish like tuna and salmon. Seeing the fish whole allows me to gauge its freshness better and gives me the opportunity to take home the bones and other trimmings for making fish stock. A whole fresh fish should appear slightly shiny, with a sheen to its skin. It should have bright, clear eyes and deep red, not muddy, rust-colored, gills. It should have a cucumber-fresh scent of the sea rather than the smell of low tide, and, in most species, should have firm flesh that springs back when poked rather than holding the indentation (ask for a plastic glove and permission before poking).

If fresh fish are hard to come by, consider the many wonderful preserved fish options, such as smoked bluefish and mackerel and high-quality canned sardines, which can be used in place of fresh ones. You can find smoked wild Alaskan salmon in many upscale stores.

Beans

I use dried beans everywhere: salads, soups, dips and spreads, stews, sauces, fillings, toppings—you name it. When soaked in advance and properly cooked, dried beans are a delicious and affordable basis for a satisfying meal. Bean varieties are easily substituted for one another. Try the heirloom varieties of beans that are becoming more available in gourmet markets and at farmers' markets (or order them online from www.heritagefoodsusa.com).

In the spring and summer, fresh shell beans, such as cranberry beans, chickpeas, and fava beans, can be prepared by simmering them until tender and silken-textured—anywhere from 5 to 20 minutes.

Canned beans are a real convenience—try different organic brands to find one you like. To freshen up tinny-tasting beans, drain the beans and rinse well under very hot tap water, or simmer with a little fresh water and a pinch of salt for a few minutes, then drain, before using.

Tofu, Tempeh, and Seitan

These high-protein, low-fat soy foods are ideal absorbers of flavors, making them a perfect addition to a tasty sauce. They have great texture, ranging from soft, creamy tofu to firm, nubby tempeh to chewy seitan. I prefer to buy locally made packaged tofu at natural food stores, which is fresher than the brands sold in most supermarkets. Chinese cooks often cook tofu with pork, and this is a nice touch—any of these vegetarian products can be combined with meat, the one adding a lighter touch and pleasing texture, the other a more savory taste that meat lovers demand.

Tofu is made by coagulating soy milk and pressing the curds, much in the way cheese is made. It is high in protein and relatively high in fat. Tempeh is made with soybeans that

Soaking and Cooking Beans

For tender, digestible beans that retain their shape, buy plump dried beans. Dried skins and shriveled or broken beans are an indication of age, and older beans take much longer to cook. Sort the beans on a plate, removing shriveled and broken ones and any stray pebbles. Then rinse and drain them.

Next, soak the beans (red lentils and split peas, which are halved and skinned, do not need soaking). You can do this in a bowl of cold water in the refrigerator overnight or speed up the process by "quick-soaking" the beans. Place the beans in a saucepan with cold water to cover by at least 1 inch, bring the water to a boil, and boil for 1 to 2 minutes, then remove from the heat, cover the pan, and let sit for at least 1 hour, or up to 3 hours, before draining and cooking.

For years I just drained my soaked beans and cooked them in fresh water, skimming off the foam. But I discovered that bringing the beans to a boil, then draining all the water, rinsing away the foam from the beans and the pot, and starting again with new water washes away much more of the complex sugars that emerge in that foam, yielding beans that are more digestible and less likely to cause intestinal gas.

After the preliminary boiling and rinsing, simmer your beans gently in water just to cover, topping up the pot if the beans begin to dry out before they are sufficiently soft. When you simmer them this way, as food scientist Harold McGee recommends, they lose less of their nutrients and flavor to the surrounding water and, surprisingly, they absorb more liquid, softening faster than they would in a larger pot of water.

Beans absorb flavors easily and benefit from the addition of aromatics to the cooking liquid. Peeled garlic cloves; chopped leek, celery, fennel, and/or carrot; and sprigs of fresh sage, rosemary, thyme, or parsley are great additions to the bean pot. Do not add salty or acidic ingredients to the beans until they have cooked halfway through, as these ingredients can toughen the bean skins.

have been inoculated with a beneficial mold that holds the beans together and makes them more digestible. Other grains may be added for flavor and texture. While tofu can be eaten raw or cooked, tempeh is bitter and indigestible unless fully cooked. Seitan, also known as wheat gluten or wheat meat, is made by washing all the starch from a glutinous dough of water and flour, leaving behind the chewy wheat protein (it is served as "mock duck" in Chinese restaurants and does have a certain poultrylike texture). The gluten is then simmered in a soy-based stock to flavor it and prolong its shelf life.

Dairy

I use cultured dairy products in many of my recipes, also adding aged cheeses such as Parmesan, Gruyère, and Asiago. And I use fresh goat cheese, ricotta, yogurt (I find Greek yogurt particularly good because it has been strained and is thick and rich), crème fraîche, and sour cream. In the market, I look for organic cheeses when possible, and I love to try the local cheeses sold at my farmers' market.

I prefer local milk from grass-fed cows that have not received growth hormones, and I look for pasteurized, rather than ultrapasteurized, products, since these have been heated less and retain more of the full flavor of raw milk (raw milk is a great product to buy from local farms when available and is sometimes sold at health-food stores). You can taste the seasonal differences in local milk and cream, noticing the rich, grassy flavor and slightly golden hue that the milk takes on when pastures are at their greenest. The breed of cow will also affect the flavor of the milk—Jersey cows give the richest milk, and whole-milk Jersey yogurt, with its creamy layer of fat on top, is wonderful.

Eggs

In the organic-versus-local debate, I choose local eggs, since freshness is paramount. The small egg farmers in my area may not have the resources to receive organic certification, but they are unlikely to rely heavily upon antibiotics, and the yolks of their eggs are pert and vivid yellow.

Choose the freshest eggs possible, and try different producers until you find one you like best. The white of a fresh egg should hold together when cracked, instead of running like liquid, and the yolk should be deep-colored and plump. There is no difference in flavor and nutritional content between white and brown eggs; the color simply depends on the breed.

Nuts and Seeds

Nuts and seeds are a great source of nutrition, flavor, and crunch. Since they have a high oil content, they're prone to rancidity. Taste your nuts and seeds to be sure they are sweet and fresh. Store them in a cool, dry place or in the refrigerator or freezer to prolong their shelf life, and don't buy them in larger quantities than necessary. Buying nuts from a store with a high turnover will help ensure they are fresh: most nuts keep from 1 to 3 months.

Toasting Nuts and Seeds

To deepen and mellow the flavor of nuts and seeds, give them a toast. Toasting them until they are lightly colored near the center will give pale nuts like almonds a richer flavor, while toasting them further, to golden brown, will give them a more pronounced roasted character.

Toast small quantities of nuts and seeds, as well as small nuts like pine nuts, in a skillet on the stovetop, since you are less likely to overtoast them if you are standing there stirring. Place them in a dry heavy skillet over medium heat. Have a plate or shallow bowl ready nearby. Toss and stir until the nuts or seeds are fragrant and lightly colored. This will take from 2 minutes, for chopped nuts and small seeds, to 10 minutes, for whole nuts. Immediately transfer the nuts or seeds to the plate or bowl to stop the cooking, and let them cool.

For larger quantities, it's easier to toast nuts in the oven. Preheat the oven to 350 degrees. Spread the nuts in a single layer on a rimmed baking sheet and toast, tossing or stirring every few minutes for even cooking, until the nuts are fragrant and have begun to color. This will take from 5 to 15 minutes, depending on size and on how toasted you want them. Transfer to a plate or bowl to cool. While hazelnuts and walnuts are still warm, you can rub them in a kitchen towel to remove their skins, if desired—these nuts tend to have papery, rather bitter skins.

Spices

Spices are an integral part of the pantry, and fresh spices make a real difference in the intensity and fragrance of a dish. Because the volatile oils that carry the flavors of such seasonings as cumin seeds and cinnamon sticks begin to lose their potency once the spice is ground, buying spices whole and grinding just what you need for a recipe will yield the freshest flavors. But you can certainly make my recipes using preground spices. Just make sure they have been purchased within the last year and stored away from air, light, and heat. If your ground spices seem a little dull, add a pinch more than the amount called for or give them a very brief toasting in a dry pan to perk them up without scorching them.

Toasting and Grinding Spices

Toasting whole spices releases their aromas and makes them easier to grind. Place them in a dry heavy skillet over medium heat. Have a plate or shallow bowl ready nearby. Toast the spices, tossing or stirring them, until they are fragrant, which will take only a minute or two; if toasted for too long, they will become dark and bitter. Transfer to the plate or bowl and cool thoroughly before grinding.

To grind small quantities of spices, use a mortar and pestle. For faster going, especially with large amounts, use an electric spice mill or clean coffee grinder. I grind coffee and spices with the same grinder, since I don't have space for two appliances. To clean a coffee grinder, grind a little raw white rice, discard, and repeat; then use a pastry brush to brush away all the rice dust. Wash the top of the grinder by hand or in the dishwasher, then dry it thoroughly before the next use. That said, when grinding more than one spice, you can often get away with just wiping your coffee grinder clean with a damp cloth when you're grinding spices that will go into the same recipe or similar spices. But if you've just ground cumin for a recipe then want to grind cinnamon for cookies, you will want to use a thoroughly clean grinder.

Cooking with the Seasons

Seeking out markets that buy from nearby sources, farmers' markets, and community-supported agriculture (CSA) groups and returning to a diet based on fresh, local foods connects you to the world around you and is better for your health and the health of the environment. Although this may mean you won't eat strawberries for most of the year, the berries you eat in season will be unforgettably sweet, juicy, and full of flavor.

To help you achieve the art of seasonal eating, here is the ingredient palette available to most of us who live in a temperate climate.

Spring

Artichokes, asparagus, avocados, shell beans, new carrots, dandelion greens, favas (broad beans), fennel, fiddleheads, lamb's-quarters, morel mushrooms, mustard greens, spinach, spring onions, peas, new potatoes, purslane, radishes, ramps, samphire, sorrel, tatsoi, young turnips, watercress.

Apricots, gooseberries, mangoes, rhubarb, strawberries.

Chives, dill, wild garlic, mint, parsley.

Cockles, crabs, soft-shell crabs, gray mullet, salmon, sardines, sea bass, shad, lemon sole, sea trout.

Duck, spring lamb.

Summer

French beans, cabbage, carrots, cauliflower, celery, corn, favas (broad beans), fennel, chanterelles and oyster mushrooms, peas, bell and chili peppers, new potatoes, summer squash and zucchini, tomatoes.

Blueberries, cherries, red currants, gooseberries, loganberries, melons, nectarines, peaches, greengage plums, raspberries, rhubarb.

Basil, lemon verbena, rosemary, sage, thyme.

Clams, fluke, John Dory, monkfish, pike, pilchards, black sea bass, trout.

Squab.

Fall

Arugula, French beans, bok choy, broccoli, Brussels sprouts, cabbage, carrots, cauliflower, chard, cucumbers, eggplant, kale, leeks, lettuce, wild mushrooms, onions, parsnips, peppers, potatoes, pumpkin, spinach, winter squash, turnips, watercress.

Almonds, apples, blackberries, cranberries, elderberries, figs, grapes, hazelnuts, melons, pears, plums, pomegranates, quinces, walnuts.

Mussels, oysters, sea bass, brown trout.

Duck, grouse, guinea fowl, partridge, wood pigeon, venison.

Winter

Beets, burdock, cabbage, cauliflower, celery, chestnuts, chicory, kale, kohlrabi, leeks, parsnips, potatoes, rutabaga, shallots, spinach, turnips.

Halibut, lobster, mussels, scallops.

Goose, guinea fowl.

Spring

MENU 1 • 18

Lentil and Rhubarb Curry with Potatoes and Peas

Cucumber Lime Raita

Naan Bread

Roasted Spring Carrots with Cumin and Lime

MENU 2 • 27

Two Dips: Dilled Yogurt Dip and Tapenade

Stuffed Eggs with Capers and Garlic

Sautéed Baby Artichokes with Garlic and Wine

Bulgur with Roasted Chickpeas, Red Onion, and Lemon

MENU 3 • 37

Crispy Pressed Chicken/Tofu with Garlic and Mint

Creamy Risotto-Style Brown Rice with Spring Greens and Asiago

Shaved Spring Vegetable and Apple Salad

MENU 4 • 46

Navy Bean, Fresh Pea, and Leek Soup

Smoked Salmon/Sun-Dried-Tomato Croque Monsieur

Spring Greens in Dill Vinaigrette

MENU 5 • 53
Gratin of Cherry Tomatoes and White Beans/Sardines
Chilled Asparagus Salad with Sherry Vinaigrette

MENU 6 • 58
Green Olive Frittata with Ricotta, Pine Nuts, and Thyme
Pan-Seared Baby Lamb Chops with Lemon and Green Olives
Butter-Braised Radishes with Their Greens
Parmesan Toasts

MENU 7 • 68
Roast Duck with Spiced Red Onion Marmalade
Goat Cheese Frittata with Spiced Red Onion Marmalade
Rice with Herbs
Sautéed Asparagus and Fiddlehead Ferns with Garlic

MENU 8 • 77
Pea Shoot, Radish, and Smoked Trout/Tofu Salad
Artichoke, Potato, and Leek Gratin

MENU 9 • 83
Asian Noodles in Broth with Vegetables and Tofu/Steak
Hiziki Salad with Sweet Sesame Vinaigrette

MENU 10 • 89
Fregola Risotto-Style with Chard and Feta Cheese
Mâche and Pea Shoots with Baby Beets and Mustard Vinaigrette

Spring

MENU 1
SERVES 4

Lentil and Rhubarb Curry with Potatoes and Peas

Cucumber Lime Raita

Naan Bread

Roasted Spring Carrots with Cumin and Lime

Anyone who likes a good curry will love this Indian-spiced meal, which happens to be vegetarian yet is so satisfying and complete that even meat-and-potato types may not notice. I'm a firm believer in using the oven as much as possible once it's on, so I make the naan, then turn down the oven, pop in the carrots, and finally rewarm the bread for a minute or two when everything else is ready. On nights when naan and raita seem above and beyond, simply warm some pita bread or steam some basmati rice and serve plain yogurt with the curry.

THE PLAN
1. Soak the lentils.
2. Make the naan dough and let rise (or make the dough up to 2 days ahead and refrigerate; bring to room temperature before proceeding).
3. Make the raita and refrigerate (or make just before serving).
4. Cook the curry.
5. Meanwhile, shape the naan and let rise.
6. Bake the naan (rewarm before serving).
7. Roast the carrots.

Lentil and Rhubarb Curry with Potatoes and Peas

SERVES 4 TO 6

With the exception of strawberry-rhubarb pie, most American cooks don't know what to do with rhubarb, but the pink-green stalks of this vegetable are tart and versatile, and there's no reason to limit them to desserts. (In Estonia and Finland, I tasted sour rhubarb sauces paired with herring and salmon.) When cooked, the stalks break down, creating a nice thick texture. The lentils in this lively curry keep their shape, providing a great contrast to the soft rhubarb.

Tip: French lentils, also called lentilles du Puy, are small whole (unpeeled) lentils that look like tiny gray-green pebbles; they are available in natural food stores and gourmet markets. Because they take longer to cook than ordinary brown lentils and can be a little harder to digest, I presoak them before cooking them. I usually start soaking them in the morning when I plan to serve them for dinner, but if you don't have time for that, you can boil the lentils in water to cover until they begin to soften, approximately 20 minutes, then drain well, rinse, and proceed with the recipe.

SPICE BLEND

1 tablespoon ground coriander, preferably toasted and freshly ground (see page 12)

2 teaspoons ground cumin, preferably toasted and freshly ground

2 teaspoons ground turmeric

1 teaspoon ground fennel, preferably toasted and freshly ground

½ teaspoon freshly ground black pepper

¼ teaspoon red pepper flakes

LENTILS

2 tablespoons ghee (opposite) or unsalted butter

1 medium onion, chopped

2 large shallots, thinly sliced

1 tablespoon chopped peeled fresh ginger

Sea salt or kosher salt

3 garlic cloves, coarsely chopped

2 **cups coarsely chopped green cabbage**

2 **cups diced (½-inch) potatoes**

1½ **cups thinly sliced rhubarb**

1 **cup French lentils, soaked for 4–6 hours and drained**

2 **teaspoons dark brown sugar**

1 **bay leaf**

1 **cup fresh or thawed frozen peas**

FOR THE SPICE BLEND: In a bowl, stir together all the ingredients.

FOR THE LENTILS: In a heavy 3- to 4-quart saucepan, melt the ghee or butter over medium heat. Add the onion, shallots, ginger, and a large pinch of salt, cover, and cook, stirring occasionally, until the onion is soft, 8 to 10 minutes. Uncover, stir in the garlic and the spice blend, and cook, stirring, for 2 minutes.

Add the cabbage, potatoes, rhubarb, lentils, brown sugar, and bay leaf, along with enough cold water to cover by 1 inch. Raise the heat to high and bring to a boil, then reduce the heat and simmer gently, uncovered, until the lentils are tender, about 30 minutes (cooking time may vary depending on the age of the lentils). Stir occasionally and add more water as necessary to keep the dish fairly soupy.

When the lentils are tender, season with salt to taste, stir in the peas, and simmer until the peas are just tender, about 4 minutes. Serve.

Ghee Whiz

Ghee, India's solution to keeping butter in a hot climate, is a great-tasting clear cooking fat that can be heated to a higher temperature than butter without burning. It is made by slowly simmering all the water out of fresh butter, a process that toasts the milk solids, giving the finished product a nutty aroma. The resulting fat is then strained to remove the milk solids. Ghee is sold in canisters in Indian food stores, or you can make your own: Heat butter gently until it no longer spits and bubbles and the milk solids that settle to the bottom are golden. Skim the foam, then remove the butter from the heat and let settle. Carefully pour off the clear fat (the ghee), leaving the toasted milk solids behind. Ghee will keep, refrigerated, for months.

Cucumber Lime Raita

MAKES ABOUT 2½ CUPS

Serve this tangy yogurt-based salad as a dip for pita bread or a condiment to cool down highly seasoned meals.

Tips: To seed the cucumber, cut the fleshy sides away in 4 long strips, and discard the square seed portion.

To strain regular yogurt, line a sieve with cheesecloth and set it over a bowl (or use a coffee filter). Spoon 1 quart plain whole-milk yogurt into the sieve and refrigerate until it has drained and reduced down to 2 cups, 2 to 3 hours.

> 1 cup finely chopped peeled and seeded cucumber
>
> 1 tablespoon extra-virgin olive oil
>
> 2 teaspoons fresh lime juice, or to taste
>
> 2 teaspoons ground cumin, preferably toasted and freshly ground (see page 12)
>
> 1 teaspoon ground coriander, preferably toasted and freshly ground
>
> Sea salt or kosher salt
>
> 2 cups Greek yogurt (or strained regular yogurt)
>
> Freshly ground black pepper
>
> ¼ cup chopped fresh cilantro

Place the chopped cucumber in a sieve and press down on it with a paper towel to squeeze out the excess liquid.

Transfer the cucumber to a medium bowl. Add the oil, lime juice, cumin, coriander, and 1 teaspoon salt and mix well. Stir in the yogurt and season with pepper and more salt and/or lime juice if desired. Serve, or cover and refrigerate for up to 3 days. Stir in the cilantro just before serving.

Naan Bread

Flatbreads are satisfying and easy to make. For this naan, I make a sponge starter of yeast, yogurt, and flour, which ferments for 2 hours before the remaining ingredients are added. Once the dough is made, it can be refrigerated for up to 2 days before baking; it will continue to develop flavor as it sits. Whenever you're ready, it's a simple matter to stretch the dough into free-form loaves and bake them for a mere 7 to 8 minutes. Creative flavorings are welcome here—sprinkle on some minced onion or poppy or cumin seeds, if you like.

1½ teaspoons active dry yeast

¾ cup warm water (100 to 110 degrees)

½ cup plain yogurt, preferably whole-milk

2½ cups unbleached all-purpose flour, or as needed

1 cup whole wheat bread flour

1½ teaspoons sea salt or kosher salt

1 tablespoon olive oil or melted ghee (see page 21) or butter, plus 1 teaspoon for greasing the bowl

Cornmeal, for dusting

In a large bowl, combine the yeast with the warm water and let stand for 5 minutes, until the yeast dissolves (it may not be bubbly).

Add the yogurt, 1 cup of the all-purpose flour, and ½ cup of the whole wheat flour to the yeast. Beat with a wooden spoon to form a smooth batter. Cover the bowl with plastic wrap or a damp kitchen towel and let stand at room temperature for 2 hours. The batter should have lots of bubbles on the surface and appear lacy and weblike when stirred.

Stir the salt and oil, ghee, or butter into the batter. Add the remaining 1½ cups all-purpose flour and ½ cup whole wheat flour and stir as much as you can (the dough will be very stiff).

Transfer the ragged mass of dough to a clean surface. Wash and dry the mixing bowl and grease it with the 1 teaspoon oil, ghee, or butter.

Knead the dough for 10 minutes, to form a smooth, shiny ball. The dough should be slightly tacky (not dry), but you can add a little more all-purpose flour, 1 tablespoon at a time, if the dough gets too sticky as you knead.

Transfer the dough to the greased bowl, turn to coat, and cover with plastic wrap or a damp towel. (The dough can be refrigerated for up to 2 days. Bring to room temperature before proceeding.) Let rise for 1 to 1½ hours, or until doubled in size.

Meanwhile, 1 hour before you plan to bake, place a pizza stone, a flat cast-iron griddle, or an inverted heavy baking sheet on the middle rack of the oven and preheat the oven to 500 degrees (note that once the risen dough has been divided and shaped, the breads need to rise for another 20 minutes).

Turn the risen dough out onto a lightly floured surface and press it lightly with your fingers to deflate. Cover with plastic wrap or a damp towel and let it rest for 5 minutes.

Cut the dough into quarters. On a floured surface, gently pull and stretch each piece of dough into an oval about 10 inches long. If the dough springs back and resists stretching, cover and let relax for a few more minutes before proceeding.

Use your fingers to dimple each piece of dough all over. Cover the dough and let rise for 20 minutes more.

Dust a pizza peel (or an overturned baking sheet) with cornmeal. Transfer 2 pieces of dough to the peel and slide them onto the preheated stone, griddle, or baking sheet—make sure they do not touch. Bake until golden brown, 7 to 8 minutes. Transfer the naan to a rack to cool, then wrap in a napkin or dish cloth. Repeat with the remaining 2 pieces dough.

These are best served within 2 hours of baking; however, they can be wrapped in plastic once cooled and kept at room temperature for up to 2 days or frozen for up to a month. Defrost before unwrapping. To reheat, wrap the breads in a slightly damp towel or in foil and heat in a 325-degree oven for 8 to 10 minutes.

Roasted Spring Carrots with Cumin and Lime

SERVES 4

Nothing says spring like tender vegetables. In season, I love to cook young market-fresh baby carrots—not to be confused with those tough, waterlogged "baby-cut" carrots sold in plastic bags. Snap a really fresh baby carrot in half and sniff it: it smells like the earth, with a faint aniselike sweetness (sniff a plastic-bagged storage carrot, organic or not, and you'll be lucky if you can detect any smell at all). If true baby carrots aren't available, peel and cut larger carrots, preferably those sold with some healthy greens still attached, a sign of freshness (be sure to snap off the greens after buying them). The tart lime dressing sets off the flavor of the carrots.

Tip: I call for Syrian Aleppo pepper flakes here, which are mild and fruity. Ordinary red pepper flakes are a fine substitute, but if you can find it, try Aleppo pepper not only here but on pizza, pasta, or beans, or anywhere you'd use red pepper flakes. You can use up to twice as much Aleppo pepper as you would regular red pepper flakes.

- 1 pound fresh baby carrots, scrubbed and trimmed, or fresh longer carrots, scrubbed, trimmed, and quartered lengthwise
- 2 tablespoons unsalted butter
- ½ teaspoon cumin seeds
- 2 tablespoons fresh lime juice
- ½ teaspoon Aleppo pepper flakes or ¼ teaspoon red pepper flakes
- Sea salt or kosher salt

Preheat the oven to 425 degrees.

Combine all of the ingredients in a large ovenproof skillet and add 2 tablespoons water. Bring to a boil.

Transfer the pan to the oven and roast, tossing halfway through, until the carrots are tender and glazed, about 15 minutes. Serve.

Spring

MENU 2
SERVES 4 AS A MEAL OR 6 TO 8 AS HORS D'OEUVRES

Two Dips: Dilled Yogurt Dip and Tapenade

Stuffed Eggs with Capers and Garlic

Sautéed Baby Artichokes with Garlic and Wine

Bulgur with Roasted Chickpeas, Red Onion, and Lemon

This is a Mediterranean-inspired spread, based on the concept of *mezze,* a communal meal of several small dishes to be eaten, usually at room temperature, with bread or another grain product. Because grains are usually neutral, the other dishes can be more strongly flavored, featuring bright, pungent ingredients—here I incorporate capers, olives, lemon, and garlic. This is a flexible mix-and-match approach, with no expectation of a central meat-based protein. Meat, fish, vegetable, legume, and egg dishes can be swapped in or out as desired, depending on the whims of the cook, the availability of ingredients, and the eating habits of the diners. You can accent this all-vegetarian collection of recipes with other prepared Mediterranean foods, such as aged goat cheese preserved in oil, *salume* (traditionally cured meats), or a tin of high-quality sardines packed in extra-virgin olive oil, brightened with a squeeze of lemon. Serve plenty of warmed pita or toasted baguette slices with the menu.

These dishes make good hors d'oeuvres as well. With the exception of the bulgur and chickpeas, they can all be served as finger foods to accompany cocktails—spear the artichokes with toothpicks, and spread the tapenade on toasts to make them easy to eat with one hand.

THE PLAN

1. Make the dips and refrigerate.
2. If making homemade mayonnaise for the eggs, make it and refrigerate.
3. Hard-cook the eggs for the stuffed eggs.
4. Stuff the eggs and refrigerate.
5. Cook the bulgur and roasted chickpeas. Serve at room temperature.
6. Prepare the artichokes. Serve hot or at room temperature.
7. Prepare the raw vegetables for the dips and refrigerate.
8. Warm the pita and make the toasts.

Dilled Yogurt Dip

MAKES ABOUT 2 CUPS; SERVES 6 TO 8

I serve this creamy dip with warm pita and raw radishes, but it has many other uses. Try a dollop in borscht or on a baked potato, or spread on dark bread and top with sliced smoked salmon. Leftover dip will keep in the refrigerator for up to 4 days.

Tip: To refresh store-bought pita breads, wrap them in a slightly damp kitchen towel and warm in a 350-degree oven for 10 minutes.

2 **cups whole-milk Greek yogurt (or strained regular yogurt; see Tip, page 22)**

2 **teaspoons grainy mustard**

1 **tablespoon chopped fresh dill**

1 **teaspoon red wine vinegar**

1 **teaspoon honey**

1 **teaspoon sea salt or kosher salt, or to taste**

Freshly ground black pepper to taste

FOR SERVING

1–2 **bunches radishes, with their tops**

Warm pita bread or toasted slices of baguette

Coarse sea salt

Rapunzel, Rapunzel

Did you know that rampion, also called rapunzel, is a type of radish, whose greens Rapunzel's mother (of fairy-tale fame) craved so fatefully? As you may remember, her concerned husband was compelled to steal the vegetables from an enchantress's garden. When caught, he had to promise the enchantress their firstborn—a baby who grew into a beauty with incredibly long hair. Radishes do indeed contain many nutrients that are beneficial to pregnant women (and everyone else), so when you can find tender young bunches of spring radishes with their greens still attached, let your hair down and eat the whole vegetable!

In a bowl, whisk together all the dip ingredients. Let sit for 10 minutes, then taste and adjust the seasoning if necessary.

Transfer the dip to a small serving dish and surround with the radishes. Serve with warm pitas or baguette toasts and a small bowl of coarse sea salt for sprinkling.

Tapenade

A combination of vinegar-cured Kalamata and oil-cured black olives balances the flavor of this tapenade and gives it a beautiful midnight color. Adding sautéed onion smooths out the assertiveness of the olives. This spread makes an excellent filling for stuffed eggs as well—try blending the mashed yolks with a few tablespoons of tapenade instead of mayonnaise.

- ¼ cup extra-virgin olive oil
- ½ cup finely chopped onion
- 1 teaspoon chopped fresh thyme
- ½ cup Kalamata olives, pitted
- ½ cup oil-cured black olives, pitted
- 1 teaspoon capers, rinsed
- Freshly ground black pepper

FOR SERVING

- 1 fennel bulb, trimmed and sliced into thin wedges
- 1–2 bunches radishes, with their tops
- 1 bunch baby carrots, peeled, green tops trimmed to 1 inch
- Toasted, sliced artisanal bread

In a small skillet, heat 2 tablespoons of the olive oil over medium heat. Add the onion and cook, stirring occasionally, until soft and pale gold, 7 to 8 minutes. Add the thyme and cook for 1 more minute. Remove from the heat and let cool slightly.

In a food processor, combine the onion mixture, olives, capers, and the remaining 2 tablespoons olive oil and pulse to a chunky puree. Season with pepper. (The tapenade will keep, covered with a thin layer of olive oil, in a sealed, refrigerated container for up to 1 month.) Transfer it to a small bowl. Serve the tapenade with the vegetable crudités and toasts.

Stuffed Eggs with Capers and Garlic

I love homemade mayonnaise so much that I had to include a recipe in this book. It's pretty simple, and it makes stuffed (aka deviled) eggs absolutely divine. Of course, if you're preparing a whole spread of dishes and you don't have time for that, go ahead and use store-bought mayo (preferably an organic brand made with eggs from free-range hens).

The mysterious smoky edge that these eggs get from a sprinkle of smoked Spanish paprika is killer, but the more traditional sprinkle of ordinary sweet paprika is also good.

8 hard-cooked large eggs (see page 56), peeled and halved lengthwise

⅓ cup mayonnaise, preferably homemade (opposite)

1 tablespoon Dijon mustard

1 tablespoon finely chopped fresh flat-leaf parsley

2 teaspoons capers, drained and chopped

2 teaspoons finely chopped scallion greens

1 small garlic clove, mashed

1 teaspoon fresh lemon juice

Sea salt or kosher salt and freshly ground black pepper

Sweet Spanish smoked paprika, for dusting

Press the egg yolks through a fine-mesh sieve into a bowl. Stir in the mayonnaise, mustard, parsley, capers, scallion greens, garlic, and lemon juice and season with salt and pepper. Pipe the mixture into the egg whites, using a pastry bag fitted with a star tip or a resealable plastic bag with a corner snipped off, or fill the whites using two teaspoons. Dust the filling with paprika and serve.

Mayonnaise

MAKES ABOUT 1 CUP

Making mayonnaise is not as mystical as it sounds—in fact, it's similar to whisking up a nice smooth vinaigrette. The secret is to start with the egg yolk at room temperature and to add the oil drop by drop, so that it emulsifies smoothly (i.e., separates into tiny invisible droplets suspended in the yolk mixture). You can make mayonnaise in a food processor or by hand, using a whisk or handheld electric mixer: stabilize the bowl of egg yolk on the counter, then whisk or beat the egg yolk mixture constantly while dribbling in the oil. My usual technique is to combine the vegetable and olive oils in a narrow-neck bottle so I can cover the opening with my thumb, thereby controlling the flow. Other ways to do this are to combine the oils in a bowl, then drizzle them in gradually using a teaspoon, or to fill a paper cup with the oil and prick a tiny hole in the bottom of the cup with a pin to allow the oil to drip through.

To use a food processor, process the egg yolk mixture while gradually pouring in the oil. Some processors even have a cup with a little hole in the bottom that fits into the feed tube, so it can be filled with oil that will slowly drip down into the whirling egg.

If you add the oil too quickly and the mayonnaise loses its smooth, creamy look and "breaks," or separates, whisk or process in a spoonful of hot water. If that doesn't work, you'll need to start again with a new egg yolk. Add the "broken" mayonnaise in place of some of the oil for this new batch.

Tip: A small risk of salmonella poisoning is associated with the consumption of raw egg yolks. To minimize this, use a farm-fresh yolk and don't serve the mayonnaise to anyone with a compromised immune system or pregnant women or the elderly.

½ cup neutral vegetable oil, such as grapeseed, canola, or sunflower

½ cup extra-virgin olive oil

1 large egg yolk, at room temperature

1 teaspoon Dijon mustard

1 garlic clove, mashed to a paste with a large pinch of salt

1 tablespoon fresh lemon juice

Sea salt or kosher salt and freshly ground black pepper

In a bottle with an opening small enough for your thumb to cover it (such as a beer bottle), combine the oils and shake together.

Anchor a small heavy bowl on the counter by placing it on top of a coiled slightly damp kitchen towel. Whisk together the egg yolk, mustard, and garlic in the bowl. Whisking this mixture constantly with one hand, dribble in the oil drop by drop until the egg yolk starts to thicken. Then gradually increase the flow of oil, still whisking constantly, until it has been completely incorporated. You should have a thick, glossy mayonnaise. Whisk in the lemon juice, taste, and season with salt and pepper. Store in the refrigerator and use within 5 days.

Sautéed Baby Artichokes with Garlic and Wine

SERVES 4

There are never enough of these, so you may want to double the recipe. In the spring, I teach a class at the Institute of Culinary Education featuring my favorite artichoke dishes—here's one I adore.

Tip: If you want to make this recipe with large globe artichokes, pare 4 to 6 artichokes down to the heart and quarter them, then proceed with the recipe.

- 16 baby artichokes, preferably with stems
- 1 lemon, halved
- ¼ cup extra-virgin olive oil
- 6 garlic cloves, peeled
- 2 sprigs fresh thyme
- ¾ cup dry white wine
- Sea salt or kosher salt and freshly ground black pepper

Artichokes of All Sizes

In addition to large globe artichokes, in the spring you can find their diminutive upstairs neighbors, baby artichokes. The term "baby" refers to nothing more than their size, however—these little cuties are the artichokes that grow higher up on the same stalk as the "grown-ups." There is a major difference in the little guys, though—they don't have that hairy, inedible choke. To prepare baby artichokes, you need only trim the base of their stems, peel a little of the stems if they feel at all woody, slice off the top third of the artichoke, and pull off any tough outer leaves, then rub all over with half a lemon to keep them from oxidizing (turning brown). The rest of the artichoke can be eaten whole, no leaf scraping and choke removal required.

Trim the artichokes (see sidebar), rubbing the cut surfaces with the lemon.

In a heavy 8- to 10-inch skillet, heat the oil over medium heat until hot but not smoking. Add the artichokes and tuck the garlic cloves and thyme sprigs among them. Cook, stirring occasionally, until the artichokes are golden brown, 8 to 10 minutes.

Pour the wine into the pan and bring to a simmer. Cover tightly, reduce the heat, and simmer gently until the artichoke stems are tender, about 15 minutes. Discard the thyme sprigs.

Raise the heat and boil, uncovered, for 2 to 3 minutes, until the juices thicken. Use a slotted spoon to transfer the artichokes and garlic to a platter, and season with salt and pepper. Drizzle the pan juices over the artichokes and serve hot or at room temperature.

Bulgur with Roasted Chickpeas, Red Onion, and Lemon

SERVES 4

Roasting, in addition to making for a streamlined cooking process, seasons the chickpeas to the core and gives them a satisfying texture. I recommend using light golden durum here—the darker varieties are heavier, and they won't take on the glorious hue of the turmeric. You can substitute couscous for the bulgur if you prefer.

> 1¼ cups water
> 1 cup medium or coarse bulgur, preferably golden durum wheat
> Sea salt or kosher salt
> 1 15-ounce can chickpeas, rinsed and drained
> 1 medium red onion, thinly sliced
> 2 tablespoons extra-virgin olive oil or unsalted butter, cut into cubes
> 2 tablespoons fresh lemon juice
> 2 bay leaves, broken in half
> 1 teaspoon cumin seeds
> ½ teaspoon ground turmeric
> ½ teaspoon sweet Spanish smoked paprika or sweet paprika
> ⅛ teaspoon cayenne pepper, or to taste
> Chopped fresh flat-leaf parsley, for garnish

Preheat the oven to 400 degrees.

In a small saucepan, bring the water to a boil over high heat. Stir in the bulgur and ½ teaspoon salt, cover, and cook for 1 minute. Take the pan off the heat and let stand, covered, until all the water has been absorbed, about 20 minutes.

Meanwhile, in an 8- to 10-inch ovenproof skillet, combine the chickpeas, onion, oil or butter, lemon juice, bay leaves, cumin seeds, turmeric, paprika, cayenne, and ¼ teaspoon salt and stir over medium heat until the chickpeas begin to sizzle. Transfer the pan to the oven and roast for 20 minutes, stirring halfway through.

Remove and discard the bay leaves and stir in the bulgur. Season with salt, if desired, and serve hot, warm, or at room temperature.

Spring

MENU 3
SERVES 4

Crispy Pressed Chicken/Tofu with Garlic and Mint

**Creamy Risotto-Style Brown Rice
with Spring Greens and Asiago**

Shaved Spring Vegetable and Apple Salad

The lemony, minty pan juices from crispy chicken or tofu make a lovely sauce for the hearty risotto in this menu, while the salad adds crunch and another level of flavor. You can serve both the chicken and the tofu, or just one of them. This is an elegant yet easy combination of main protein, starchy side, and fresh salad, and the traditional protein-grain-veg presentation may make even the tofu-wary relax.

THE PLAN
1. Soak the rice and salt the chicken.
2. Marinate the chicken and tofu.
3. Cook the rice. Make the salad and refrigerate.
4. Finish cooking the rice and greens and keep warm.
5. Cook the chicken and tofu.

Crispy Pressed Chicken/Tofu
with Garlic and Mint

SERVES 4: 2 SERVINGS CHICKEN, 2 SERVINGS TOFU

Pressing the chicken thighs with something heavy not only speeds up the cooking time but also forces out the fat, resulting in supremely crispy skin, one of the great joys of eating chicken. Pressing the water out of the tofu results in a similar crispness. The chicken and tofu are covered by the weight throughout the cooking, so use your ears to keep tabs on their progress—you should hear a calm, friendly sizzle, not an intense hiss. Adjust the heat if things sound either too crazy or suspiciously quiet.

Note: To serve just one choice for 4 people, double the quantity of chicken or tofu.

Tip: To weight the chicken or tofu, I place a smaller pan on top (making sure it has a clean bottom), then weight it down with a full kettle, a heavy can of tomatoes, or a brick. The chicken and tofu can be cooked in two skillets simultaneously—monitor the heat under both pans to keep them cooking at the same rate.

GARLIC-MINT MARINADE

- 4 large garlic cloves, smashed
- 1½ teaspoons sea salt or kosher salt
- ½ cup packed chopped fresh mint
- Finely grated zest of 1 lemon
- 3 tablespoons fresh lemon juice
- 1 teaspoon Aleppo pepper flakes (see Tip, page 25) or ½ teaspoon red pepper flakes, or to taste
- ¼ cup extra-virgin olive oil

- 4 chicken thighs, preferably salted in advance (see sidebar, page 40)
- Sea salt or kosher salt if necessary
- 12–14 ounces extra-firm tofu, sliced crosswise into four ½-inch-thick slabs and pressed (see page 279)

FOR THE MARINADE: Mash the garlic to a paste with the salt. In a bowl, whisk together the mint, lemon zest, lemon juice, garlic paste, and pepper flakes. Whisking constantly, drizzle in the olive oil. Divide the marinade between two bowls or resealable plastic bags.

MARINATE THE CHICKEN: If the chicken has been presalted, pat it thoroughly dry. Otherwise, season the chicken well with salt. Toss the chicken with half the marinade and let sit for 30 minutes at room temperature, or cover and refrigerate for up to 12 hours.

MARINATE THE TOFU: Toss the tofu with half the marinade and let sit for 30 minutes at room temperature, or cover and refrigerate for up to 4 hours.

TO COOK THE CHICKEN: Preheat a large cast-iron skillet over medium-high heat for several minutes. Lift the chicken from the marinade, gently pat it dry with a paper towel, and lay skin side down in the pan. Reserve the marinade. Weight the chicken (see Tip) and cook for 5 minutes, then reduce the heat to medium and continue to cook until the chicken skin is well browned, about 5 more minutes. Flip the chicken, put the weight back on top, and cook until the chicken is browned on the second side and cooked through, 6 to 8 more minutes.

Transfer the chicken to a serving platter. Pour the oil out of the pan, then add the reserved marinade to the pan. Stir and simmer for 1 to 2 minutes, scraping up the browned bits from the bottom of the pan, then pour over the chicken and serve.

TO COOK THE TOFU: Preheat a large cast-iron skillet over medium-high heat for several minutes. Lift the tofu from the marinade, gently pat it dry with a paper towel, and lay in the pan. Reserve the marinade. Weight the tofu (see Tip) and cook for 5 minutes, then reduce the heat to medium and continue to cook until the tofu is golden brown on the bottom, about 5 more minutes. Flip the tofu, put the weight back on top, and cook until the tofu is browned on the second side, 6 to 8 more minutes.

Transfer the tofu to a serving plate. Pour the oil out of the pan, then add the reserved marinade to the pan. Stir and simmer for a few seconds, scraping up the browned bits from the bottom of the pan, then pour over the tofu and serve.

The Season for Poultry

For the moistest, most flavorful chicken and duck, I like to rub the skin and the inside of the cavity of a whole bird with kosher salt, then wrap and refrigerate it overnight (or up to 2 days in advance of cooking), which firms the meat and seasons it to the bone. I use ¾ teaspoon kosher salt for every pound of meat. Incidentally, this is similar to the koshering process—so if you are using kosher chicken, it won't be necessary.

Creamy Risotto-Style Brown Rice with Spring Greens and Asiago

SERVES 4 TO 6

If someone served me this rice with a crisp white Sancerre or Pouilly-Fumé and nothing else, I'd be thoroughly happy. The cooking water from the mixed greens imbues the rice with the fresh flavors of spring.

This risotto-style brown rice requires advance planning and makes good leftovers. You'll need to soak and cook the brown rice before starting the risotto. You can use this same approach with other grains too, such as millet, quinoa, barley, or farro.

Tips: Cook the brown rice following the directions for your rice cooker, or cook it on the stovetop: First soak 1½ cups rice in 2¼ cups water with a pinch of salt for 4 to 12 hours in the refrigerator. Then bring the whole thing to a boil, add another ½ teaspoon salt, reduce the heat, cover, and simmer gently until the water is absorbed, 40 to 45 minutes.

If you have leftover rice, make delicious croquettes by dredging patties of the rice in beaten egg, coating them with dry bread crumbs, and panfrying in olive oil until crisp.

> Sea salt or kosher salt
>
> 12 ounces (about 12 cups) mixed spring greens, such as tatsoi, baby mustard greens, lamb's-quarters, and arugula
>
> 1 tablespoon extra-virgin olive oil
>
> 1 large bunch scallions or ramps (wild leeks), trimmed and thinly sliced (about 1½ cups)
>
> 1 teaspoon finely chopped peeled fresh ginger
>
> 1 teaspoon finely chopped garlic
>
> 3½ cups cooked brown rice, preferably basmati (from 1½ cups raw rice)
>
> 1 tablespoon unsalted butter
>
> 2 ounces Asiago cheese, finely grated (about ½ cup), plus additional for serving
>
> Freshly ground black pepper

Bring a large pot of salted water to a boil. Add the greens and cook until they are just wilted, about 1 minute. Use a mesh skimmer or slotted spoon to transfer the greens to a colander and let cool slightly; reserve the cooking water.

Press the greens to remove excess water, then transfer them to a board and coarsely chop.

In a large skillet, heat the olive oil over medium-high heat. Add the scallions or ramps with the ginger, garlic, and a pinch of salt and cook, stirring, until softened, about 2 minutes.

Stir in the rice, chopped greens, butter, and 1½ cups of the reserved cooking water and cook, stirring, until the water is almost absorbed, 3 to 4 minutes. Stir in the cheese and season with salt and pepper. Serve, passing additional grated cheese at the table.

The Nicest Rices

The fastest-cooking rices are white, but even if you're in a rush, don't limit yourself to plain long-grain. Try scented jasmine or basmati for a little more flavor in pilafs, soups, and rice salads, or use plump, medium-grain Arborio rice from Italy's Po River Valley for chewy, creamy risottos. The many varieties of brown rice are twice the rice in terms of taste, texture, and nutrition. Nutty, fragrant brown basmati and jasmine are standbys in my kitchen, but I also love to use exotic varieties like black rices from Asia and red rice from the French Camargue.

Shaved Spring Vegetable and Apple Salad

SERVES 6 TO 8

Even when the season for apples has long passed, I can't resist making use of one of the fine varieties of organic storage apples still available in early spring. When other fruits are barely buds on the trees, apples add a sweet, crunchy note to this sophisticated salad. The salad is even better the day after it's made, so the recipe makes enough for leftovers.

Sunchokes, also known as Jerusalem artichokes, are actually a relative of the sunflower plant, not the artichoke—hence my preference for the former name. A tuber native to the Americas, they resemble little knobs of ginger. Served raw, they have a crisp texture and sweet, nutty flavor. Roasted, they become silken. It's easiest to use a mandoline or Benriner to shave the ingredients for this salad, though you can always thinly slice them with a good sharp knife.

2 fennel bulbs, trimmed, fronds reserved, cored, and shaved or sliced paper-thin

½ cup extra-virgin olive oil

2 tablespoons rice vinegar

2 tablespoons fresh lemon juice

2 tablespoons chopped fresh chives

2 red apples, such as Gala, Winesap, or Red Delicious, quartered, cored, and shaved or sliced paper-thin

6 large or 8 small radishes, trimmed and shaved or sliced paper-thin

4 large or 6 small sunchokes, peeled and shaved or sliced paper-thin

Sea salt or kosher salt and freshly ground black pepper

Chop enough of the reserved fennel fronds to make 2 tablespoons (discard the rest).

In a medium bowl, whisk together the oil, rice vinegar, lemon juice, chives, and fennel fronds. Add the apples and vegetables to the vinaigrette, toss well, and season with salt and pepper. Cover and refrigerate for at least 30 minutes, or up to 1 day, to allow the flavors to meld.

Taste the salad again and add additional salt if necessary before serving.

Spring

MENU 4
SERVES 4

Navy Bean, Fresh Pea, and Leek Soup

Smoked Salmon/Sun-Dried-Tomato Croque Monsieur

Spring Greens in Dill Vinaigrette

Rainy spring days just beg for soup and grilled sandwich meals. This soup is hearty enough to serve on its own or with bread and cheese. But if you've got bread and cheese, why not do something fun with it, as I do in these playful takes on the classic pressed ham and cheese, the croque monsieur? The smoked salmon version was inspired by Eric Ripert, the chef of New York's renowned Le Bernardin.

THE PLAN
1. Make the soup, cool, and refrigerate.
2. Wash the salad greens and refrigerate.
3. Make the vinaigrette.
4. Make the sandwiches.
5. Meanwhile, reheat the soup.
6. Toss the salad with the vinaigrette.

Navy Bean, Fresh Pea, and Leek Soup

SERVES 6

Navy beans and fresh peas complement each other in both size and flavor in this warming soup. A little sauerkraut, a preserved vegetable that traditionally would have been left over from the winter stores, perks up the soup just before serving.

Tip: Use the larger amount of sauerkraut if you have the raw, naturally fermented kind and the smaller quantity if your sauerkraut is harsh (you can also give it a quick rinse if it is really biting).

> 1 tablespoon unsalted butter
>
> 1 tablespoon extra-virgin olive oil, plus additional for drizzling
>
> 2 large leeks, white and tender green parts only, cleaned and thinly sliced (about 2 cups)
>
> 1 tablespoon chopped fresh mint
>
> Sea salt or kosher salt
>
> 1 pound fresh peas, shelled (1¾ cups fresh or frozen peas)
>
> 1 cup cooked navy beans (see page 9), with their cooking liquid, or 1 cup canned organic navy beans, with their liquid
>
> ½–1 cup drained sauerkraut, to taste

In a large saucepan, heat the butter and oil over medium-high heat. Add the leeks, mint, and ½ teaspoon salt, reduce the heat to medium-low, cover, and cook until the leeks are tender, 4 to 5 minutes.

Add the peas, beans, and 4 cups of the bean liquid (top it up with water or vegetable stock if you don't have enough cooking liquid left or are using canned beans). Cover, bring the soup to a simmer, and cook until the peas are tender, 5 to 7 minutes, or 3 to 4 minutes for frozen peas.

Add the sauerkraut and simmer for 2 more minutes. Season with salt to taste. Serve the soup with a drizzle of olive oil.

Speaking of Leeks

Long, many-layered leek stalks are an ideal hiding place for grit. To prepare leeks, cut off the tough green upper third, then peel away the outer layer if it is dark green. Carefully trim a thin slice from the bottom to remove the dangling roots, leaving enough of the base to hold the leek together. Hold it upright on your work surface and, starting at the green top, cut the leek lengthwise into quarters, cutting down into but not through the white base (you want the leek to stay together). Holding the base, swish the leek through a bowl of water; change the water and swish again, repeating as necessary until there is no grit in the bottom of the bowl. Pat dry before slicing (or slice, then spin-dry in a salad spinner).

Smoked Salmon/Sun-Dried-Tomato Croque Monsieur

SERVES 4: 2 SALMON SANDWICHES, 2 SUN-DRIED-TOMATO SANDWICHES

If you want to keep the fish and vegetarian sandwiches separate, use two medium skillets.

If you prefer, double the ingredients for one type of sandwich and leave out the other.

SALMON SANDWICHES

4 ½-inch-thick slices whole-grain artisanal bread

Grainy mustard

1 teaspoon minced fresh chives

1 teaspoon finely grated lemon zest

Freshly ground black pepper

2–3 ounces sliced smoked salmon, preferably wild

3 ounces Comté or Emmenthaler cheese, coarsely grated or thinly sliced

SUN-DRIED-TOMATO SANDWICHES

6 oil-packed sun-dried tomatoes, drained

4 ½-inch-thick slices whole-grain artisanal bread

1 teaspoon minced fresh chives

Freshly ground black pepper

4 ounces Comté or Emmenthaler cheese, coarsely grated or thinly sliced

4 tablespoons (½ stick) unsalted butter, melted

FOR THE SALMON SANDWICHES: Spread 2 slices of the bread with mustard and sprinkle with the chives, lemon zest, and pepper. Cover with the smoked salmon and top each sandwich with half of the cheese and then another slice of bread.

FOR THE SUN-DRIED-TOMATO SANDWICHES: Lay 3 sun-dried tomatoes each on 2 slices of the bread and sprinkle with the chives and pepper. Top each with half of the cheese and then another slice of bread.

TO COOK THE SANDWICHES: Heat a very large cast-iron skillet or cast-iron griddle over medium heat for several minutes, until hot. Brush the pan with half the melted butter and place all the sandwiches in the pan or cook them in batches. Weight the sandwiches with another heavy pan (with a clean bottom), press down firmly, and cook until the sandwiches are golden on the bottom, about 2 minutes.

Remove the top pan and brush the tops of the sandwiches with the remaining butter. Flip them over, set the pan back onto the sandwiches, press down, and cook until the cheese is melted and the sandwiches are golden brown and crispy on the second side, 2 to 3 more minutes. Cut in half and serve.

Spring Greens in Dill Vinaigrette

Many people don't season salads with enough salt. I always sprinkle a little salt on the leaves at the very last minute before dressing them (any earlier, and they will wilt).

> 2 tablespoons fresh lemon juice
>
> ½ teaspoon honey
>
> 1 tablespoon chopped fresh dill
>
> 1 teaspoon finely chopped shallot
>
> Sea salt or kosher salt and freshly ground black pepper
>
> ¼ cup extra-virgin olive oil
>
> 4 large handfuls (about 4 ounces) spring salad greens

In a salad bowl, whisk together the lemon juice, honey, dill, shallot, and salt and pepper to taste. Whisking constantly, drizzle in the olive oil until it is thoroughly combined. Just before serving, add the greens and toss to coat.

Spring

MENU 5
SERVES 4

Gratin of Cherry Tomatoes and White Beans/Sardines

Chilled Asparagus Salad with Sherry Vinaigrette

This menu can accommodate vegans if you make the gratin with only beans (bake it in two gratin dishes or in one 2-quart baking dish) and leave the Parmesan out of the bread crumbs. The crumbled egg garnish on the asparagus is optional as well.

THE PLAN
1. Assemble and bake the gratins.
2. Meanwhile, cook the asparagus and marinate it.
3. If desired, boil the egg and make the mimosa for the salad.
4. Assemble the salad.

Gratin of Cherry Tomatoes and White Beans/**Sardines**

SERVES 4: 2 TO 3 SERVINGS BEANS, 2 TO 3 SERVINGS FISH

This appealing gratin is a great way to prepare white beans or flavorful fish. Hands down, my favorite sardines are the ones fresh-caught in New England in the spring—they are smaller and milder in flavor than those imported from Spain and Portugal. That said, you could substitute any small firm-fleshed fish, such as rouget or whiting, or even high-quality oil-cured whole Spanish sardines, rinsed well. Or use the same weight of Boston (Atlantic) or Spanish mackerel, or fresh herring fillets if you can find them.

Note: If you like, double the amount of beans or fish and make a single gratin of either variety.

½ cup extra-virgin olive oil, plus additional for the baking dish

2 cups tightly packed fresh sourdough bread crumbs (see page 263)

½ cup freshly grated Parmesan cheese (about 2 ounces)

¼ cup finely chopped fresh flat-leaf parsley or cilantro

Freshly ground black pepper

2 cups thinly sliced spring onions (white parts only) or finely chopped red onions

Sea salt or kosher salt

2 tablespoons chopped garlic

4 teaspoons chopped fresh thyme

½ teaspoon red pepper flakes

3 cups halved cherry tomatoes

1 cup dry white wine

1 pound fresh sardines (6–8), filleted

1 15-ounce can white beans, rinsed and drained, or 1¾ cups cooked white beans (see page 9)

Set a rack in the upper third of the oven and preheat the oven to 350 degrees. Drizzle a little olive oil over the bottom of two 1-quart gratin dishes or 9-inch glass pie plates.

In a bowl, combine the bread crumbs, Parmesan, parsley or cilantro, ¼ cup of the olive oil, and black pepper to taste.

In a large skillet, heat the remaining ¼ cup oil over high heat. Add the onions and a large pinch of salt and cook, stirring, until the onions are soft, 3 to 4 minutes. Reduce the heat to medium, add the garlic, thyme, and red pepper flakes, and cook, stirring, for 2 more minutes, until the garlic is softened.

Add the tomatoes and wine and bring to a boil. Season with salt to taste and remove from the heat.

FOR THE SARDINES: Season the fish all over with salt and pepper. Lay the fish skin side up in one of the gratin dishes and pour half the tomato-wine mixture over it. Spread half the bread crumbs on top. Bake until the fish is cooked through, the juices are bubbling, and the bread crumbs are nicely browned, 25 to 30 minutes. Serve.

FOR THE BEANS: Stir the beans into the remaining tomato-wine mixture and pour into the second gratin dish. Spread the remaining bread crumbs over the top. Bake until the juices are bubbling and the bread crumbs are nicely browned, 25 to 30 minutes. Serve.

Chilled Asparagus Salad
with Sherry Vinaigrette

While thick asparagus are great for roasting, I like to turn thin ones into a simple salad. I cook them very briefly, so they retain their crunch. The optional sieved hard-cooked egg, called mimosa, is a traditional spring topping for this chic dish.

Tip: After cooking, drain the asparagus well and pat thoroughly dry so the vinaigrette won't get watered down.

    1 pound thin asparagus, bottom 1 inch trimmed
      Sea salt or kosher salt
    1½ tablespoons sherry vinegar
    2 teaspoons Dijon mustard
    ⅛ teaspoon honey or maple syrup
    1 tablespoon minced scallion white
    1½ tablespoons extra-virgin olive oil
      Freshly ground black pepper
    1 hard-cooked egg (optional)
    1 tablespoon finely chopped fresh chives

How *Not* to Hard-Boil an Egg

Since you're aiming for a moist, bright yellow yolk without that ugly blue-green tinge, and a firm but not rubbery white, hard-*boiling* is exactly what you don't want to do to an egg. To hard-*cook* eggs, place them in a pot with cold water to cover, turn the heat to high, and bring to a boil. Lower the heat and simmer for 1 minute. Cover the pot, turn off the heat, and let the eggs sit, covered, for 10 minutes. Pour off the water, keeping the eggs in the pot, then swirl and shake the pot until the eggs crack all over. They will virtually pop out of their shells with just a minimum of peeling.

Fill a bowl with water and ice. If you have time, peel the lower 2 inches of the asparagus stalks to make them more tender and the salad greener.

In a large skillet or a saucepan wide enough to accommodate the asparagus, bring 6 cups water to a boil, and add 2 tablespoons salt. Add the asparagus and cook for 2 minutes, adjusting the heat if necessary. Drain the asparagus and immediately transfer to the ice bath to chill. Drain well and blot thoroughly dry with paper towels.

In a large bowl, whisk together the vinegar, mustard, honey, and scallion. Whisking constantly, drizzle in the oil until thoroughly combined. Season with salt and pepper. Toss the asparagus with the vinaigrette and arrange on a platter. Chill for 30 minutes to allow the asparagus to absorb the vinaigrette.

If using the hard-cooked egg, halve it, remove the yolk, and press the yolk through a coarse sieve into a small bowl. Finely chop the egg white and add it to the yolk, along with the chives. Season with pepper and a little salt. Sprinkle the egg, or just the chives, over the asparagus before serving.

Spring

MENU 6
SERVES 4

Green Olive Frittata with Ricotta, Pine Nuts, and Thyme

**Pan-Seared Baby Lamb Chops with Lemon
and Green Olives**

Butter-Braised Radishes with Their Greens

Parmesan Toasts

This company-worthy menu offers a fresh take on two iconic foods of spring: lamb and egg. Please give the radishes a chance too. In late spring and early summer, they're surprisingly sweet, mild, and charming, with none of the aggressive pungency you may associate with older radishes. Parmesan toasts are a favorite flourish of mine whenever I have day-old bread (I *always* have Parmesan)—they're quick to make and bursting with flavor.

THE PLAN
1. Make the frittata.
2. Meanwhile, braise the radishes.
3. Cook the lamb.
4. Turn down the oven and bake the Parmesan toasts and reheat the radishes if necessary.

Green Olive Frittata with Ricotta, Pine Nuts, and Thyme

SERVES 2 AS A MAIN COURSE, 4 AS AN APPETIZER

This frittata is good hot or warm, so when you're making the whole menu, you can make it first and let it sit until the lamb is finished or serve it as an appetizer if everyone is having the lamb. Ricotta gives the eggs a light yet substantial texture that puts it squarely in the main-course category for vegetarians.

- 2 tablespoons extra-virgin olive oil
- 1 large or 2 small leeks, white part only, cleaned and thinly sliced (about 1 cup)
- 1 teaspoon sea salt or kosher salt
- 6 large eggs
- 1 cup whole-milk ricotta cheese
- ¼ cup green olives, pitted and finely chopped
- 3 tablespoons pine nuts, lightly toasted (see page 11)
- 2 tablespoons chopped fresh flat-leaf parsley
- 2 teaspoons chopped fresh thyme
- ½ teaspoon chopped fresh rosemary

Set a rack in the middle of the oven and preheat the oven to 400 degrees.

In an 8- to 10-inch ovenproof skillet, heat 1 tablespoon of the oil over medium-high heat. Add the leeks and ½ teaspoon of the salt and cook, stirring, until the leeks are softened and lightly browned, 6 to 8 minutes.

Meanwhile, in a medium bowl, combine the eggs, ricotta, olives, pine nuts, parsley, thyme, rosemary, and the remaining ½ teaspoon salt. Beat lightly with a fork until just combined (do not overmix).

With a rubber spatula, scrape the leeks into the egg mixture and stir to combine. Wipe out the skillet with a paper towel.

Return the skillet to medium heat for a minute, then add the remaining 1 tablespoon oil and heat it. Pour in the egg mixture and immediately transfer to the oven. Bake until the eggs are just barely set in the middle, about 20 minutes.

Take the pan out of the oven and turn on the broiler. Place the frittata about 4 inches from the heat source and broil, watching carefully, until golden brown, 2 to 3 minutes. Serve hot or warm.

Pan-Seared Baby Lamb Chops with Lemon and Green Olives

SERVES 4

Recipes often warn of the pitfalls of overcooking tender, lovely little lamb chops like these, and while I agree, serving them so rare they're barely warm in the middle isn't much better. For me, lamb is most enjoyable when it's cooked medium-rare.

¼ cup extra-virgin olive oil, plus more if needed

1 cup chopped onion

¾ cup chopped celery

Sea salt or kosher salt

⅔ cup dry white wine

½ cup green olives, pitted and finely chopped

2 garlic cloves, finely chopped

2 teaspoons chopped fresh thyme

½ teaspoon chopped fresh rosemary

12 baby lamb rib chops, frenched (you can have the butcher do this)

Freshly ground black pepper

Lemon wedges, for serving

Center a rack in the oven and preheat the oven to 400 degrees.

In a small saucepan, heat 3 tablespoons of the olive oil over medium-high heat. Add the onion, celery, and a pinch of salt and cook, stirring occasionally, until the vegetables are softened, about 5 minutes. Stir in the wine, olives, garlic, thyme, and rosemary, turn off the heat, and cover to keep warm.

Season the lamb all over with salt and pepper. Heat a large heavy ovenproof skillet over high heat for a few minutes. Add the remaining 1 tablespoon olive oil, place the lamb chops in the pan, and sear them in batches, adding more oil if necessary, until nicely browned on the first side, about 3 minutes. Flip the chops and cook for 2 minutes on the second side.

Remove the chops to a plate and pour the fat from the pan. Pour in the olive mixture, then bring to a boil.

Return the chops to the pan. Transfer to the oven and roast until the chops are done to taste, about 3 minutes for medium-rare. Allow the chops to rest in the pan for a few minutes to reabsorb their juices, then serve with lemon wedges.

Butter-Braised Radishes with Their Greens

SERVES 4

Served whole, cooked radishes are a real treat. Small white baby turnips with their greens are lovely prepared this way too. Be aware that these cook fast, going from tender to mush in a blink.

Tip: Layer the greens on top of the radishes and don't stir them in, so that you can remove them first and squeeze some of their liquid back into the pot without mashing the radishes.

1 large or 2 small bunches radishes (about 2 pounds) with greens

3 tablespoons unsalted butter

1 teaspoon brown sugar, plus more if needed

Sea salt or kosher salt

⅔ cup water

1 tablespoon white wine vinegar

Freshly ground black pepper

Freshly grated nutmeg

Cut the leaves from the radishes, leaving about ½ inch of green attached. Scrub the radishes. Wash the greens well, coarsely chop them, and keep separate.

In a 10- to 12-inch skillet with a tight-fitting lid, melt the butter with the brown sugar and ½ teaspoon salt over medium-high heat. Add the water and radishes and bring to a boil. Reduce the heat to medium-low, cover, and simmer gently until the radishes can be easily pierced with a knife but are not completely soft, about 3 minutes.

Spread the greens over the radishes and raise the heat to return the liquid to a boil. Reduce the heat to medium-low, cover, and simmer gently until the greens are emerald colored and tender, about 5 more minutes.

Use tongs to transfer the greens to a large bowl or serving dish, first pressing the excess liquid out of the greens against the side of the pan. Transfer the radishes to the bowl or dish.

Add the vinegar, pepper to taste, and a few gratings of nutmeg to the liquid remaining in the pan and bring to a boil over high heat. Boil, uncovered, until the liquid has turned syrupy (you'll end up with about 2 tablespoons), about 2 minutes. Taste and add a little more salt and/or brown sugar if needed.

Return the radishes and greens to the pan and fold gently with a rubber spatula to coat them without mashing the radishes. Serve.

Parmesan Toasts

SERVES 4

Crunchy and cheesy, these are a great accompaniment to soups and salads. Served with a dish of olives and a glass of sparkling wine, they make a simple, elegant hors d'oeuvre.

> 1 8-ounce loaf country bread (or half a 1-pound loaf), sliced ½ inch thick
> Extra-virgin olive oil, for brushing
> Freshly ground black pepper
> ¾ cup lightly packed freshly grated Parmesan cheese (about 3 ounces)

Set a rack in the middle of the oven and preheat the oven to 375 degrees.

Arrange the bread on a rimmed baking sheet. Brush the tops liberally with olive oil and season with pepper. Bake until toasted and golden, about 10 minutes.

Sprinkle the cheese over the toasts. Continue to bake until the cheese is golden brown, about 5 minutes. Serve immediately.

Spring

MENU 7
SERVES 4

Roast Duck with Spiced Red Onion Marmalade

Goat Cheese Frittata
with Spiced Red Onion Marmalade

Rice with Herbs

Sautéed Asparagus and Fiddlehead Ferns with Garlic

This satisfying spring menu is lovely enough for a dinner party, but don't save it just for company—it's not out of the realm of everyday cooking. In place of the duck, you could serve the red onion marmalade with steak or lamb, or roast a rich fish like bluefish, mackerel, or salmon (leaving out the frittata if everyone eats fish).

Note: If you prefer, make either the duck or the goat cheese frittata, doubling the recipe to serve 4.

THE PLAN

1. Salt the duck.
2. Make the red onion marmalade.
3. Roast the duck.
4. Meanwhile, cook the rice.
5. Sauté the asparagus and fiddleheads and reheat the marmalade if desired.
6. Make the frittata.

Roast Duck with Spiced Red Onion Marmalade

SERVES 2 TO 3

Cooking duck can seem intimidating, but roasting duck isn't much more difficult than roasting chicken. The key is gently browning the duck on the stovetop first, rendering out a lot of the fat and leaving the skin nice and crisp. Then the meat is cooked through in the oven and finished under the broiler to further crisp the skin. The Red Onion Marmalade nicely counterpoints the rich duck.

I use Long Island duck, also called Pekin duck; these are smaller and leaner than Muscovy duck. Salting overnight seasons the meat to the bone, but if you're in a hurry, you can skip this step and just season the duck well before cooking. The legs take longer to cook, so they go in the oven first.

> 2 Long Island (Pekin) duck legs, preferably presalted (see page 40)
>
> 2 skin-on boneless Long Island (Pekin) duck breasts, preferably presalted
>
> Freshly ground black pepper
>
> Sea salt or kosher salt
>
> 1 teaspoon extra-virgin olive oil
>
> ¼ cup water
>
> 1 teaspoon finely chopped fresh rosemary
>
> Spiced Red Onion Marmalade (page 72), for serving

Center a rack in the oven and preheat the oven to 425 degrees.

If you presalted the duck, pat it very dry. Cut away the excess fat and some of the excess skin from the duck. Season with pepper, and with salt if it wasn't presalted.

Heat a large ovenproof skillet over high heat, and add the oil. When the oil is very hot but not smoking, swirl it to coat the bottom of the pan. Add the duck skin side down and sear, without moving, for 1 minute. Reduce the heat to medium and cook undisturbed until the skin is crisp but not scorched (reduce the heat if it starts to sizzle violently), about 10 minutes.

Transfer the duck to a plate and pour off the fat from the pan. Add the water to the pan and bring to a simmer over high heat, stirring and scraping up the browned bits from the bottom. Place the duck legs back in the pan skin side up, transfer the pan to the oven, and roast for 10 minutes.

Add the duck breasts skin side up to the pan, along with any juices that have collected on the plate. Roast for 6 more minutes, or until medium-rare.

Remove the duck from the oven and turn on the broiler. Sprinkle the rosemary over the duck, place the duck about 6 inches from the heat source, and broil, watching carefully, until the skin is sizzling and crisp, 1 to 2 minutes. Serve with the marmalade.

Making the Most of Duck

You can buy duck breasts and legs separately in many stores, but I usually just buy a whole duck. To make use of the whole duck, cut it up (or have your butcher do this, and ask for the carcass as well), and pan-sear the breasts and the legs (see opposite). Render the golden fat, which has a high smoke point and is one of the most flavorful cooking fats available. The cracklings, bits of crispy skin, are a by-product of rendering the fat. They are a treat scattered over soup or mashed root vegetables, or just snack on them with a glass of crisp white wine.

Make a rich stock by combining the carcass with chopped onions, carrots, celery, and some fresh herbs in a pot. Cover with cold water and simmer for 1 to 2 hours; strain. Chill the broth, then skim the fat. The broth can be refrigerated for up to 3 days or frozen for up to 3 months.

To make them, trim the excess skin and fat from the duck breasts and legs, and pull off any remaining fat left on the carcass. Slice the skin into 1-inch pieces. Put the skin and fat in a heavy skillet, cover with cold water, and bring to a simmer over medium-high heat. Skim away any scum that rises to the surface, reduce the heat to low, and cook until all the water has evaporated. You'll start to hear crackling sounds when the water is gone, and at this point the skin will begin to render the fat. Reduce the heat so the fat simmers gently—do not rush this; it will take 45 minutes to an hour. Turn the chunks of fat over every 15 minutes or so. You will wind up with crisp, golden brown cracklings from the skin and about a cup or so of clear golden fat. Strain the fat through a coffee filter or paper towel, transfer to a clean glass jar, and cool to room temperature, then cover and refrigerate; the rendered fat will keep for up to 6 months. Drain the cracklings on paper towels and season with salt and pepper.

Serve right away or store tightly covered for up to 3 days in the refrigerator.

Spiced Red Onion Marmalade

MAKES 2 CUPS

This is a wine-friendly condiment with a taste as bright and rich as its plummy color. Use a red wine similar to or the same as what you'll be drinking with the meal—a fruity Cru Beaujolais such as Morgon or Fleurie or a California Pinot Noir is ideal if you're serving the roast duck. The recipe makes plenty, so you will have leftovers even if you are making the frittata too. I particularly like it as a topping for goat cheese crostini.

Every Onion and Its Cousin

Onions are part of the aromatic Amaryllidaceae family. In addition to the familiar papery-skinned yellow, white, and red onions, known as storage onions, are various fresher, greener family members. Spring onions are the teenagers. These bulbous fresh white onions with their greens still attached can be found in farmers' markets and specialty produce shops in the spring and are often sold year-round in markets with a Mexican clientele. Both the white bulb and the tender green part are used. Scallions are an onion variety that does not develop a bulb. Chives are the delicate herbal cousin, perfect for snipping fresh over dishes for a mildly onion-flavored garnish. Chinese chives, or garlic chives, are tougher, flatter, and more pungent than regular, and they benefit from cooking. With their thick, layered stalks, leeks must be trimmed and carefully cleaned (see page 49) before cooking.

1 tablespoon extra-virgin olive oil

1 tablespoon unsalted butter

2 pounds red onions, thinly sliced

Sea salt or kosher salt

1 750-ml bottle fruity red wine

¼ cup red wine vinegar

6 tablespoons honey

1 tablespoon minced peeled fresh ginger

1 teaspoon minced fresh sage

½ cinnamon stick, broken in half

Freshly ground black pepper

In a large skillet, heat the oil and butter over medium heat. Add the onions and a pinch of salt and cook, stirring, until the onions are softened, 8 to 10 minutes.

Add the wine, vinegar, honey, ginger, sage, and cinnamon and bring to a boil. Reduce the heat to medium-low, partially cover and simmer, stirring occasionally and adjusting the heat if the marmalade starts to stick to the bottom of the pan, until the onions are meltingly tender and the liquid is reduced to a syrupy glaze, about 1 hour. Discard the cinnamon stick.

Season the marmalade with ½ teaspoon salt and a generous grinding of pepper. Serve hot or warm. The marmalade keeps for up to 2 weeks, refrigerated.

Goat Cheese Frittata with Spiced Red Onion Marmalade

SERVES 2 TO 3

When my cowriter, Zoe, sampled this unusual egg dish, she realized that I had channeled the taste memory of our respective Jewish grandmothers' eggy kugel, made with sweet onions, cottage cheese, and noodles. In this menu, the elegant, burnished frittata makes a great vegetarian counterpart to the duck.

Tip: To make the frittata when you don't have the marmalade on hand, cook ½ cup chopped red onion in a little olive oil with a pinch of salt until softened, about 5 minutes over medium heat. Use in place of the marmalade.

4 large eggs

⅔ cup Spiced Red Onion Marmalade (page 72)

½ cup crumbled fresh goat cheese (about 4 ounces)

¼ cup freshly grated Parmesan cheese

1 tablespoon unsalted butter, cut into tiny cubes

Sea salt or kosher salt and freshly ground black pepper

1 teaspoon extra-virgin olive oil

2 tablespoons finely chopped fresh flat-leaf parsley

Position an oven rack about 6 inches from the heat source and preheat the broiler to high.

In a medium bowl, beat together the eggs, red onion marmalade, goat cheese, Parmesan, and butter. Season with salt and pepper.

In a 6-inch ovenproof skillet, heat the oil over medium-high heat. Add the egg mixture and cook, undisturbed, for about 3 minutes, until the bottom is set.

Transfer the pan to the oven and broil, watching carefully, until the top is browned and the middle is barely set, about 3 minutes. Slip a rubber spatula under the frittata and run it around the sides, then slide the omelet onto a serving plate. Sprinkle with the parsley and cut into wedges to serve.

Rice with Herbs

This verdant rice packs a punch. It's spicy, redolent of fresh herbs, and very pretty.

½ cup packed baby spinach leaves

½ cup packed fresh cilantro leaves and tender stems

¼ cup packed fresh flat-leaf parsley leaves

¼ cup packed fresh mint leaves

1 small jalapeño, finely chopped

1¾ cups water

2 tablespoons unsalted butter

2 scallions, white and light green parts only, thinly sliced

1 cup basmati rice

¼ cup pine nuts

1 teaspoon sea salt or kosher salt

In a blender, combine the spinach, cilantro, parsley, mint, jalapeño, and water. Puree until smooth.

In a medium saucepan, melt the butter over medium-high heat. Add the scallions and cook, stirring, until softened, 1 to 2 minutes. Add the rice and pine nuts and cook, stirring, for 3 minutes.

Stir in the green puree. Raise the heat, add the salt, and bring to a boil. Cover, reduce the heat to low, and cook until the water has been absorbed and the rice is tender, about 20 minutes. Serve.

Sautéed Asparagus and Fiddlehead Ferns with Garlic

SERVES 6

The curled-up young shoots of ostrich and cinnamon ferns grow wild in the deciduous forests of the Northeast in the spring and are foraged by those in the know, who tend to guard their sources vigilantly—though they may offer their treasure at farmers' markets. The sweet green fiddleheads are similar to asparagus in taste, so I combine the two vegetables here in a big spring jumble. If you can't get fiddleheads, just use twice the amount of asparagus (skip the blanching step). Leftovers are great in eggs or tossed with pasta.

To rid fiddleheads of any unwelcome dirt or bacteria, you must blanch them in boiling water for a few minutes before sautéing.

Sea salt or kosher salt

1 pound fiddlehead ferns

1 tablespoon extra-virgin olive oil

2 garlic cloves, thinly sliced

1 pound thin asparagus, bottom 1 inch trimmed, cut on the diagonal into 1-inch lengths

Lemon wedges, for serving

In a large pot, bring 4 quarts water to a boil, and add 2 tablespoons salt. Fill a large bowl with water and ice. Add the fiddleheads to the boiling water and blanch for 2 minutes, then drain and transfer to the ice water to stop the cooking. Drain well and blot dry with paper towels.

In a large skillet, heat the oil over high heat until it shimmers. Add the garlic and cook, stirring, until it is just colored but not browned, about 30 seconds. Add the fiddleheads, asparagus, and a healthy pinch of salt and cook, tossing frequently, until the fiddleheads and asparagus are crisp-tender, 3 to 4 minutes. Serve with lemon wedges.

Spring

MENU 8
SERVES 4

Pea Shoot, Radish, and Smoked Trout/Tofu Salad

Artichoke, Potato, and Leek Gratin

While either of these recipes could be a glorious one-dish lunch, the crisp, bright salad and sumptuous gratin combine for a two-course supper of supreme elegance. You can make the salad with all trout or all tofu if everyone falls on the same side of the fish-eating question. Both smoked trout and smoked tofu are sold ready to eat, no preparation required.

THE PLAN

1. Make the gratin.
2. Meanwhile, make the salad.

Pea Shoot, Radish, and Smoked Trout/Tofu Salad

SERVES 4: 2 SERVINGS TROUT, 2 SERVINGS TOFU

This salad was inspired by a smoked trout and daikon radish salad I had at Ici, a great little place in Fort Greene, Brooklyn. I loved the pairing of the smoky protein and crunchy radish, so I created my own version with smoked tofu or smoked trout, or both. The soft texture and rich flavor of the protein are offset by the crisp, refreshing radish. I use toasted sesame oil in the dressing, which has a complementary smokiness. When I tested the recipe, Emma, my teenage daughter, devoured about three quarters of the bowl, so I knew I was on to something.

Tip: If you have a mandoline or Benriner, it will make short work of slicing the radish and julienning the daikon and carrot. Otherwise, use your sharpest knife—thin radish slices will make the salad much more elegant.

SALAD

- 1 cup red radish matchsticks
- 1 cup daikon radish matchsticks
- 1 cup carrot matchsticks
- ¾ teaspoon sea salt or kosher salt
- 1 3½-ounce package (about 3 cups) sweet pea shoots or large mild sprouts, such as sunflower
- 2 teaspoons finely chopped fresh mint
- 2 teaspoons finely chopped fresh chives

- 1 fillet smoked trout (about 4 ounces), skin removed and coarsely chopped
- 3 ounces (half a standard package) smoked tofu, cut into matchsticks

VINAIGRETTE

2 tablespoons plus 2 teaspoons extra-virgin olive oil

2 tablespoons rice vinegar

1 tablespoon fresh lemon juice

2 teaspoons soy sauce, preferably naturally brewed

1 teaspoon sugar

1 teaspoon toasted sesame oil

2 teaspoons sesame seeds, lightly toasted (see page 11), for garnish

FOR THE SALAD: In a medium bowl, toss together the red radishes, daikon, carrots, and salt. Transfer to a strainer, set it over the bowl, and refrigerate for 30 minutes to drain.

Squeeze the excess water from the salted vegetables and transfer them to a large bowl. Toss with the pea shoots or sprouts, the mint, and the chives. Divide the salad between two bowls. Add the trout to one bowl and the tofu to the other and toss well.

FOR THE VINAIGRETTE: In a small bowl, whisk together all the ingredients.

Pour half the vinaigrette over each salad and toss well. Garnish with the sesame seeds and serve immediately.

Artichoke, Potato, and Leek Gratin

The artichoke is not easy—you have to work to get the best out of it, and you might prick your fingers on its thorny leaves in the process—but once you get through its complex layers, it is the most satisfying and succulent of foods. In this unusual gratin, firm, nutty artichokes, leeks, and meltingly tender potatoes are offset by a crunchy topping. If everyone present eats poultry, chicken stock is tasty in this recipe.

Tip: Use lemon juice to keep artichokes from browning once cut.

    4 large artichokes, stems snapped off
    1 lemon, halved
    ½ cup extra-virgin olive oil
      Sea salt or kosher salt and freshly ground black pepper
    1 tablespoon unsalted butter
    3 leeks, white and tender green parts only, cleaned and thinly sliced
    3 garlic cloves, finely chopped
    2 teaspoons finely chopped fresh thyme
 1½ pounds russet (baking) or yellow-fleshed potatoes
    ¾ cup vegetable or chicken stock or water, brought to a boil
    1 cup packed fresh bread crumbs (see page 263)
    ½ cup packed freshly grated Parmesan cheese (about 2 ounces)

Preheat the oven to 425 degrees.

Peel off the tough outer green leaves from each artichoke until you reach the tender lighter-colored inner leaves. Slice the top third off each artichoke, halve lengthwise, and scoop out all the choke with a melon baller or a sharp spoon. Use a paring knife to trim the dark green leaf bits from the base of the artichokes, then rub the artichokes all over with half of the lemon.

In a bowl, combine the juice from the remaining lemon half with 2 tablespoons of the olive oil. Thinly slice the artichokes crosswise, adding them to the bowl as you work. Season with salt and pepper, and toss to coat.

In a medium skillet, heat 1 tablespoon of the olive oil and the butter over medium heat. When the butter has melted, add the leeks, garlic, thyme, and ½ teaspoon salt and cook, stirring, until the leeks are softened, 6 to 8 minutes. Take the pan off the heat.

Peel and thinly slice the potatoes. Place them in a bowl with 2 tablespoons of the olive oil, season with salt and pepper, and toss to coat.

Grease a 2-quart gratin dish with 1 tablespoon of the olive oil. Transfer the leeks to the dish, spreading them evenly, and smooth with a spatula. Spread the artichokes in an even layer over the leeks and top with the potatoes, patting to level them. Pour the boiling stock or water over the top.

In a small bowl, toss the bread crumbs and cheese with the remaining 2 tablespoons olive oil. Season with salt and pepper. Spread the topping over the vegetables. Bake for 45 minutes, or until the vegetables are tender and the topping is golden brown and crisp. Serve.

MENU 9
SERVES 4

Asian Noodles in Broth with Vegetables and Tofu/Steak

Hiziki Salad with Sweet Sesame Vinaigrette

Along with stir-frying, simmering in a broth is perhaps the easiest way to combine lots of vegetables with a protein source; it's also a streamlined technique for cooking a healthy, delicious meal, whether you're feeding red-meat eaters or vegans. A bowl of noodles is a great one-dish supper, but little bowls of sea vegetable salad on the side add textural contrast and nutrition. Make the hiziki salad first so you can chill it.

THE PLAN
1. Soak the hiziki.
2. Make the salad and chill it.
3. Make the noodles in broth.
4. Toss the salad.

Asian Noodles in Broth
with Vegetables and Tofu/Steak

SERVES 4: 2 SERVINGS TOFU, 2 SERVINGS STEAK

This is a soup for all seasons—in the summer, try adding baby bok choy leaves; in the fall, add chopped pumpkin and broccoli; and in the winter, use diced root vegetables and sliced cabbage. You can substitute shrimp or cubed firm fish such as halibut for the steak and/or tofu if you like.

Note: To make an all-tofu or all-meat meal, double the quantity of either one and use one saucepan.

Tips: Make a double batch of broth and freeze half (for up to 3 months), and you'll have an instant base for a one-pot meal.

Mirin is a sweet Japanese rice wine for cooking, available in Asian markets, natural food stores, and some supermarkets.

1 8-ounce package udon or soba noodles

BROTH
½ cup soy sauce, preferably naturally brewed
⅓ cup mirin
3 tablespoons rice vinegar
1 tablespoon finely grated peeled fresh ginger

1 cup snow peas, strings removed and halved crosswise on the diagonal
1 cup thinly sliced mushrooms

6 ounces flank steak, sliced against the grain into short thin strips
8 ounces soft tofu, cubed

GARNISHES
1 romaine lettuce heart, shredded
½ cup thinly sliced red radishes or daikon matchsticks
½ cup carrot matchsticks
2 scallions, white and light green parts only, thinly sliced
Toasted sesame oil, for serving (optional)
Hot sauce, for serving (optional)

Strings Attached

Although string beans are now grown to be so tender that they don't need to be "destringed" (and are probably ready to lose that name), older varieties had a fibrous thread running along their seams, as snow peas and sugar snaps still do. Removing this is a simple matter of snapping the stem end and pulling away the string.

Bring a large pot of water to a boil. Add the noodles and cook until al dente, about 8 minutes. Drain and divide among four large soup bowls.

FOR THE BROTH: In each of two small saucepans, combine 1½ cups of water with half of the soy sauce, mirin, vinegar, and ginger and bring to a simmer over medium heat. Add half the snow peas and half the mushrooms to each pan, then add the steak to one pan and the tofu to the other. Simmer until the snow peas are crisp-tender, the meat is cooked, and the tofu is heated through, 3 to 5 minutes.

Divide the vegetable garnishes among the bowls and ladle the hot soup over the noodles. Drizzle each serving with a few drops of sesame oil and hot sauce, if desired. Serve immediately.

Hiziki Salad with Sweet Sesame Vinaigrette

SERVES 4

Hiziki is a beautiful black ribbonlike seaweed. This salad is a fresher, more succulent version of the standard seaweed salad found on many sushi menus.

- ½ cup hiziki
- 4 cups warm water
- 1 tablespoon extra-virgin olive oil, plus additional for drizzling
- 1 scallion, trimmed, white and pale green parts thinly sliced and kept separate
- 2 tablespoons maple syrup
- 2 tablespoons rice vinegar
- 1 tablespoon soy sauce, preferably naturally brewed
- ½ teaspoon toasted sesame oil
- 1 teaspoon finely grated peeled fresh ginger
- 1 star anise (optional)
- ⅛ teaspoon cayenne pepper, or to taste (optional)
- 2 tablespoons sesame seeds, lightly toasted (see page 11)
- 1 bunch watercress, tough stems discarded
- Juice of ½ lemon

In a medium bowl, combine the hiziki with 3 cups of the water. Let soak until the hiziki has plumped, 30 minutes to 1 hour. Drain, rinse well, and drain again thoroughly.

What Exactly Is Hiziki?

Sold dried in health-food stores, this seaweed looks like black twigs. The strands become plump and toothsome when soaked in warm water for 30 minutes to 1 hour. The distinct sea-vegetable taste of hiziki can stand up to strong flavors like soy, sesame, ginger, and citrus or vinegar.

In a medium skillet, heat the olive oil over medium heat. Add the hiziki and scallion whites and cook, stirring occasionally, for about 5 minutes, or until the hiziki smells nutty and toasted. Add the maple syrup, vinegar, soy sauce, sesame oil, and ginger and star anise and cayenne (if using). Add the remaining 1 cup water, or enough to barely cover the hiziki, raise the heat, and bring to a boil. Reduce the heat to medium and simmer, uncovered, until nearly all the cooking liquid has evaporated and the hiziki is tender, about 20 minutes.

Transfer the salad to a bowl and refrigerate until well chilled, at least 30 minutes.

Just before serving, toss the salad with the sesame seeds and scallion greens.

In a serving bowl, toss the watercress with the lemon juice and a drizzle of olive oil. Mound the hiziki on top and serve.

Spring

MENU 10
SERVES 4

Fregola Risotto-Style with Chard and Feta Cheese

**Mâche and Pea Shoots with Baby Beets
and Mustard Vinaigrette**

This meatless menu is a jubilee of earthy, briny, sharp, and sweet flavors, full of
crunchy, tender vegetables and chewy little nuggets of the Sardinian pasta called
fregola. It's a colorful spring meal that takes the old standby of pasta and a salad
to new heights.

THE PLAN
1. Roast the beets.
2. Make the vinaigrette.
3. Toss the beets in the vinaigrette and refrigerate.
4. Make the fregola.
5. Finish the salad.

Fregola Risotto-Style with Chard and Feta Cheese

A small round pasta from Sardinia, fregola consists of charming, irregularly shaped nubs of toasted durum wheat about the size of peppercorns. Like risotto rice, it will slowly absorb the liquid it's cooked in while retaining its resilient texture, without turning to mush. Here I cook the fregola in a quick herb and vegetable stock, which I consider indispensable for any risotto-style vegetarian dish. Kombu seaweed adds a depth of flavor that you don't find in most vegetable stocks. If you're not a vegetarian, you could substitute 4 cups of chicken, seafood, or fish broth (preferably homemade). If fregola is not available, you can substitute an equal amount of farro (see Tip, page 139), medium-grain bulgur, or Israeli couscous—just start testing for doneness after 10 minutes of covered cooking for bulgur, or be prepared to add an extra 5 minutes for farro.

Chard meshes perfectly with the cheese, but you can substitute spinach with good results; add a little more chopped celery to make up for the absence of the crunchy chard stems.

Tips: Creamy, mild French feta is great just as is, but Greek feta tends to be quite salty. You can remove some of the salt by soaking it in milk for a few hours in the fridge, then draining away the salty liquid and proceeding with the recipe. Adjust the seasoning if your feta still seems quite salty.

After simmering the stock, the vegetables will have given up much of their flavor; however, they can still be enjoyed in various ways. Discard the thyme, lemon, and kombu and toss the vegetables with extra-virgin olive oil, sea salt, and freshly ground black pepper, then sprinkle with a little wine vinegar and serve as a side dish. Or simply season with salt and pepper and use as a filling for an omelet.

VEGETABLE STOCK

1 medium onion, thinly sliced

1 medium carrot, peeled and thinly sliced

1 celery stalk with leaves, thinly sliced

Reserved mushroom stems (from below), sliced

2 sprigs fresh thyme

2 lemon slices, seeds removed

1 4-inch piece kombu (optional)

6 cups water

FREGOLA

2 tablespoons unsalted butter

2 tablespoons extra-virgin olive oil

1 cup finely chopped onion

½ cup finely chopped peeled carrots

1 bunch Swiss chard, trimmed, stems thinly sliced, leaves shredded (about 8 cups loosely packed leaves) and kept separate

½ cup finely chopped celery

8 ounces white button mushrooms or cremini mushrooms, stems removed and reserved for the stock, caps thinly sliced (about 2 cups)

2 garlic cloves, finely chopped

2 teaspoons finely chopped fresh thyme

1 cup fregola

7 ounces feta cheese, preferably French, crumbled (about 1⅓ cups)

Sea salt or kosher salt and freshly ground black pepper

Extra-virgin olive oil, for drizzling

FOR THE STOCK: In a large saucepan, combine all the ingredients and bring to a boil over high heat. Reduce the heat and simmer, uncovered, for 30 minutes, or until the liquid has reduced to 4 cups. Strain the stock through a sieve, pressing down hard on the solids to extract as much liquid as possible. Set aside.

FOR THE FREGOLA: In a heavy 3- to 4-quart saucepan or a small Dutch oven, heat the butter and oil over medium heat. Add the onion, carrots, chard stems, and celery and cook, stirring, until the vegetables soften, about 3 minutes. Add the mushroom caps, garlic, and thyme, raise the heat a bit, and cook, stirring occasionally, until the mushrooms have given up their juices and the vegetables are lightly browned, 7 to 8 minutes.

Add the fregola and stir until it smells toasty, 1 to 2 minutes. Pour in the stock and bring to a boil. Cover, reduce the heat, and simmer gently until the fregola is al dente, about 15 minutes.

Stir in the chard leaves and simmer, uncovered, until tender, 2 to 3 minutes. Stir in the feta cheese and heat through. Season with salt if needed and plenty of pepper.

Serve the fregola in wide soup plates, drizzled with your finest extra-virgin olive oil.

Mâche and Pea Shoots with Baby Beets and Mustard Vinaigrette

SERVES 4

Mâche, a tender, buttery baby lettuce, and pea shoots, the crunchy, nutty first shoots of the pea plant, combine with chilled baby beets for a fresh version of the classic bistro beet salad. The slightly bitter edge of toasted mustard seeds counterbalances the sweetness of the beets.

Tip: The beets should be completely chilled for this salad. You can roast and peel them up to 3 days in advance. With the beets ready and chilled, the rest of the salad will come together quickly. Large storage beets are fine to use here if baby beets are unavailable; they will take 5 to 10 minutes longer to cook.

1 pound baby beets

DRESSING

2 teaspoons mustard seeds

1 tablespoon white wine vinegar

1 tablespoon fresh lemon juice

1 tablespoon Dijon mustard

5 tablespoons extra-virgin olive oil

Sea salt or kosher salt and freshly ground black pepper to taste

1 3½-ounce package pea shoots, halved if very long

1½ cups (1½ ounces) mâche or other tender salad leaves, such as baby arugula

Snipped fresh chives, for garnish

Preheat the oven to 450 degrees.

Wrap the beets in foil and set them on a baking sheet in case the juices run. Roast until they can be easily pierced with a knife, about 50 minutes. Let cool slightly.

MEANWHILE, FOR THE DRESSING: In a small dry skillet, toast the mustard seeds over medium heat, shaking the pan, until they are fragrant and beginning to pop, 1 to 2 minutes. Transfer to a medium bowl and let cool.

Add the remaining vinaigrette ingredients to the mustard seeds and whisk well.

Holding the beets under cold running water, rub off their skins. Then pat dry. Trim both ends of each beet away and thinly slice, then cut the slices into thin matchsticks.

In a large bowl, toss the beets with half of the vinaigrette. Season with salt and pepper. Refrigerate for 30 minutes, or until completely chilled. (The beets can be prepared up to 3 days ahead, covered, and refrigerated.)

TO FINISH THE SALAD: Taste the beets and adjust the seasoning if necessary. Add the pea shoots and toss well, then add the mâche and the remaining vinaigrette and toss again. Sprinkle with chives and serve.

Summer

MENU 1 • 99

Charmoula Lamb/Tempeh Kebabs

Summer Vegetable Simmer

Couscous with Dried Fruit and Pine Nuts

MENU 2 • 104

Summer Bean Ratatouille

Portobello Mushrooms/Steak with Bread Crumb Salsa

Arugula Salad with Mustard Vinaigrette

MENU 3 • 111

Grilled Shrimp in Harissa

Fresh Corn Polenta with Sautéed Cherry Tomatoes

Grilled Zucchini with Mint Oil

MENU 4 • 117

Chilled Melon Soup

Salade Niçoise with Many Possibilities

MENU 5 • 123

Tofu with Lemon, Soy, White Wine, and Butter Sauce

Striped Bass with Lemon, White Wine, and Butter Sauce

Quinoa Salad with Green Beans, Corn, and Tomatoes

MENU 6 • 130

Seafood/Tofu Ceviche with Quick-Pickled Red Onion

Zucchini-Rice Soup with Basil and Parmesan

MENU 7 • 137

Gazpacho with Crumbled Feta Cheese

Farro with Corn, Red Beans, and Scallops/Avocado

MENU 8 • 141

Chilled Curried Red Lentil and Peach Soup

Spicy Grilled Chicken Wings with Lemon and Garlic

Baked Baby Eggplants Stuffed with Rice, Feta, and Rosemary

Panzanella

MENU 9 • 151

Cannelloni with Ricotta, Parmesan, and Mint

Summer Vegetable Ragout

Chopped Salad with Sherry Vinaigrette

MENU 10 • 157

Spicy Roasted Pepper Soup with Goat Cheese and Chives

Whole Wheat Pita Bread

Spiced Lamb Croquettes

Falafel

Two Traditional Sauces: Hot Sauce (Zhoug) and Sesame Tahini Sauce

Cucumber, Red Onion, and Tomato Salad

Summer

MENU 1
SERVES 4

Charmoula Lamb/Tempeh Kebabs
Summer Vegetable Simmer
Couscous with Dried Fruit and Pine Nuts

Serve this festive menu by mounding some of the pretty, bejeweled couscous on the middle of each plate, then topping it with lamb or tempeh and spooning the colorful summer vegetables over and around. Conveniently, the majority of the cooking can be done in advance, so that you need only put the kebabs on the grill just before you're ready to eat. The couscous and vegetables are both great warm or at room temperature, and if it's a hot day, the vegetables can be chilled before serving.

Greek yogurt (or strained regular yogurt—see Tip, page 22), seasoned with salt, pepper, and chopped cilantro, would be a cooling accompaniment to the meal.

THE PLAN
1. Make the charmoula.
2. Marinate the lamb.
3. Simmer the vegetables.
4. Simmer the tempeh.
5. Make the couscous.
6. Grill the kebabs.

Charmoula Lamb/Tempeh Kebabs

SERVES 4: 2 SERVINGS LAMB, 2 SERVINGS TEMPEH

Charmoula is a Moroccan mix of spices and lemon—if you've ever eaten in North African restaurants, you'll recognize its bright, savory flavor. Lamb from the neck, which is often sold for kebabs, will work well here, but I prefer to buy boneless leg of lamb and cut it into cubes myself, as the meat is leaner and will absorb the seasonings more quickly.

Note: Double either the tempeh or the lamb to serve only one kind of kebab.

Tip: There's no such thing as medium-rare tempeh—it becomes palatable only when it's fully cooked—so simmering is necessary before the final grilling, which gives the tempeh a charred, smoky flavor.

CHARMOULA

⅓ cup fresh lemon juice

½ cup packed coarsely chopped fresh flat-leaf parsley

½ cup packed coarsely chopped fresh cilantro

4 garlic cloves, peeled

2½ teaspoons sea salt or kosher salt

2 teaspoons ground cumin, preferably toasted and freshly ground (see page 12)

1 teaspoon ground coriander, preferably toasted and freshly ground

1 teaspoon sweet paprika

⅛ teaspoon cayenne pepper

½ cup extra-virgin olive oil

12 ounces boneless lamb, cut into 1½-inch cubes

⅔ cup water

8 ounces tempeh, cut into 1½-inch cubes

Assorted vegetables, such as summer squash, bell peppers, cherry tomatoes, and onions (optional)

FOR THE CHARMOULA: In a food processor, combine the lemon juice, parsley, cilantro, garlic, salt, cumin, coriander, paprika, and cayenne and process to a smooth paste. Add the oil and process until thoroughly combined.

FOR THE LAMB: Place the cubed lamb in a bowl, add half the charmoula, and toss to coat. Cover and refrigerate for at least 2 hours, or overnight.

Soak four 10- to 12-inch or eight 4- to 6-inch wooden skewers in cold water for at least 1 hour, or use metal skewers.

Light a grill fire.

FOR THE TEMPEH: Whisk the remaining charmoula with the water. Arrange the tempeh cubes in one layer in a large skillet and pour the charmoula mixture over them. Bring to a simmer over high heat, cover, reduce the heat to medium, and cook until most of the liquid is absorbed and the white streaks in the tempeh have disappeared, so it is uniform in color all the way through, about 15 minutes. If the pan looks dry before the tempeh is cooked through, add a little more water.

Thread the lamb and tempeh (separately) onto the skewers, alternating with the optional vegetables, if desired. Grill the kebabs, turning occasionally, until well charred on all sides, 8 to 12 minutes. Serve.

Summer Vegetable Simmer

SERVES 4

You can also serve this ragout over pasta or plain grilled fish or chicken. Or combine it with a little yogurt or cream and puree it, and you'll have a great soup to serve hot or chilled.

⅓ cup extra-virgin olive oil

1 medium onion, halved and thinly sliced

Sea salt or kosher salt

2 garlic cloves, chopped

1 small jalapeño, seeded and chopped, or a large pinch of red pepper flakes, or to taste

3 medium zucchini (about 1½ pounds), halved, seeded, and sliced ½ inch thick

3 large ripe tomatoes (about 1½ pounds), peeled, seeded, and chopped

Freshly ground black pepper

2 tablespoons torn fresh mint leaves

In a large skillet, heat the olive oil over medium-high heat. Add the onion and a pinch of salt and cook, stirring occasionally, until the onion is softened but not browned, about 5 minutes. Add the garlic and jalapeño or pepper flakes and cook, stirring, for another minute or two.

Tomato Tactics

Often the extra step of peeling and seeding tomatoes noticeably improves the taste and texture of a dish. The skins separate from the flesh during cooking and end up as tough little bits, while the pulpy seeds can water down a sauce and give a bitter edge to cooked dishes. To peel tomatoes, core them, score an X in the bottom of each one, and plunge them into a large pot of boiling water just until the skins loosen, about 30 seconds. Drain and peel under cool running water. To seed a tomato, halve it and use your fingers to scrape out the seedy pulp. You'll be left with the dense, fruity tomato flesh.

Add the zucchini and tomatoes and season with another pinch of salt and a few grinds of pepper. Raise the heat to high and bring to a boil, then cover, reduce the heat slightly, and simmer rapidly for 5 minutes, stirring occasionally.

Uncover the pan, add the mint, and simmer, stirring, until the liquid has thickened, 4 to 5 more minutes. Season with additional salt and pepper to taste, remove from the heat, and let cool. Serve at room temperature or chilled.

Couscous with Dried Fruit and Pine Nuts

SERVES 4

Making couscous is as easy as boiling water. Here the tiny grains of pasta gain texture, color, and flavor from the dried fruit, which plumps up as the couscous softens.

> 1½ **cups water**
> 2 **tablespoons extra-virgin olive oil or unsalted butter**
> **Sea salt or kosher salt**
> 1 **cup quick-cooking couscous (regular or whole wheat)**
> ⅓ **cup chopped mixed dried fruit, such as sour cherries, apricots, raisins, and dates**
> ¼ **cup chopped fresh mint, flat-leaf parsley, or cilantro, or a combination**
> 3 **tablespoons pine nuts, toasted (see page 11)**

In a small saucepan, combine the water, olive oil or butter, and ½ teaspoon salt and bring to a boil. Turn off the heat and stir in the couscous and dried fruit. Cover and set aside until all the water is absorbed, about 15 minutes.

Fluff the couscous and transfer to a serving bowl. Stir in the herbs and pine nuts and serve hot or warm.

Summer

MENU 2
SERVES 4

Summer Bean Ratatouille

Portobello Mushrooms/Steak with Bread Crumb Salsa

Arugula Salad with Mustard Vinaigrette

The ratatouille in this menu is more substantial than the traditional Niçoise ver-sion, thanks to the addition of fresh shell beans. Served with slices of charred steak or mushrooms, a tangy bread crumb salsa, and a crisp, slightly peppery salad, it makes a robust meal. Use a hearty red wine for the ratatouille, and then serve the rest of the bottle.

THE PLAN
1. Make the ratatouille (rewarm before serving, if desired).
2. Marinate the onions for the salsa.
3. Toast the bread crumbs for the salsa.
4. Prepare the salad ingredients (refrigerate the arugula).
5. Grill or roast the mushrooms.
6. Meanwhile, grill or pan-roast the steak.
7. Finish the salsa.
8. Toss the salad.

Summer Bean Ratatouille

SERVES 4 TO 6

In this ratatouille, the eggplant and shell beans absorb the flavors of the zucchini and tomatoes. The final step of reducing the vegetable cooking liquid gives the finished dish a lustrous, jammy sheen and an earthy intensity.

Tip: A standard chef's knife is 10 inches long and most paring knives are 3 to 4 inches, but I often find myself reaching for a 6-inch knife for cutting vegetables. It's more precise and flexible than a chef's knife, yet long enough to make it all the way through an onion or eggplant. I am fond of the Japanese-made knives of this size, usually called fish or vegetable knives, which serve the purpose beautifully.

1 pound fresh shell beans, such as cranberry beans, black-eyed peas, or chickpeas, shelled (about 1½ cups), or one 15-ounce can pinto beans, rinsed and drained

2–3 sprigs fresh thyme

1 bay leaf if using fresh beans

Sea salt or kosher salt

⅓ cup extra-virgin olive oil

2 medium red onions, chopped

1 teaspoon cumin seeds

1 pound plum tomatoes (5–6), cored, seeded (see page 102), and coarsely chopped

1 1-pound eggplant, cut into 1-inch cubes

1 red bell pepper, cored, seeded, and cut into 1-inch pieces

1 yellow bell pepper, cored, seeded, and cut into 1-inch pieces

1 large sprig fresh flat-leaf parsley

1 pound small zucchini, diced

3 garlic cloves, coarsely chopped

½ teaspoon red pepper flakes, or to taste

1 cup dry red wine, such as Côtes du Rhône or Shiraz

If using fresh beans, place them in a pot with 1 thyme sprig, the bay leaf, and cold water to cover by ½ inch. Bring to a boil over high heat, then reduce the heat and simmer, partially covered, until just tender, about 15 minutes, adding a little more water if needed to keep the beans covered. Season with ½ teaspoon salt and simmer, uncovered, for 5 more minutes. Drain the beans (reserve their liquid for soup, if desired) and discard the thyme and bay leaf.

In a large heavy pot, heat the olive oil over medium-high heat until shimmering. Add the onions, cumin, and 2 teaspoons salt and cook, stirring, until the onions are soft but not browned, about 10 minutes.

Add the tomatoes, eggplant, bell peppers, parsley sprig, and the remaining 1 or 2 thyme sprigs. Stir to combine, cover, and simmer, covered, for 8 to 10 minutes, stirring occasionally. Stir in the zucchini, garlic, red pepper flakes, wine, and drained beans or canned beans. Reduce the heat to medium-low and simmer, covered, until the vegetables are tender, about 20 minutes.

Transfer the ratatouille to a large bowl, then set a large strainer over the pot and pour the ratatouille into the strainer (set the bowl aside). Discard the herb sprigs. Let drain for 10 minutes, then shake the strainer to release as much liquid as possible into the pot. Return the ratatouille to the bowl.

Bring the strained liquid to a simmer over high heat and simmer until it reduces to a glaze, about 5 minutes (you will have about ⅓ cup liquid). Use a rubber spatula to scrape the liquid into the ratatouille and stir to combine. Serve warm or at room temperature.

Portobello Mushrooms/**Steak** with Bread Crumb Salsa

You certainly don't *need* to embellish this menu with the bread crumb topping—there's plenty to enjoy without it—but it adds an enticing textural element, and the same flavors of garlic, herbs, and red onion weave through the rest of the meal. This crispy mixture is equally good sprinkled over roasted or grilled rich fish such as salmon, mackerel, or sardines, over dark-meat chicken, and over bean dishes or grilled zucchini and eggplant.

You can roast the mushrooms and pan-roast the steak or light the grill and take your cooking outside.

Note: You can serve either the mushroom or the steak version and double it if serving 4.

Tip: Whenever you sear a protein in a pan, it's important that the protein be absolutely dry so you get a golden brown sear—that nicely browned exterior gives the protein its rich savor. Use a few paper towels to pat the meat or other protein dry after you unwrap it.

BREAD CRUMB SALSA

⅓ cup finely chopped red onion

1 small garlic clove, finely chopped

¾ teaspoon sea salt or kosher salt

Red wine vinegar

1½ cups packed bread crumbs made from fresh or day-old bread (see page 263)

¼ cup extra-virgin olive oil

⅓ cup packed chopped mixed fresh herbs, such as flat-leaf parsley, thyme, tarragon, cilantro, basil, and/or mint

MUSHROOMS

2 large portobello mushroom caps, wiped clean with a damp towel

Extra-virgin olive oil, for brushing

Sea salt or kosher salt and freshly ground black pepper

STEAK

1 14- to 16-ounce strip steak, 1 inch thick

2 teaspoons sea salt or kosher salt

1 teaspoon freshly ground black pepper

1 tablespoon extra-virgin olive oil if pan-roasting

Preheat the oven to 400 degrees. Light a grill if grilling the mushrooms and steak.

FOR THE SALSA: In a small bowl, combine the onion, garlic, and ¼ teaspoon of the salt. Pour in enough red wine vinegar to barely cover the onion.

Spread the bread crumbs on a rimmed baking sheet and drizzle the olive oil over them, tossing to coat. Bake, tossing well halfway through, until the crumbs are golden brown and crisp, about 12 minutes. Use a rubber spatula to scrape the crumbs onto a plate and let cool. Leave the oven on if you are not going to grill the mushrooms and steak.

FOR THE MUSHROOMS: Brush the mushrooms generously with olive oil and season them on both sides with salt and pepper.

To grill, place the mushrooms on the hot grill and cook, turning once, until they are cooked through and slightly charred, about 15 minutes.

To roast, place the mushrooms gill side down in a baking dish and roast until cooked through, about 15 minutes.

FOR THE STEAK: Pat the steak dry with paper towels. In a small dish, combine the salt and pepper. Season the meat on both sides with this mixture.

To grill, place the steak on a medium-hot grill and cook, turning once, until done to taste, about 4 minutes per side for medium-rare.

To pan-roast, heat a large heavy skillet, preferably cast-iron, over high heat for several minutes. Add the olive oil, and when it just begins to smoke, add the steak. Cook until well browned on the first side, about 3 minutes. Flip the steak and sear for another 2 minutes.

Transfer the pan to the oven and roast until done to taste, about 2 minutes for medium-rare. Transfer to a cutting board and let rest for 5 to 10 minutes.

TO FINISH THE SALSA: Drain the onion mixture well. In a medium bowl, toss the onion with the bread crumbs, herbs, and the remaining ½ teaspoon salt.

Slice the mushrooms and steak and serve sprinkled with the salsa.

Arugula Salad with Mustard Vinaigrette

The kick of peppery arugula and mustard wakes up the rich, deep flavors of the ratatouille, mushrooms, and steak in this menu.

> **1 tablespoon fresh lemon juice**
>
> **1 tablespoon Dijon mustard**
>
> **2 tablespoons extra-virgin olive oil**
>
> **2 bunches arugula (about 8 ounces), trimmed and torn**
>
> **Sea salt or kosher salt and freshly ground black pepper**

In a bowl, beat the lemon juice and mustard together with a fork. Beating constantly, drizzle in the oil and beat until thoroughly blended.

Place the arugula in a large salad bowl, season it with a pinch of salt and pepper to taste, and toss with the dressing to coat. Serve.

Take Your Greens for a Spin

If your greens aren't thoroughly dry, the dressing won't cling to them and your salad will be soggy and tasteless. Avoid this by firing up your salad spinner not once, but twice: spin the greens dry, pour the water out of the spinner bowl, shake the greens to wake them from their spun torpor, and then spin again—you'll be amazed by how much more water you will get the second time around.

Summer

MENU 3
SERVES 4

Grilled Shrimp in Harissa

Fresh Corn Polenta with Sautéed Cherry Tomatoes

Grilled Zucchini with Mint Oil

Warm, sunny corn polenta is topped with a fresh, quick tomato sauce, to serve with the shrimp and zucchini in this menu. Vegetarians can add a fried egg or two if they want. The vivid colors and flavors of the meal are a reflection of the season's vibrant energy. The cool, refreshing mint balances the spicy, smoky shrimp and zucchini.

Note: You can double the shrimp recipe if everyone is having some.

THE PLAN
1. Salt the zucchini and make the mint oil.
2. Make the polenta and keep warm.
3. Meanwhile, marinate the shrimp.
4. Sauté the tomatoes.
5. Grill or broil the zucchini and shrimp.
6. Fry the eggs, if desired.

Grilled Shrimp in Harissa

SERVES 2

Harissa is a spicy North African condiment that is simple to make at home and far better than the canned version sold in Middle Eastern stores. Toasting and then grinding the whole spices allows their aromas to bloom. When the shrimp is marinated in the spice paste and grilled, the heat of the grill continues the process, bringing out the depth of the cumin, caraway, fennel, cayenne, and garlic. The harissa also contains lemon juice, and the acid will firm up the shrimp; it's important not to overmarinate here, as the acid will eventually toughen the shrimp.

Harissa has many other uses. Try brushing it on just-grilled artisanal bread, top with a slice of tomato and an anchovy if desired, and serve as an appetizer. Or dress warm potatoes and green beans with a spoonful for a racy potato salad. In cooler weather, toss potatoes with a little harissa before roasting them.

If you can't get excellent shrimp for this recipe, substitute scallops or chunks of firm-fleshed fish such as swordfish, monkfish, or halibut.

Tip: If grilling the shrimp, use a grilling rack to keep them from falling through the grate, or skewer them before grilling.

HARISSA

2 teaspoons ground cumin, preferably toasted and freshly ground (see page 12)

½ teaspoon ground fennel, preferably toasted and freshly ground

½ teaspoon ground caraway, preferably toasted and freshly ground

½ teaspoon cayenne pepper, or to taste

1 teaspoon sea salt or kosher salt

5 tablespoons extra-virgin olive oil

¼ cup fresh lemon juice

2 large garlic cloves, finely chopped

1 pound large shrimp, peeled, leaving the tail section on, and deveined

Light a grill if grilling the shrimp.

FOR THE HARISSA: In a medium bowl, stir together the cumin, fennel, caraway, cayenne, and salt. Whisk in the olive oil, lemon juice, and garlic.

Toss the shrimp in the harissa, and marinate for 10 to 15 minutes.

Preheat the broiler if not grilling the shrimp.

Place the shrimp on the broiler pan if broiling, and broil or grill, turning once, until cooked through, about 3 minutes per side. Serve.

Fresh Corn Polenta with Sautéed Cherry Tomatoes

SERVES 4

This polenta is a great way to savor corn in both dried and fresh forms, the whole corn kernels adding sweet flavor and texture. A mix of different small tomatoes, such as pear, grape, orange, and cherry tomatoes, in various colors (check the farmers' market) will make it a real showstopper. The tomatoes are tossed with garlic and herbs and cooked until they begin to break down and become a sauce, while still retaining their color. An egg on top rounds things out for anyone who doesn't eat shrimp—I use the recipe for Spanish-Style Eggs on page 300, but you can prepare the eggs however you prefer, whether over easy, poached, or hard-cooked and sliced.

POLENTA

- 3 cups water
- 2 tablespoons unsalted butter
- 1 teaspoon sea salt or kosher salt
- 1 cup medium corn grits
- 1 cup corn kernels (from 1 large or 2 small ears)
- 1 scallion, trimmed, green part thinly sliced, white part chopped and reserved for the tomatoes

CHERRY TOMATOES

- ¼ cup extra-virgin olive oil
- 2 pints cherry tomatoes
- 2 garlic cloves, finely chopped
- ½ teaspoon red pepper flakes
- ¼ cup chopped mixed fresh herbs, such as oregano, tarragon, basil, and flat-leaf parsley
- Sea salt or kosher salt and freshly ground black pepper

- Fried eggs (see headnote above; optional)
- Freshly grated Parmesan cheese, for serving

Preheat the oven to 200 degrees.

FOR THE POLENTA: In a medium ovenproof saucepan, bring the water to a boil over high heat. Add the butter and salt, then stir in the grits and the corn and continue to stir until the water returns to a boil. Reduce the heat and simmer, stirring occasionally, until the polenta is thick, 5 to 7 minutes. Stir in the scallion green. Cover the pan and transfer to the oven to keep warm.

FOR THE TOMATOES: In a 12- to 14-inch skillet or large enameled cast-iron casserole dish, combine the oil, tomatoes, garlic, reserved scallion white, and the red pepper flakes and cook over high heat, stirring, until the tomatoes soften and begin to release their juices, 3 to 4 minutes. Stir in the herbs and cook for 2 more minutes. Season with salt and pepper, and remove from the heat.

Divide the polenta among four shallow soup plates. If serving with the eggs, slide them onto the polenta. Spoon the tomatoes on top. Serve sprinkled with Parmesan.

Grilled Zucchini with Mint Oil

Salting draws out moisture and firms up the zucchini, but if you're short on time, you can skip this step and allow for a slightly longer cooking time.

Leftover mint oil is great for grilling fish. Or use it in a salad dressing, brush on crostini, or drizzle over fresh mozzarella or warm pasta.

> 3 medium zucchini (1½ pounds), sliced lengthwise ½ inch thick
> Sea salt or kosher salt
> ½ cup extra-virgin olive oil
> 3 garlic cloves, thinly sliced
> ¼ teaspoon red pepper flakes
> 2 tablespoons coarsely chopped fresh mint
> 2 teaspoons red wine vinegar
> Freshly ground black pepper

Sprinkle the zucchini slices all over with salt. Lay them out flat on kitchen or paper towels to drain for 30 minutes.

Meanwhile, in a small saucepan, combine the oil, garlic, and red pepper flakes, bring just to a simmer, and simmer gently until the garlic is golden, 5 to 7 minutes. Add the mint and take the pan off the heat.

Light a grill or preheat the broiler.

Pat the zucchini dry and lightly brush the tops of the slices with mint oil. Place them oiled side down on the grill or broiler pan and lightly brush the tops of the slices with mint oil. Grill or broil, turning once, until softened and nicely browned, 4 to 5 minutes per side.

Transfer the zucchini to a platter. Drizzle with 3 tablespoons of the remaining mint oil and the vinegar, season with salt and pepper, and serve.

Summer

MENU 4
SERVES 4

Chilled Melon Soup

Salade Niçoise with Many Possibilities

This casual menu is easy on the cook and ideal for steamy summer days. The chilled soup takes minutes to prepare, and the salad is set out buffet-style, so diners can assemble their own, choosing tuna, eggs, cheese, or beans, or a little of everything. Add a good loaf of bread and a bottle of dry rosé for a lovely meal that can even be packed up and taken on a picnic.

THE PLAN

1. Make the soup and chill it.
2. Hard-cook the optional eggs and make the red onions, if serving.
3. Make the vinaigrette.
4. Make the salad.

Chilled Melon Soup

This simple soup depends entirely on the quality of your ingredients. Because both the sweetness of the melon and the heat of the jalapeño can vary considerably, the measurements for the chili and honey, as well as the fresh lime juice, are all to taste. Ripe mango makes a nice addition to this soup, either blended in or cubed as a garnish instead of the optional crab. I've made the soup using habanero pepper, Tabasco, or cayenne pepper instead of the jalapeño, spicing it to taste.

Tip: Filling the blender one-quarter full with melon and pureeing it, then adding the remaining melon piece by piece, results in the smoothest soup.

> 1 large cantaloupe (about 4 pounds), halved, seeded, peeled, and coarsely chopped
> ¼ cup heavy cream
> 1 tablespoon chopped fresh mint
> ½ small jalapeño, seeds and veins removed, minced, or to taste
> Fresh lime juice to taste (from up to 1 lime)
> 1–2 teaspoons honey, or to taste
> Sea salt or kosher salt
>
> **Optional garnishes**
> 8 ounces lump crabmeat, picked over for shells and cartilage
> Crème fraîche
> Diced mango

Fill a blender a quarter full with melon chunks and pulse to puree. With the motor running, add the remaining melon piece by piece, pureeing until smooth (you may need to blend in two batches). Blend in the cream and mint.

Add the jalapeño a little at a time, blending and tasting until the heat level is right for you. Season with lime juice, honey, and salt to taste.

Pour the soup into a bowl, cover, and refrigerate until thoroughly chilled (see Tip, page 144 for a quick-chill technique).

Serve garnished with the crabmeat, crème fraîche, and/or mango, if desired.

Salade Niçoise with Many Possibilities

SERVES 4: 2 SERVINGS WITH TUNA, 2 SERVINGS WITH CHEESE

Niçoise salad is traditionally prepared with canned tuna, but I like to use a seared fresh tuna steak here, which makes the dish feel more like an entrée. The tuna is optional—the salad is substantial even without it—and a serving of cheese is equally delicious.

A big composed salad like this is ripe for improvisation and flexible eating, since each diner composes the meal to his or her liking. Tofu marinated with garlic and mint (page 38), grilled instead of being cooked under the pan on the stovetop, would be a great addition, with or without the tuna and eggs. Just be sure to include the small, briny black Niçoise olives, or you'll have to make up another name for the salad!

Note: Diners can choose tuna and/or cheese for their salads—many will want both.

CAPER VINAIGRETTE

¾ cup extra-virgin olive oil

¼ cup white wine vinegar

2 tablespoons Dijon mustard

4 teaspoons capers, rinsed and drained

2 medium garlic cloves, peeled

2 teaspoons fresh thyme leaves

SALAD

1 pound new red potatoes (about 4 medium), peeled and sliced ½ inch thick

8 ounces green beans, trimmed

Sea salt or kosher salt and freshly ground black pepper

8 ounces fresh cranberry beans, shelled (about ¾ cup) and cooked (see page 8), or half a 15-ounce can chickpeas, rinsed and drained

TUNA (OPTIONAL)

1 8-ounce tuna steak, about ½ inch thick

Olive oil, for searing

Sea salt or kosher salt and freshly ground black pepper

12 ounces (about 12 cups) young lettuce, torn

    4 **hard-cooked eggs, quartered (see page 56; optional)**

    Pickled Red Onions (recipe follows; optional)

    Cured anchovies (optional)

    2 **ounces cheese, such as fresh mozzarella, French feta, Monterey Jack, or young pecorino, cubed**

    4 **plum tomatoes, sliced, or 1 cup cherry tomatoes, halved**

12–16 **Niçoise olives**

    Sliced cucumbers

FOR THE VINAIGRETTE: In a blender, combine all the ingredients and blend until smooth.

If grilling the optional tuna, light a grill.

FOR THE SALAD: Fit a pot with a steamer rack, add an inch or two of water to the pot, and bring to a boil. Place the potatoes on the steamer rack, cover, and steam for 6 minutes. Arrange the green beans on top of the potatoes and steam until the potatoes are tender and the beans are crisp-tender, about 4 minutes.

Spread a kitchen towel on a baking sheet and spread the green beans and potatoes on the towel to drain for a minute or two; leave the water in the steamer at a simmer.

Transfer the green beans to a bowl and season them with salt and pepper. Toss with 1 tablespoon of the vinaigrette.

Transfer the potatoes to another bowl, season with salt and pepper, and toss with 1 tablespoon of the vinaigrette.

Place the cranberry beans or chickpeas on the steaming rack, cover, and steam for 2 minutes to warm them. Transfer to a bowl, season with salt and pepper, and toss with 1 tablespoon of the vinaigrette.

FOR THE OPTIONAL TUNA: If not grilling the tuna, heat a heavy skillet over high heat until very hot, about 2 minutes.

Rub the tuna lightly on both sides with oil and season it with salt and pepper. Grill or sear until lightly browned on the first side, about 1 minute. Flip and cook until browned on the second side and done to taste, about 1 minute more for rare. Transfer to a cutting board and let rest for a few minutes, then slice the tuna against the grain into ⅓-inch-thick slices.

In a large bowl, season the lettuce with salt and pepper and toss with 2 tablespoons of the vinaigrette.

TO ASSEMBLE THE SALAD: Place the eggs, pickled onions, and anchovies (if using), the cheese, tomatoes, olives, cucumbers, and tuna, if using, on a platter. Mound the lettuce in four shallow salad bowls. Surround the lettuce with the potatoes, mound the cranberry beans or chickpeas on the lettuce, and pile the green beans on top. Let your guests add their own ingredients as desired. Pass the remaining vinaigrette at the table.

Pickled Red Onions

MAKES ABOUT 1 CUP

Tangy red onion slices are great on salads and sandwiches.

> 2 tablespoons white wine vinegar
>
> 1 tablespoon sugar
>
> 1 tablespoon sea salt or kosher salt
>
> 1 cup water
>
> 1 medium red onion, thinly sliced

In a 16-ounce jar or covered container, combine the vinegar, sugar, salt, and water. Add the onion, press it down into the liquid to submerge it, cover, and refrigerate for at least 30 minutes. The onions will keep refrigerated for up to 1 month.

Summer

MENU 5
SERVES 4 TO 6

Tofu with Lemon, Soy, White Wine, and Butter Sauce

Striped Bass with Lemon, White Wine, and Butter Sauce

Quinoa Salad with Green Beans, Corn, and Tomatoes

This is one of those meals that I'd never have thought of if I hadn't been feeding fish eaters and vegetarians at the same time. The classic combination of lemon, wine, and butter with fish is the inspiration for a similar treatment, incorporating soy sauce, for tofu. Add a jubilee of a grain salad, bursting with bright colors and flavors, and you've got a meal that will satisfy everyone—especially the proud cook.

Note: If you're serving 4 to 6 diners with the same preferences, you can double either the fish or the tofu and leave the other dish out.

THE PLAN
1. Cook the quinoa.
2. Blanch the corn and green beans.
3. Make the salad.
4. Bake the fish and tofu.

Tofu with Lemon, Soy, White Wine, and Butter Sauce

SERVES 2 TO 3

The combination of butter and soy sauce is unexpected and delicious. This preparation is a luscious fusion of Asian ingredients and French technique that creates a new way to enjoy the texture of tofu.

1 pound firm tofu, sliced into six ½-inch-thick slabs

¼ cup dry white wine

2 tablespoons soy sauce, preferably naturally brewed

2 tablespoons fresh lemon juice

2 teaspoons honey

3 tablespoons unsalted butter, cubed

2 tablespoons finely chopped shallot

1 ½-inch slice fresh ginger, peeled and finely chopped

½ teaspoon sea salt or kosher salt

Pinch of red pepper flakes

3–4 sprigs fresh thyme or rosemary

Set a rack in the upper third of the oven and preheat the oven to 400 degrees.

Lay the tofu in a small ovenproof skillet that will hold it comfortably without overlapping.

In a small bowl, stir together the wine, soy sauce, lemon juice, and honey. Scatter the butter cubes, shallot, and ginger over the tofu, pour the wine mixture over and around, and season the tofu with the salt and red pepper flakes. Scatter the thyme or rosemary sprigs over the tofu.

Bring to a boil over high heat, then transfer the pan to the oven and bake for 10 minutes.

Place the pan over high heat, bring the sauce to a simmer, and simmer until it begins to thicken, 3 to 5 minutes. Discard the herbs and serve the tofu drizzled with the pan sauce.

Striped Bass with Lemon, White Wine, and Butter Sauce

SERVES 2 TO 3

The fast pan sauce is a traditional technique that you can memorize, to pull out whenever you have fillets of firm white fish, whether it be striped bass, cod, hake, halibut, or snapper.

Tip: Warming the serving platter or dinner plates is a nice touch here, since the cooked fish spends a couple minutes out of the pan while the sauce is finished. You can warm the plates in a low oven. Or, if you need to warm a lot of dinner plates for a party, put them in an empty dishwasher and set the machine to the hot air drying cycle.

> 1 1-pound striped bass fillet
>
> 3 tablespoons unsalted butter, cubed
>
> 2 tablespoons finely chopped shallot
>
> ⅓ cup dry white wine
>
> 2 tablespoons fresh lemon juice
>
> Sea salt or kosher salt
>
> Pinch of red pepper flakes
>
> 3–4 sprigs fresh thyme or tarragon

Set a rack in the upper third of the oven and preheat the oven to 400 degrees.

Lay the fish in an ovenproof skillet that will hold it comfortably (cut it in half if necessary). Scatter the butter cubes and shallot over the fish, pour the wine and lemon juice over and around, and season the fish with salt and the red pepper flakes. Scatter the thyme or tarragon sprigs over the fish.

Bring to a boil over high heat, then transfer the pan to the oven and bake until a thermometer inserted into the center of the fish registers 125 to 130 degrees, about 10 minutes, or until the fish is cooked through but still moist. Discard the herbs and transfer the fish to a warm platter.

Place the pan over high heat, bring the sauce to a simmer, and simmer until it begins to thicken, 2 to 3 minutes. Pour the sauce over the fish and serve.

Quinoa Salad with Green Beans, Corn, and Tomatoes

SERVES 4 TO 6

If you have tender young green beans that are so sweet you could eat them raw, just blanch them briefly along with the corn. They'll take the same amount of time. But try a bean first—if it seems a little tough, boil the beans separately, as described below, to be sure they cook through. I like to use red quinoa here, which is nutty-tasting and has a striking mahogany color, but you can use any kind.

>   1 cup red quinoa
>   Sea salt or kosher salt
>   2 ears corn, shucked
>   8 ounces green beans, trimmed and cut into 1-inch lengths
>   1 cup cherry or grape tomatoes, quartered, or halved if small
>   ¼ cup extra-virgin olive oil, plus 1 teaspoon if using pumpkin seeds
>   ¼ cup pumpkin seeds (optional)
>   2 tablespoons fresh lemon juice
>   ½ cup fresh flat-leaf parsley leaves
>   2 tablespoons chopped fresh chives

In a small pot, combine the quinoa with 2 cups water and ½ teaspoon salt and bring to a boil over high heat. Reduce the heat slightly, cover, and simmer until the water is absorbed, about 15 minutes. Take the pan off the heat and let sit, still covered, for 5 minutes.

Spread the quinoa on a rimmed baking sheet and let cool to room temperature.

Bring a large pot of salted water to a boil. Add the corn and boil, uncovered, until tender, 3 to 5 minutes. Lift the corn from the water, leaving the water over the heat, and rinse under cold water until cool. Drain well.

Add the green beans to the water and boil, uncovered, until crisp-tender, 3 to 5 minutes, or longer if necessary. Drain the beans and spread them on a towel-lined baking sheet to cool.

One at a time, hold each ear of corn upright on a cutting board and slide a knife down the cob from top to bottom to slice off the kernels.

In a large serving bowl, toss together the quinoa, green beans, corn, and tomatoes.

If using pumpkin seeds, heat the 1 teaspoon olive oil in a small skillet over medium-high heat. Add the seeds and toast, tossing, until the seeds begin to make popping sounds and are golden brown, 2 to 3 minutes. Transfer to a plate to cool.

Toss the salad with the ¼ cup olive oil, the lemon juice, and ½ teaspoon salt, or to taste. Sprinkle with the pumpkin seeds (if using), parsley, and chives and serve.

Don't Shock Me

Most salad recipes that include green beans instruct you to blanch the beans by plunging them into boiling water until crisp-tender, then draining and "shocking" them in an ice water bath to stop the cooking before draining again. I'm not thrilled about this multistep procedure, since the beans tend to lose flavor and become waterlogged. Instead, I drain the warm beans while they're still quite crisp and spread them on a baking sheet lined with a kitchen towel, which absorbs water and helps them cool more quickly than they would piled up in a colander. The slightly warm, very dry beans take to the dressing like a cat takes to a sunny windowsill. Once they're dressed, I chill the beans in the refrigerator.

Summer

MENU 6
SERVES 4

Seafood/Tofu Ceviche with Quick-Pickled Red Onion

Zucchini-Rice Soup with Basil and Parmesan

These recipes make it easy on the cook and are cooling to eat. The zucchini soup can be served warm or at room temperature, in the Mediterranean style, and the zesty ceviche, which you can make with fish or tofu or both, is served chilled, so think of this light yet sustaining combination for scorching nights.

THE PLAN
1. Marinate the onions.
2. Cook the soup.
3. Meanwhile, marinate the seafood and tofu.
4. Make the ceviche.

The Appeal of Peeling Peppers

You may have grilled or roasted bell peppers to remove their skins (see page 160), which gives them a smoky taste and melting texture, but did you know you can also just peel them with a vegetable peeler? First quarter the pepper and trim away its seeds and veins, then flatten the slices on your work surface and peel them. Pepper peeling is hardly obligatory, but when you have the time, the results are crisp yet tender peppers if left raw, or absolutely melting if they're cooked.

Seafood/Tofu Ceviche
with Quick-Pickled Red Onion

SERVES 4: 2 SERVINGS FISH, 2 SERVINGS TOFU

Ceviche, which essentially uses a brief pickling technique, is a South American coastal approach to raw fish. The fish is tossed with an acid, usually citrus juice, which quickly renders it opaque, as though it had been cooked. Whereas mixing raw fish with acid firms its flesh, when you mix raw tofu with acid, its texture begins to break down and soften. Giving both fish and tofu the ceviche treatment means the two proteins end up with a similar pleasing texture.

If you soak the hiziki as soon as you start cooking this dish, it will be ready to toss in by the time the ceviche is prepared. Sea beans, also called samphire, are a fresh, crunchy, twiglike green sea vegetable with a briny taste. If you come across them, they can be substituted for the dried hiziki.

Always confirm with your fishmonger that the fish you're using can be eaten raw (any labeled "sushi-grade" is good to go, but there may be other options).

When you're working with raw fish, cold is key. Keep the fish in the refrigerator for all but the minute you spend rinsing, drying, and chopping it.

Note: Double the amount of fish or tofu, if you like, to serve just one version to your guests.

PICKLED ONIONS

3 tablespoons red wine vinegar

3 tablespoons water

1 tablespoon sugar

2 teaspoons sea salt or kosher salt

¾ cup very thinly sliced red onion

SEAFOOD

8 ounces skinless fluke fillets (or other mild white-fleshed fish, such as flounder, red snapper, or black sea bass), any thin dark central portion removed, cut into ½-inch cubes, or sea scallops, halved, or quartered if large

8 ounces firm tofu, rinsed well, gently pressed dry, and cut into ½-inch cubes

6 tablespoons fresh lime juice (from 2–3 limes)

3 tablespoons soy sauce, preferably naturally brewed

2 plum tomatoes, cored, halved lengthwise, seeded (see page 102), and diced

2 medium Kirby cucumbers, peeled if desired, seeded (see page 22), and cut into ½-inch cubes

1 medium yellow bell pepper, cored, quartered, ribs removed, peeled if desired (see page 131), and thinly sliced crosswise

¼ cup hiziki (see page 87), soaked in 1 cup warm water for 15 minutes

¼ cup chopped fresh cilantro

1 jalapeño, seeds and veins removed if desired, minced, or to taste

¼ cup extra-virgin olive oil

Freshly ground black pepper

1 head Bibb lettuce, separated into leaves

Sea salt or kosher salt

1 large avocado, pitted, peeled, quartered lengthwise, and sliced crosswise into ½-inch slices

Toasted sliced sourdough bread, for serving

FOR THE PICKLED ONIONS: Combine the vinegar, water, sugar, and salt in a bowl and whisk to dissolve the sugar and salt. Place the onion in a narrow jar and pour the pickling liquid over it. Cover, shake well, and refrigerate for at least 20 minutes.

TO MARINATE THE SEAFOOD/TOFU: Place the seafood and tofu in separate bowls and pour 3 tablespoons of the lime juice over each. Add 2 tablespoons of the soy sauce to the tofu and toss well. Add the remaining 1 tablespoon soy sauce to the seafood and toss well. Cover and refrigerate for 15 minutes.

Drain the onions, reserving the pickling liquid.

Divide the onions, tomatoes, cucumbers, and bell pepper between the bowls of ceviche. Add 2 tablespoons of the reserved onion marinade to each bowl.

Drain the hiziki, rinse it well, and then drain thoroughly. Toss half the hiziki into each bowl of ceviche. Divide the cilantro, jalapeño, and olive oil between the two bowls, season with pepper, and toss well.

Make a bed of lettuce leaves on each of four plates and season the lettuce lightly with salt. Top the lettuce with the ceviche. Garnish with the avocado, and serve with sourdough toast.

Zucchini-Rice Soup
with Basil and Parmesan

SERVES 4 TO 6

This easy, delectable Italian soup is made from water rather than stock, so the flavor of the garden-fresh vegetables shines through. You might think that the recipe calls for an enormous amount of zucchini, but the watery vegetable nearly melts, thickening the surrounding broth. Besides, there's so much zucchini around this time of year! For a pretty, summery look, I like to use a mix of zucchini and yellow summer squash.

I think the sweet, subtle flavor of this soup is best appreciated when it's warm, rather than piping hot. For anyone who doesn't eat cheese, sprinkle on a pinch of extra sea salt instead of the Parmesan.

Tip: To grate large quantities of a hard cheese, cut the cheese into chunks, place it in a food processor fitted with the regular blade, and pulse until the cheese is pulverized. While the texture will be slightly different than if you had finely grated the cheese by hand, it will sprinkle and melt just as well, and the processor method takes a fraction of the time.

¼ cup extra-virgin olive oil

1 large onion, finely chopped

Sea salt or kosher salt

1½ pounds zucchini (or half zucchini and half yellow summer squash), cut into ½-inch cubes

¼ cup thinly sliced garlic (6–8 cloves)

4 cups water

⅓ cup basmati rice

½ cup loosely packed fresh basil leaves, thinly sliced, plus additional thinly sliced leaves for garnish

⅓ cup freshly grated Parmesan cheese, plus additional for serving

Freshly ground black pepper

In a 4- to 5-quart Dutch oven or other heavy pot, heat 2 tablespoons of the oil over medium-high heat until shimmering. Add the onion and 1 teaspoon salt and toss well.

Cover and cook for 5 minutes. Add the zucchini and garlic and cook, stirring, until softened, about 2 minutes.

Pour in the water, raise the heat to high, and bring to a boil. Add the rice and basil, return to a boil, and simmer, covered, over low heat for 30 minutes, until the rice is tender.

Stir in the cheese and the remaining 2 tablespoons olive oil and season with salt and pepper to taste. Serve warm or at room temperature, garnished with sliced basil leaves. Pass additional grated Parmesan at the table.

Summer

MENU 7
SERVES 6

Gazpacho with Crumbled Feta Cheese

Farro with Corn, Red Beans, and Scallops/Avocado

This casual meal has a beach-house feel. Both the soup and grain salad are served cool, and the menu incorporates plenty of fresh farm stand offerings like corn, tomatoes, and herbs. The farro is a great accompaniment for seared scallops (or steamed lobster or crab), or top the vegetarian version with creamy cubes of avocado. Both the gazpacho and salad can be made in advance.

THE PLAN
1. Make the gazpacho and chill it.
2. Cook the farro.
3. Make the farro salad.

Gazpacho with Crumbled Feta Cheese

SERVES 6

Gazpacho is as full of vegetables as a big tossed salad. Seek out a bottle of high-quality tomato juice at a natural food store or specialty market rather than using the canned stuff, and you'll end up with a brighter-tasting soup. Be sure to chill the gazpacho thoroughly before serving, even chilling the soup bowls, if you like. If you prefer, skip the feta—the gazpacho is great unadorned too.

2 pounds tomatoes, peeled (see page 102), seeded, and chopped

2 cups tomato juice

2 tablespoons extra-virgin olive oil

1 cup seeded (see Tip, page 22) and finely diced peeled cucumber

1 cup finely diced yellow bell pepper

¼ cup finely diced red onion

2–3 tablespoons chopped mixed fresh herbs, such as basil, dill, cilantro, chives, and/or mint

1 jalapeño, ribs removed, seeded and finely chopped

1 large garlic clove, minced

2 teaspoons ground cumin, preferably toasted and freshly ground (see page 12)

1 tablespoon balsamic vinegar

Fresh lemon or lime juice to taste

Sea salt or kosher salt and freshly ground black pepper to taste

½ cup crumbled feta cheese, for serving

In a blender, combine the tomatoes with the tomato juice and olive oil, and puree. Transfer to a bowl and stir in the remaining ingredients (except the feta). Refrigerate until cold (or see Tip, page 144 for a quick-chill technique).

Serve the gazpacho garnished with crumbled feta cheese.

Farro with Corn, Red Beans, and Bacon/Soy Sauce and Scallops/Avocado

Dill awakens this hearty grain dish, which is smoky and rich if seasoned with the bacon and has a complex, subtle flavor if seasoned with the soy sauce. Leftovers are good served chilled.

Note: The recipe calls for putting the farro in two separate bowls and topping it with scallops or avocado or make one large bowl if you prefer. If you are so inclined, save the bacon fat to cook the scallops.

Tip: Farro, the partially hulled spelt grain, is an ancient relative of wheat that has been grown for food in Italy for centuries, and it is often safe for people who can't tolerate wheat gluten. Look for it in gourmet or Italian food markets. You can substitute pearl barley or whole unpolished wheat berries; whole wheat berries should be soaked overnight and will need to be simmered for up to 2 hours before they become tender.

FARRO

4 cups water

1 teaspoon sea salt or kosher salt

1 cup farro

¼ cup extra-virgin olive oil

2 cups corn kernels (from 3–4 ears)

1 15-ounce can red beans, rinsed and drained

1 cup chopped scallions (white and pale green parts)

¼ cup chopped fresh dill

Freshly ground black pepper

BACON AND SCALLOPS

6 slices bacon (4 ounces), cut crosswise into ¼-inch strips

1 pound sea scallops

Olive oil, for searing

Sea salt or kosher salt

Freshly ground black pepper

Squeeze of lemon juice

AVOCADO

2–3 teaspoons soy sauce, preferably naturally brewed, or to taste

1 avocado pitted and peeled

Squeeze of lime juice

Lime wedges, for serving

FOR THE FARRO: In a medium saucepan, bring the water to a boil over high heat. Add ½ teaspoon of the salt, then add the farro and boil until it is just tender, about 20 minutes. Drain in a colander or sieve, rinse under cold water to stop the cooking, and drain well.

FOR THE BACON: In a large heavy skillet, cook the bacon over medium-high heat, stirring occasionally, until it renders its fat and begins to crisp, 8 to 10 minutes. Transfer to a paper-towel-lined plate to drain. If desired, strain the bacon fat and save for cooking the scallops.

TO FINISH THE FARRO: In a large skillet, heat the oil over high heat. Add the corn, beans, and scallions and cook, stirring, until the vegetables begin to soften, 1 to 2 minutes. Stir in the farro. Add the dill and season with the remaining ½ teaspoon salt and pepper to taste.

Divide the farro between two serving bowls and stir the bacon into one of the bowls and the soy sauce into the other.

FOR THE SCALLOPS: Pat the scallops completely dry. Heat a large heavy skillet over medium-high heat until hot. Add a film of olive oil (or reserved bacon fat) to the pan, then add the scallops and sear, turning once, until nicely colored on each side, about 2 minutes. Season with salt, pepper, and a squeeze of lemon and remove from the heat.

FOR AVOCADO: Cube the avocado and toss with a little lime juice.

Top one bowl of farro and bacon with the seared scallops and the other with the avocado. Serve with lime wedges.

Scallop Sense

Buy scallops labeled "dry," which will vary slightly in color, rather than bleached white "wet" scallops, which have been soaked in preservatives and have a burstingly plump appearance. Dry scallops sear much better; wet scallops give off their liquid as they cool and will not brown well. If you can, smell the scallops before you bring them home to be sure they are fresh and sweet, without any ammoniac off aromas.

Summer

MENU 8
SERVES 4

Chilled Curried Red Lentil and Peach Soup

Spicy Grilled Chicken Wings with Lemon and Garlic

Baked Baby Eggplants Stuffed with Rice,
Feta, and Rosemary

Panzanella

This spread is a flexible feast, designed to be tailored to your needs. For a buffet or picnic, serve the eggplant and chicken wings with a sturdier salad and some bread instead of the panzanella (bread salad), since it will get mushy if prepared in advance. For a leisurely dinner al fresco, start with the soup, then toss the panzanella together and serve it with the eggplant and chicken wings. Close the meal with fresh summer fruits and sorbets.

You'll need to marinate the chicken wings at least 2 hours ahead (or preferably the night before) and make the soup in advance so it chills.

Note: The eggplant is the vegetarian main course here; for an entirely vegetarian menu to serve 4 to 6, double the recipe and omit the chicken wings. Alternatively, make a double or triple recipe of the chicken wings to serve 4, and skip the eggplant.

THE PLAN

1. Marinate the chicken wings.
2. Make and chill the soup.
3. Make the rice for the eggplant.
4. Make the curry powder if desired.
5. Stuff and bake the eggplant.
6. Prepare the ingredients for the panzanella.
7. Grill the chicken wings.
8. Assemble the panzanella.

Chilled Curried Red Lentil and Peach Soup

SERVES 6

In the early nineties, as the chef of Angelica Kitchen Restaurant, I contributed to an event to raise money for the homeless and hungry sponsored by Share Our Strength and American Express. Chefs from participating restaurants in New York City gathered at the Cathedral Church of St. John the Divine to offer up their specialties to the dining public. Peter Hoffman, the talented and passionate chef-owner of Savoy Restaurant, served a glorious chilled red lentil and peach soup with sheep's-milk yogurt. Here is my interpretation of that soup.

I use my own curry powder, which is mellow and highly aromatic. If you are using a purchased curry powder, be sure it is fresh and of high quality—the curry sold in plastic jars in most supermarkets doesn't offer much flavor. Madras-style curry, sold in tins, is a good option.

Dice the flesh of an extra peach or two to sprinkle on top of the soup as a pretty garnish if you like.

Tip: Want to chill a cold soup quickly? Fill a large bowl with water and ice. Pour the hot soup into a smaller bowl and set it in the ice water to cool, stirring the soup frequently and changing the ice water as it warms. Once the soup is cool, place it in the freezer for 20 or 30 minutes to chill it, stirring every 10 minutes so it doesn't start to freeze.

1½ cups split red lentils (available in health-food stores or Indian markets)

1 pound ripe peaches

2 tablespoons unsalted butter

1 large onion, chopped

Sea salt or kosher salt

1 tablespoon Mellow Curry Powder (recipe follows) or store-bought curry powder

2 teaspoons finely chopped peeled fresh ginger

1 cup dry white wine

1 tablespoon honey, or to taste

Finely grated zest of 1 lime

Squeeze of lime juice

Greek yogurt (or strained regular yogurt; see Tip, page 22), for serving

Chopped fresh cilantro, for garnish

Pick over the lentils and discard any pebbles or other foreign material. Put them in a strainer and rinse briefly under cold running water. In a medium saucepan, combine the lentils with 6 cups water and bring to a boil over high heat. Skim off and discard any foam that has risen to the surface, reduce the heat to low, and simmer, partially covered, until the lentils are tender, 25 to 30 minutes.

Meanwhile, bring a large pot of water to a boil. Add the peaches and blanch just until the skins loosen, 30 seconds to 1 minute. Drain the peaches in a colander and cool under cold running water. Peel and halve the peaches. Discard the pits and chop the flesh.

In a medium heavy pot, melt the butter over medium heat. Add the onion and ½ teaspoon salt, and cook, stirring, until the onion is translucent, 5 to 7 minutes. Stir in the peaches, curry powder, ginger, wine, and honey. Reduce the heat to low, cover, and cook for 15 minutes.

When the lentils are tender, add them (with their liquid) to the onion mixture and simmer, uncovered, for 5 more minutes.

With an immersion blender (or working in batches in a regular blender), puree the soup until smooth. Season with salt to taste. Let cool, then cover and refrigerate until cold, at least several hours, or overnight.

Add the lime zest to the soup and season with a squeeze of lime juice. Taste and add additional honey and/or salt if desired. Garnish each bowl of soup with a dollop of yogurt and a sprinkling of chopped cilantro.

Mellow Curry Powder

2 tablespoons coriander seeds

1 tablespoon cumin seeds

½ cinnamon stick

1 teaspoon caraway seeds

1 teaspoon fennel seeds

1 teaspoon whole black peppercorns

1½ tablespoons ground turmeric

1 teaspoon ground ginger

¼ teaspoon cayenne pepper

Combine the coriander, cumin, cinnamon, caraway, fennel seeds, and black peppercorns in a small skillet over medium heat and toast for 1 to 2 minutes until fragrant. Transfer to a mortar or spice mill. Add the turmeric, ginger, and cayenne and grind to a powder.

In a small bowl, whisk together all the spices. Store in a tightly sealed jar in a cool, dark place for up to 1 month.

Spicy Grilled Chicken Wings
with Lemon and Garlic

SERVES 2

Whenever I'm grilling chicken on the bone (a moister way to cook it), I partially cook it first both to speed the grilling and to prevent the exterior from drying out and overcharring before the meat has cooked through. Scoring the wings and simmering them in the marinade also infuses them with flavor.

You can multiply this recipe easily to serve as an hors d'oeuvre for a crowd.

- 8 chicken wings (about 2 pounds), wing tips removed
- ¼ cup fresh lemon juice
- 3 tablespoons soy sauce, preferably naturally brewed
- 1 red jalapeño pepper, finely chopped (ribs and seeds removed if you prefer a milder dish)
- 2 teaspoons finely chopped peeled fresh ginger or 1 teaspoon finely grated peeled fresh ginger
- 1 garlic clove, chopped
- 1 teaspoon chopped fresh rosemary
- Oil, for brushing
- Lemon wedges, for serving

Using a sharp knife, score the chicken wings diagonally several times on each side. In a bowl or large resealable plastic bag, combine the wings, lemon juice, soy sauce, jalapeño, ginger, garlic, and rosemary and toss or mix well. Cover or seal and refrigerate for at least 2 hours, or up to 8 hours.

Light a grill, or heat a grill pan until very hot.

Meanwhile, pour the chicken and its marinade into a large saucepan and bring to a simmer over medium-high heat. Cover and simmer for 3 minutes. Turn the wings over and simmer, uncovered, until all the marinade has been absorbed, 2 to 3 more minutes.

Lightly brush the grill grate or grill pan with oil. Place the chicken wings, fleshier sides down, on the grill or in the pan and cook, turning once, until nicely charred and cooked through, 4 to 5 minutes per side. Serve with lemon wedges.

Baked Baby Eggplants Stuffed
with Rice, Feta, and Rosemary

SERVES 2 TO 3

Historians have traced the birthplace of the eggplant to India. It arrived in Spain with the Moorish invasion and spread through the Mediterranean thanks to medieval Italian merchants who traded with the East. Early varieties were small and egg-shaped (hence their name). The vegetable was originally considered purely an ornamental attraction, but Mediterranean cooks gradually took to frying, pickling, roasting, mashing, or stuffing eggplants, as I do here.

Tip: Fresh eggplants have smooth, shiny, tight skin, a sparkling complexion, and bright green stems; they should feel heavy in the hand. Avoid spongy, dull-looking eggplants with wrinkled skin and brownish green stems. Their flesh will be seedy and acrid.

4–6 Italian or other small eggplants (1 pound total)
 Sea salt or kosher salt

FILLING

2 tablespoons extra-virgin olive oil

1 cup finely chopped onion

1 cup diced (¼-inch) yellow bell pepper

2 garlic cloves, finely chopped

1 teaspoon sea salt or kosher salt

1 small jalapeño, finely chopped

1 tablespoon finely chopped fresh rosemary

1 tablespoon chopped fresh basil

1 cup cooked white or brown basmati rice

½ cup crumbled feta cheese (about 3 ounces)

1 tablespoon finely chopped fresh flat-leaf parsley

2½ cups (8–10 ounces) peeled (see page 102), seeded, and chopped tomatoes

¼ cup dry white wine

½ teaspoon sugar

½ teaspoon sea salt or kosher salt

Preheat the oven to 350 degrees.

Trim the eggplants and halve them lengthwise. Scoop out the flesh, leaving ½-inch-thick shells, and dice the flesh. Sprinkle the eggplant shells lightly with salt.

FOR THE FILLING: In a large skillet, heat the oil over medium heat. Add the onion, bell pepper, garlic, and salt and cook, stirring, until the vegetables are softened, 3 to 4 minutes. Add the diced eggplant, jalapeño, rosemary, and basil, cover, reduce the heat, and cook, stirring occasionally, until all the vegetables are tender, about 10 minutes.

Scrape the vegetables into a bowl, add the rice, and stir to combine. Stir in the feta cheese and parsley.

Combine the tomatoes, wine, sugar, and salt in a baking dish large enough to hold the eggplant halves in a single snug layer.

Stuff the eggplant halves with the filling, loosely mounding it, and arrange on top of the tomatoes. Bake until the eggplant shells are tender when pierced with a knife, 30 to 40 minutes. Serve hot or at room temperature.

Panzanella

SERVES 4

One of those dishes invented by cooks who valued yesterday's bread too much to toss it, this salad can be made with fresh or day-old bread—the better the bread, the better the salad. Once the toasted bread has been tossed with the juicy tomatoes and oil and vinegar, the panzanella should be served immediately so the bread remains crisp.

> 6 tablespoons extra-virgin olive oil
>
> 3 cups ½-inch cubes sourdough bread (with crust)
>
> 2 tablespoons balsamic vinegar or red wine vinegar
>
> 4 medium tomatoes (about 1½ pounds), cut into wedges
>
> 1 medium cucumber, peeled, seeded (see Tip, page 22), and diced
>
> 1 small red onion, thinly sliced
>
> ¼ cup pitted Kalamata olives, coarsely chopped
>
> ½ cup fresh basil leaves, torn
>
> 2 tablespoons capers, rinsed
>
> Sea salt or kosher salt and freshly ground black pepper

In a large skillet, heat 3 tablespoons of the oil over medium heat. Add the bread cubes and cook, stirring occasionally, until golden brown on all sides, 3 to 4 minutes. Transfer to a large serving bowl and let cool.

Add the remaining 3 tablespoons oil, the vinegar, tomatoes, cucumber, onion, olives, basil, and capers to the bread, season with salt and pepper to taste, and toss well. Serve immediately.

Summer

MENU 9
SERVES 3 TO 4

Cannelloni with Ricotta, Parmesan, and Mint

Summer Vegetable Ragout

Chopped Salad with Sherry Vinaigrette

Making pasta by hand is rewarding because the result is especially fresh and tender. Moreover, whenever you knead a dough, it develops a texture unique to your hands alone, making the meal memorable. Double these recipes and invite friends—you'll be glad you did.

THE PLAN
1. Prepare the pasta dough and let it rest.
2. Prepare the cannelloni filling.
3. Roll, cut, and cook the pasta.
4. Assemble the cannelloni and refrigerate.
5. Cook the ragout.
6. Meanwhile, bake the cannelloni.
7. Make the salad.

Cannelloni with Ricotta, Parmesan, and Mint

SERVES 3 TO 4

Fresh pasta is stuffed with a sprightly herbaceous filling. If you prefer a heartier pasta, substitute up to ⅔ cup semolina or whole wheat bread flour for some of the white flour. As ricotta cheese varies a lot in quality and consistency, I recommend buying the cheese a day ahead, ideally from a store that sells it fresh, and checking it when you get home. If it seems overly moist, drain it in a cheesecloth-lined sieve set over a bowl in the refrigerator for at least 6 hours, or up to 24 hours. This will keep the cannelloni from getting watery.

I use a pasta machine, but you can also roll the pasta out by hand, using a wooden rolling pin. You want to end up with sheets that are about ¹⁄₁₆ inch thick. To test whether the pasta is thin enough, place your hand underneath it—when you've rolled it to the right thickness, you will be able to see the outline of your hand clearly.

This recipe makes 8 cannelloni, so everyone can have at least 2, but you may well want more—the quantities can be increased proportionally if desired. After you have assembled the cannelloni and brushed them with butter, you can refrigerate them while you make the Summer Vegetable Ragout.

Tips: If you don't have almond flour, pulse unblanched almonds in a food processor until you have a coarse meal (don't overprocess, or you'll end up with a paste).

The pasta dough can be made in a food processor. Pulse all the ingredients together until combined. Transfer the dough to a lightly floured surface, and knead for 2 to 3 minutes. Let the dough rest, wrapped in plastic wrap, for 30 minutes.

PASTA

2 cups unbleached all-purpose flour

Sea salt or kosher salt

3 large eggs

FILLING

2 cups ricotta, preferably fresh, drained if watery

⅔ cup freshly grated Parmesan cheese (about 3 ounces)

¼ cup almond flour

1 large egg, lightly beaten

Finely grated zest of 1 lemon

2 teaspoons fresh lemon juice

2 tablespoons finely chopped fresh mint

2 tablespoons finely chopped fresh chives

Freshly ground black pepper to taste

Melted unsalted butter, for brushing

Summer Vegetable Ragout (page 155)

Freshly grated Parmesan cheese, for serving

FOR THE PASTA: Measure the flour into a large bowl, then sprinkle 2 tablespoons of the flour onto a clean work surface. Whisk ¼ teaspoon salt into the flour in the bowl. Use your fingers to make a well in the center of the flour. Crack the eggs into the well and beat them lightly with a fork, then slowly draw the surrounding flour into the eggs with the fork until you have a ragged mass of dough. Continue to mix the dough with your hands, then form it into a ball. The dough is ready for kneading when a clean, dry finger inserted into the center of the dough comes out clean.

Wash and dry your hands. Transfer the dough to the floured work surface and knead until it is shiny and supple, 8 to 10 minutes. Wrap the dough in plastic and let it rest at room temperature for 30 minutes.

Lay several clean kitchen towels on a work surface. Unwrap the dough and divide it into 4 equal pieces. Work with one piece of dough at a time, keeping the remainder covered in plastic wrap. Adjust the rollers on your pasta machine to the widest setting. Flatten the first piece of dough and run it through the machine. Fold the dough into thirds, insert a narrower end into the machine, and roll it through again. Lay the rolled dough flat on a towel. Repeat the process until all 4 pieces of dough have been rolled twice. Make sure the pieces do not touch each other when you lay them on the towel or they may stick together.

Bring the rollers of the pasta machine one notch closer together. Insert a narrower end of the first piece of dough into the machine and roll it through. Repeat with the remaining pieces, always rolling them in the same order to prevent uneven drying and to ensure consistent texture and color in the finished pasta. Continue rolling, narrowing the rollers one notch at a time, until you have passed all the sheets of dough through the next-to-the-last setting.

Cut each sheet of dough crosswise in half and trim the edges so they are straight.

Bring a large pot of water to a boil and add a small handful of salt. Fill a large bowl with ice water.

Add the pasta sheets to the boiling water and cook until just al dente, about 1 minute. Use tongs to gently transfer the sheets to the ice water. When the pasta is cool, drain well, and lay the sheets out on the towels to drain—do not let them overlap, or they may stick to each other.

Preheat the oven to 425 degrees.

FOR THE FILLING: In a bowl, stir together all the filling ingredients until smooth.

Liberally brush one large or two small baking dishes with melted butter.

Lay 1 sheet of pasta on your work surface and spread ⅓ cup of the filling across the bottom of the sheet, stopping 1 inch short of the edge. Roll the pasta up into a tube shape and transfer to the baking dish, seam side down. Repeat with the remaining pasta sheets and filling. Brush the tops of the cannelloni with melted butter. (At this point, the cannelloni can be covered and refrigerated until ready to bake.)

Bake the cannelloni until golden brown on top and crisp around the edges, about 18 minutes, or 20 to 25 minutes if the cannelloni have been refrigerated. Serve the cannelloni accompanied by the ragout and with Parmesan cheese for sprinkling.

Summer Vegetable Ragout

SERVES 4

A garden in a saucepan, this simple sauce can double as a topping for bruschetta or a cool dip for toasted wedges of pita bread.

   ¼ cup extra-virgin olive oil

   ½ cup ¼-inch-diced onion

   ½ cup ¼-inch-diced carrot

   2 pounds ripe tomatoes, peeled (see page 102), seeded, and chopped

   2 pounds red or yellow bell peppers, peeled (see page 131) and cut into ¼-inch dice

   2 garlic cloves, chopped

   2 sprigs fresh thyme, summer savory, or oregano

   1 jalapeño, finely chopped

   2 tablespoons chopped fresh basil or flat-leaf parsley

   Sea salt or kosher salt

In a medium saucepan, heat the olive oil over medium heat. Add the onion and carrot and cook, stirring, until the vegetables soften, 4 to 5 minutes, adjusting the heat if necessary to keep them from browning. Stir in the tomatoes, bell peppers, garlic, herb sprigs, and jalapeño. Raise the heat to high and bring to a simmer, then lower the heat, cover, and simmer until the peppers are meltingly tender, 15 to 20 minutes.

Uncover, raise the heat, and simmer until the juices have thickened, 3 to 4 minutes. Stir in the chopped basil or parsley and season with salt. Serve.

Chopped Salad with Sherry Vinaigrette

SERVES 6

With some bread and cheese, this is a hearty lunch salad. If you don't have sherry vinegar, use half balsamic and half red wine vinegar.

2 ears corn, shucked

1 garlic clove, halved

1 small red onion, halved and very thinly sliced

3 tablespoons sherry vinegar

1 tablespoon fresh lemon juice

1 teaspoon honey

½ cup extra-virgin olive oil

 Sea salt or kosher salt and freshly ground black pepper

4 hearts of romaine, coarsely chopped

4 medium tomatoes, diced

3 medium Kirby cucumbers, peeled, quartered lengthwise, and cut into bite-sized pieces

2 ripe avocados, pitted, peeled, and diced

½ cup walnuts, lightly toasted and skins rubbed off (see page 11)

12 fresh mint leaves, torn

7 fresh basil leaves, torn

Boil or steam the corn until just tender, then cool the ears under cold running water and pat dry.

Rub the inside of a large salad bowl with the garlic; discard the garlic. Add the onion, vinegar, lemon juice, and honey to the bowl, stirring to coat the onion. Set aside for 5 minutes.

Hold each ear of corn upright on a cutting board. Slide a sharp knife down the cob from top to bottom to slice off the kernels.

Whisk the oil into the onion mixture and season with salt and pepper. Add the corn and the remaining ingredients to the dressing and toss well. Taste and season with additional salt and pepper if needed. Serve immediately.

Summer

MENU 10
SERVES 6

Spicy Roasted Pepper Soup with Goat Cheese
and Chives

Whole Wheat Pita Bread

Spiced Lamb Croquettes

Falafel

Two Traditional Sauces: Hot Sauce (Zhoug) and
Sesame Tahini Sauce

Cucumber, Red Onion, and Tomato Salad

If you love a falafel sandwich, you'll find this menu is transporting. The soup makes it a full meal, and the sauces and fresh pita elevate each bite far above the falafel stand. Serve everything together, or serve the soup separately as a first course. Diners can assemble their own pita sandwiches, adding falafel or lamb, salad, zhoug, and tahini sauce as they wish.

Making pita is easy, even if you're normally shy about baking bread (and the actual baking takes mere minutes). The soup and sauces can be made ahead.

Form the falafel and lamb croquettes in advance, then cook them right before serving. The salad can be tossed together in minutes, and the baked pita kept warm. Feel free to make substitutions, using a bottled hot sauce, substituting hummus or yogurt for the tahini sauce, and/or warming up some good purchased whole wheat pita. The soup, falafel, and lamb will still be a treat.

Note: Double the falafel recipe if meat eaters will want some too, or if you're serving six vegetarians. Or double the lamb and leave out the falafel.

THE PLAN
1. One to 2 days ahead, prepare the dough for the pita. Up to 1 day ahead, soak the chickpeas.
2. Make the zhoug and refrigerate.
3. Make the tahini sauce and refrigerate (bring to room temperature before serving).
4. Make the soup (reheat before serving).
5. Make the falafel and lamb mixtures and refrigerate.
6. Shape the pitas and let rest.
7. Bake the pitas.
8. Prepare the salad.
9. Cook the falafel and lamb.

Spicy Roasted Pepper Soup
with Goat Cheese and Chives

SERVES 6

This satisfying soup is spiced up with a little fresh chili pepper—I like to use a moderately hot, fruity chili, such as a ripe red jalapeño; remove the seeds and veins for a milder flavor. The color is essentially an aesthetic decision—if only green jalapeños are available, they will be fine. The goat cheese rounds out the flavor of the soup, making it truly luxurious.

½ cup extra-virgin olive oil

2 medium onions, chopped

6 garlic cloves, peeled and left whole

1 tablespoon finely chopped red chili pepper or ½ teaspoon red pepper flakes, or to taste

1 teaspoon ground cumin, preferably toasted and freshly ground (see page 12)

1 teaspoon ground fennel, preferably toasted and freshly ground

1 teaspoon sweet paprika

Sea salt or kosher salt

3 large red bell peppers (about 2 pounds), roasted (see page 160), peeled, seeded, and chopped

4 cups water

Juice of ½ lemon, or to taste

4 ounces fresh goat cheese, crumbled (about ½ cup)

Snipped fresh chives, for garnish

In a large heavy pot, heat the olive oil over medium heat. Add the onions, garlic, chili or red pepper flakes, cumin, fennel, paprika, and 1 teaspoon salt and cook, stirring frequently, for 5 minutes. Reduce the heat to very low, cover, and cook, adding a tablespoon or two of water if the vegetables begin to stick, until the garlic is meltingly tender, 20 to 30 minutes.

Add the bell peppers and water and bring to a boil, then reduce the heat and simmer, uncovered, for 10 minutes. Remove from the heat.

Puree the soup using an immersion blender, or in batches in a regular blender, until smooth. Rewarm if necessary before serving.

Season the soup with the lemon juice and salt to taste. Serve topped with the crumbled goat cheese and chives.

Roasting Peppers

Bell peppers, fresh poblanos, Anaheim chilies, and even large jalapeños can be charred until their skins blacken and blister, covered tightly so they steam as they cool, and then peeled. This process rids the pepper of its tough, sometimes bitter skin and brings out the flavor of the flesh, as well as adding a slight smokiness.

To roast a whole fresh pepper on a gas stove, use tongs to turn the pepper over the flame until well charred all over, about 5 minutes. Transfer the pepper to a bowl, cover with a plate, and let steam for about 15 minutes to loosen the skin. Remove the skin with your fingers or a damp towel, then cut the pepper open and pull or cut away the seeds and veins (wear rubber gloves when handling chilies to avoid a burn).

To roast more than one pepper, I prefer to cut the peppers into large pieces that will lay flat on a baking sheet, remove the stems and seeds, and then broil them skin side up, watching and rearranging the peppers as needed, until they are well charred. The steaming method is the same as above.

Whole Wheat Pita Bread

MAKES 6 PITAS

These fluffy rounds are best the day they are baked; however, they can be stored in a plastic bag at room temperature for up to 2 days or frozen, well wrapped, for up to a month. Defrost them without unwrapping, then rewarm in a 350-degree oven.

The dough benefits from an overnight rise in the refrigerator; the slow, cool rise develops the bread's flavor. But you can skip this step if you like and let the dough rise at room temperature for about an hour, or until doubled in size, then shape the pitas and bake them.

This recipe calls for a pizza stone; using a stone is a great way to get a nice crust if you bake often. Pizza stones are available at kitchenware stores; clean unglazed quarry tiles, sold at flooring or hardware stores, can also be used. Or you can simply preheat a cast-iron griddle or an overturned baking sheet—the sturdiest you have—in the oven and use that.

> ½ **teaspoon active dry yeast**
> 1¼ **cups warm water (100 to 110 degrees)**
> 1¼ **cups whole wheat bread flour, plus additional for dusting**
> 1½ **teaspoons sea salt or kosher salt**
> **About 1 tablespoon olive oil**
> **About 1½ cups unbleached all-purpose flour**

Place the yeast in a large mixing bowl and stir in the warm water. Let stand until the yeast has dissolved, about 5 minutes.

Add the whole wheat flour and stir with a wooden spoon until you have a smooth batter. Cover the bowl with plastic wrap or a damp kitchen towel and set aside to proof at room temperature for about 2 hours. The batter should have lots of bubbles on the surface and should appear lacy and weblike when stirred.

Stir in the salt and 1½ teaspoons of the oil. Mix in enough white flour to form a ragged mass of dough.

Scoop up the dough and transfer it to a clean work surface. Knead for about 10 minutes, adding additional white flour as necessary, until you have a smooth, shiny dough that is only slightly tacky.

Smear the inside of a 1-gallon resealable plastic bag with a teaspoon or two of olive oil or use a large bowl. Transfer the dough to the bag or bowl and seal or cover. Refrigerate for at least 12 hours, or up to 2 days.

About 1 hour before you plan to bake (note that once the dough has been shaped into balls, it needs to rest for 30 minutes to 1 hour), place a pizza stone on the bottom of the oven and position a rack in the top third of the oven. Preheat the oven to 500 degrees.

Transfer the dough to a lightly floured work surface and gently shape it into a 12-inch-long log. Cut the log crosswise into 6 equal pieces. Form each piece into a ball, dust lightly with whole wheat flour, and cover with a kitchen towel. Let rest for at least 30 minutes, or up to 1 hour.

With a rolling pin or an empty wine bottle, roll each piece of dough from the center outward, rotating it a quarter turn with each roll, into a 6-inch round. Place 3 rounds of dough on the pizza stone and bake for 5 minutes. The pitas will puff up. Transfer them to the top oven rack and bake for 2 more minutes. Remove the pitas from the oven and cool for a few minutes, then wrap them in a clean towel to keep them warm. Repeat with the remaining dough. Serve warm.

Spiced Lamb Croquettes

SERVES 3 TO 4

These lemon-and-cumin-seasoned lamb patties get nice and crisp outside but stay moist and fragrant within. Here is a good place to use up a last serving of leftover cooked rice. In the event that there isn't any leftover rice around, cook some up—you'll need ¼ cup uncooked rice. But why not make an entire pot and use the rest for another purpose (such as the fried rice on page 280)?

12 **ounces ground lamb**

½ **cup cooked rice, preferably basmati or jasmine, at room temperature**

1 **large egg**

2 **tablespoons finely chopped fresh cilantro or flat-leaf parsley**

1 **garlic clove, finely chopped**

Finely grated zest of ½ lemon

1 **teaspoon fresh lemon juice**

1 **teaspoon ground cumin, preferably toasted and freshly ground (see page 12)**

1 **teaspoon ground coriander, preferably toasted and freshly ground**

¼ **teaspoon freshly ground black pepper**

½ **teaspoon sweet Spanish smoked paprika or sweet paprika**

¼ **teaspoon cayenne pepper**

1½ **teaspoons sea salt or kosher salt**

Olive oil, for panfrying

In a large bowl, combine the lamb, rice, egg, cilantro or parsley, garlic, lemon zest and juice, spices, and salt and toss until just combined. Divide the mixture into 12 even portions. Gently form them into balls, and press down on them to form ½-inch-thick patties.

Line a platter with paper towels. Heat a large skillet over medium-high heat for a minute or two, then pour in ⅛ inch oil to heat until it shimmers. Add the patties, working in batches if necessary, and fry, turning once, until browned on both sides and cooked through, about 3 minutes per side. Drain on the paper-towel-lined platter and serve hot.

Falafel

SERVES 3

Falafel is crispy, nutritious, and addictive. The baking soda in this recipe not only lightens the finished falafel, but also makes the chickpeas more digestible. Because the beans are never boiled, it's up to the soda to break down the indigestible phytic acids in the skin.

½ cup lightly packed fresh cilantro or flat-leaf parsley leaves, coarsely chopped

¾ cup dried chickpeas, soaked and drained (see page 9)

1½ teaspoons fresh lemon juice

3 tablespoons finely chopped red onion

1 garlic clove, chopped

1 teaspoon ground cumin, preferably toasted and freshly ground (see page 12)

¾ teaspoon sea salt or kosher salt

½ teaspoon ground coriander, preferably toasted and freshly ground

½ teaspoon baking soda

⅛ teaspoon cayenne pepper, or to taste

4 grinds black pepper

4–6 cups vegetable oil, for deep-frying

In a food processor, pulse the cilantro or parsley until finely chopped. Add the chickpeas and pulse until they are finely ground (they should have the consistency of cracker crumbs). Add the lemon juice, onion, garlic, cumin, salt, coriander, baking soda, cayenne, and black pepper and pulse to combine. The mixture should hold its shape when squeezed. If not, process for a few more seconds. Transfer to a large bowl and toss well.

Fill a medium heavy saucepan or a Dutch oven with at least 3 inches of oil, attach a deep-frying thermometer to the side of the pot, and heat the oil to 360 degrees (the temperature will drop when the falafel is added but should never dip below 350 degrees). Line a platter with paper towels.

Moisten your hands and divide the falafel mixture into 12 equal portions (about 2 scant tablespoons each). Form each into an oval about 2 inches long and ½ inch thick, moistening your hands as needed while you work.

Fry the falafel a few at a time, turning halfway through, until well browned, about 4 minutes per batch. Transfer to the paper-towel-lined platter to drain. Return the oil to 360 degrees before adding each batch. Serve warm.

Hot Sauce (Zhoug)

MAKES ½ CUP

This Israeli hot sauce will perk up both the lamb and falafel. It has a fresh, full flavor in addition to its peppery heat—which you can adjust by choosing to include the seeds and veins of the chilies or not. It's a simply made food processor sauce, best prepared within a few hours of serving.

> 1 cup packed coarsely chopped fresh cilantro leaves and tender stems
>
> 2 tablespoons chopped fresh mint
>
> 2 tablespoons coarsely chopped medium-spicy chili peppers (about 2 peppers), such as red and/or green jalapeños or serranos
>
> ⅓ cup fresh lemon juice (from about 2 lemons)
>
> 1 tablespoon extra-virgin olive oil
>
> ½ teaspoon kosher salt or sea salt

In a food processor, combine all the ingredients and process until smooth. Transfer to a small bowl. Refrigerate until ready to serve.

Sesame Tahini Sauce

MAKES ABOUT 1¾ CUPS

Tahini, Middle Eastern sesame paste, is sold in jars in Middle Eastern and natural food stores and many supermarkets. It should be stirred well before using, as it separates easily. Once opened, tahini keeps best in the refrigerator. If you've had your tahini for a while, taste it to make sure it's fresh, without any bitter aftertaste.

Leftover sauce is great served as a dip with vegetables and pita bread.

¾ cup tahini

5 tablespoons fresh lemon juice (from about 2 lemons)

1 garlic clove, mashed with ¾ teaspoon sea salt or kosher salt (see page 286)

¼ teaspoon cayenne pepper, or to taste

¾ cup water

In a bowl, whisk together the tahini, lemon juice, garlic paste, and cayenne. Whisk in the water until smooth. Transfer to a small bowl. The sauce can be made up to 3 days in advance and refrigerated, covered. Bring to room temperature before serving.

Cucumber, Red Onion, and Tomato Salad

MAKES 3 CUPS

This chopped salad is more than an optional flourish—tucked into the pitas, it is an essential fresh counterpoint to the falafel or lamb.

- **2 Kirby cucumbers, peeled and chopped**
- **2 plum tomatoes or a handful of cherry tomatoes, chopped**
- **1 small red onion, chopped**
- **Sea salt or kosher salt and freshly ground black pepper**

In a small bowl, toss together the cucumbers, tomatoes, and onion. Season to taste with salt and pepper and serve.

Fall

MENU 1 • 171
Giant Lamb/Seitan Turnovers
Golden Split Pea Dal
Carrot-Yogurt Chutney

MENU 2 • 178
Black Bean Enchiladas with Chicken/Smoked Tofu and Mole Verde
Avocado, Cucumber, and Hiziki Salsa
Chive Sour Cream

MENU 3 • 186
Roasted Squash Potage with Spiced Crème Fraîche
Baked Fish/Ricotta Dumplings over French Lentils
Sautéed Escarole with Red Pepper and Garlic

MENU 4 • 195
Lemon-Thyme Roast Chicken
Lemon-Thyme Tofu
Spicy Roasted Winter Squash
Toasted Millet Pilaf
Kale with Cremini Mushrooms

MENU 5 • 204
Chestnut Apple Soup
Penne with Beets, Beet Greens, Goat Cheese, and Walnuts

MENU 6 • 210
White Beans/Shrimp with Brown Butter and Tons of Herbs
Soft Polenta
Roasted Broccoli with Parmesan

MENU 7 • 217
Autumn Stew with Miso and Duck/Tofu
Napa Cabbage Salad with Sweet Peppers and Sesame Vinaigrette
Sweet Brown Rice

MENU 8 • 225
Lasagna with Fall Vegetables, Gruyère, and Sage Béchamel
Roasted Brussels Sprouts with Fennel Seeds and Balsamic

MENU 9 • 232
Pan-Seared Seitan with Thyme, Lemon, and Mustard
Pan-Seared Lamb Steak with Thyme, Lemon, and Mustard
Carrots with Black Olives and Mint
Spicy Lentils with Pumpkin and Greens over Couscous

MENU 10 • 243
Stuffed Dumpling Squash/Poussin with Quinoa, Dried Fruit,
and Pumpkin Seeds
Pinto Beans with Chipotle and Melted Garlic
Mustard Greens with Shallots and Vinegar

Fall

MENU 1
SERVES 4

Giant Lamb/Seitan Turnovers

Golden Split Pea Dal

Carrot-Yogurt Chutney

A satisfying departure from the ordinary, this visually delightful meal celebrates the gold, orange, and brown tones of the season. To serve, spoon the golden dal onto plates. Cut the crisp, bronzed turnovers in half to reveal the savory filling and place two halves on top of the dal on each plate. Sprinkle with some bright green cilantro leaves, and serve with the colorful carrot chutney on the side.

You can assemble the turnovers up to 1 day in advance and refrigerate them, well wrapped in plastic. Then, as they bake, you'll have time to put together the chutney. If you've got any mango chutney in the fridge, serve some of that here too.

THE PLAN

1. Make the chutney and refrigerate.
2. Simmer the peas for the dal.
3. Prepare the filling for the turnovers.
4. Assemble and bake the turnovers.
5. Meanwhile, finish the dal and keep warm.

Giant **Lamb**/Seitan Turnovers

I brush the tops of these crisp, flaky triangles with a mixture of oil and curry powder, which gives them a golden color and adds flavor. If you have ghee on hand, you can use it instead of the oil, or use half oil and half melted butter for a similar effect (ghee or butter will brown the turnovers nicely and add more flavor). I also like to sprinkle the tops of the different turnovers with a few pinches of nigella (black onion), sesame, or poppy seeds, both to decorate them and to make it easier to distinguish between the seitan and lamb. (Nigella seeds are available in Middle Eastern markets.)

If you know how to fold a flag, then you'll be familiar with the technique used for folding the phyllo.

Note: If you want to make 4 turnovers of either lamb or seitan, use a pound in all, double the salt (½ teaspoon in all for the seitan, 1 teaspoon for the lamb), and work in one bowl rather than two.

Tip: If you have a meat grinder, buy 8 ounces of boneless lean lamb from the leg and grind it yourself—it will be fresher and leaner than store-bought ground lamb. Otherwise, ask your butcher for the leanest ground lamb available.

> 2 small Yellow Finn or Yukon Gold potatoes (about 8 ounces)
>
> Sea salt or kosher salt
>
> 10 ounces spinach leaves (one 10-ounce bag, or leaves from about 2 bunches)
>
> 6 tablespoons plus 1 teaspoon extra-virgin olive oil
>
> 1 cup chopped onion
>
> 2 teaspoons chopped seeded red or green chili pepper or ¼ teaspoon cayenne pepper, or to taste
>
> 1 garlic clove, finely chopped
>
> 1 teaspoon finely chopped peeled fresh ginger
>
> 1 tablespoon ground cumin, preferably toasted and freshly ground (see page 12)
>
> 1 tablespoon plus 1 teaspoon mild curry powder
>
> ¼ teaspoon ground cinnamon
>
> 1 cup fresh or thawed frozen peas (about 10 ounces)
>
> 1 teaspoon fresh lemon juice

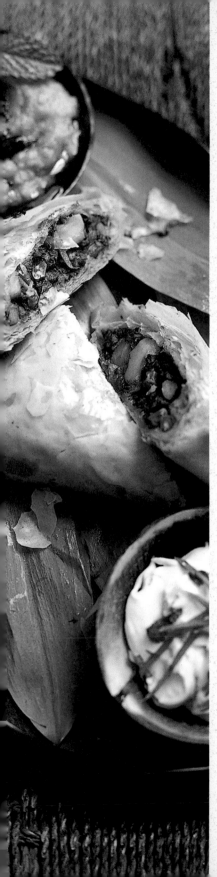

8 ounces lean ground lamb

8 ounces seitan

12 8-by-13-inch sheets organic phyllo (about 8 ounces), thawed if frozen, or regular phyllo, trimmed to the same size

Sesame, nigella, and/or poppy seeds, for garnish (optional)

Chopped fresh cilantro, for garnish

Place the potatoes in a saucepan with water to cover, salt the water well, and bring to a boil. Boil the potatoes until just tender, about 15 minutes. Drain and peel under cold running water. Cut into ½-inch cubes (you'll end up with about 1½ cups).

Rinse the spinach, drain, and place it in a saucepan with the water still clinging to the leaves. Cover and cook over medium heat, stirring a few times, until the spinach has wilted, about 3 minutes. Transfer to a sieve and cool under cold running water. Drain well, and squeeze out all of the excess liquid. Chop the drained spinach (you'll end up with about ⅔ cup).

In a large skillet, heat 2 tablespoons of the oil over high heat. Add the onion and cook, stirring occasionally, until soft, about 3 minutes. Add the chili or cayenne, garlic, ginger, cumin, 1 tablespoon of the curry powder, and the cinnamon and cook, stirring occasionally, for 5 minutes.

Add the potatoes, peas, and 1 cup water to the pan and bring to a simmer. Season with 1 teaspoon salt, reduce the heat to medium-low, cover, and simmer gently until the peas are tender, about 5 minutes, or 3 minutes for frozen peas. Uncover the pan and simmer, stirring, until the liquid has evaporated, 3 to 4 minutes more. Stir in the spinach and lemon juice. Remove from the heat.

Set a rack in the lower third of the oven and preheat the oven to 400 degrees.

FOR THE LAMB: In a small skillet, heat 1 teaspoon of the oil over high heat. Add the lamb and cook, stirring, until well browned, about 3 minutes. Season with ½ teaspoon salt and remove from the heat.

FOR THE SEITAN: In a food processor, combine the seitan and ¼ teaspoon salt and pulse until finely ground (it should resemble ground meat).

Divide the potato mixture between two medium bowls. Add the lamb to one bowl and the seitan to the other, tossing well.

In a small bowl, mix the remaining ¼ cup olive oil with the remaining 1 teaspoon curry powder. Brush your work surface with some of the oil. Stack 2 sheets of phyllo on the work surface, with a shorter edge facing you, and brush the top sheet with oil (keep the remaining phyllo covered with a damp kitchen towel as you work). Top with 2 more sheets and brush with more oil. Repeat once more, for a total of 6 sheets. Cut the rectangle lengthwise in half (leaving the short ends facing you).

Mound half the lamb filling in the lower left corner of one rectangle, leaving a border of at least 1 inch. Fold the bottom right corner diagonally over the filling. Lift up the filled triangle from the bottom left corner and flip it over, keeping the edges flush on the left side. Now fold the bottom left corner of the filled triangle diagonally over so that the edges are flush on the right side. Flip the filled triangle over again. Gently place the package seam side down on a rimmed baking sheet. Repeat with the second strip of phyllo and the rest of the lamb filling.

Repeat the process with the remaining phyllo and the seitan filling, to make 2 more turnovers.

Brush the tops of the triangles with more curry oil, and garnish each with a pinch of seeds, if desired, using different seeds to indicate lamb and seitan. Bake until crisp and golden, 20 to 25 minutes. Serve hot or warm, cut in half and sprinkled with cilantro.

Please Freeze the Peas

Unless you can find super-fresh peas in the pod in the spring, use frozen ones. Frozen organic peas are darn good. They're quick-frozen at peak freshness, and their flavor is concentrated by freezing.

Golden Split Pea Dal

SERVES 4 TO 6

A dal is a thick sauce of spiced dried legumes served with Indian meals. Here I use yellow split peas (sold as channa dal in Indian markets), which retain a little of their shape, giving the sauce a pleasing texture. The peas are simmered with a fragrant mix of spices, then seasoned at the end with spiced ghee or oil, which adds another layer of flavor as well as heat. Use leftover dal to give body and oomph to a soup of simmered vegetables such as cabbage, peas, and root vegetables.

1 cup yellow split peas (channa dal)

4 cups water

1 large shallot, thinly sliced

2 garlic cloves, peeled and left whole

3 quarter-sized slices peeled fresh ginger

1 teaspoon ground cumin, preferably toasted and freshly ground (see page 12)

½ teaspoon ground coriander, preferably toasted and freshly ground

½ teaspoon cayenne pepper, or to taste

¼ teaspoon ground turmeric

1 small bay leaf

Sea salt or kosher salt

2 tablespoons ghee (see page 21) or vegetable oil

2 teaspoons brown mustard seeds

2–3 small dried red chilies

A handful of fresh cilantro leaves, chopped

In a medium saucepan, combine the split peas and the water and bring to a boil over medium-high heat. Reduce the heat to maintain a slow simmer, skim off the foam that rises to the top, and add the shallot, garlic, ginger, cumin, coriander, cayenne, turmeric, and bay leaf. Cover and simmer gently, stirring occasionally, until the peas are very tender and falling apart, 1 hour or longer (depending on the age and dryness of the peas).

Remove and discard the ginger and bay leaf. Crush the garlic against the side of the pan with the back of a wooden spoon and stir it back into the dal. Season with salt, and remove from the heat.

In a small skillet or saucepan, heat the ghee or oil over medium heat until shimmering. Add the mustard seeds and chilies. As soon as the mustard seeds begin to pop and the chilies puff and blister, pour the contents of the pan into the dal and stir well. Let stand, covered, for a few minutes.

Stir the dal and taste again for salt. Serve garnished with cilantro.

Carrot-Yogurt Chutney

SERVES 4

The balance of sweet, savory, and tangy flavors in this cool chutney makes it an ideal wake-up for warm, spicy foods.

- 2 medium carrots, peeled and grated
- 1 cup Greek yogurt (or strained regular yogurt; see Tip, page 22)
- 2 tablespoons coarsely chopped golden raisins
- 2 tablespoons fresh lemon juice
- 1 tablespoon finely chopped fresh cilantro
- 1 teaspoon finely chopped scallion or fresh chives, plus additional for garnish
- 1 teaspoon finely chopped fresh mint
- 1 teaspoon honey
- Sea salt or kosher salt and freshly ground black pepper to taste

In a bowl, stir together all the ingredients. Serve immediately, or cover and refrigerate for up to 3 hours. Taste for seasoning before serving, and garnish with scallions or chives.

Fall

MENU 2
SERVES 4

**Black Bean Enchiladas with Chicken/Smoked Tofu
and Mole Verde**

Avocado, Cucumber, and Hiziki Salsa

Chive Sour Cream

Enchiladas are great party food. Both the filling and the mole can be made up to 1 day in advance, then brought to room temperature before you assemble and bake the dish.

If making the tofu enchiladas for vegans, leave out the cheddar cheese. The salsa is a lively touch, but for a simpler meal, the enchiladas are satisfying served with just some sliced avocado, or even on their own.

THE PLAN

1. Make the mole and the filling for the enchiladas.
2. Meanwhile, soak the hiziki for the salsa.
3. Assemble and bake the enchiladas.
4. Prepare the sour cream.
5. Finish the salsa.

Black Bean Enchiladas with
Smoked Tofu/Chicken and Mole Verde

SERVES 4: 2 SERVINGS TOFU, 2 SERVINGS CHICKEN

Inspired by a Mexican snack of tortillas dipped in chili sauce and fried (*enchilada* essentially means "chilied"), the Tex-Mex version of enchiladas is thought to have been invented in the 1950s. Like cannelloni or stuffed crepes, the idea is a winner—roll chewy tortillas around a savory filling, cover with sauce and cheese, bake, and you have a cheesy, saucy, bubbling casserole that's both delicious and comforting.

Flavorful Tex-Mex ingredients like chilies, beans, and cheese are equally at home in vegetarian or meat-centered preparations. When I make these, meat eaters always enjoy the smoked tofu version as much as the chicken. (Smoked chicken breast is available in gourmet stores, or you can order it online at www.dartagnan.com.) The mole verde, a sauce of tangy tomatillos and rich, nutty pumpkin seeds, is lighter than the more familiar deep brown mole poblano made from chilies and chocolate.

Note: I bake the chicken and tofu enchiladas in one large roasting pan, marking the chicken ones with toothpicks for ease of serving. If you prefer, you can bake the two types separately in two 8-inch square pans. Start checking the smaller pans 10 minutes earlier, as they will cook a bit faster. Of course, you can always make double of one filling and skip the other if you prefer.

If you want to make the recipe with all chicken or all tofu, you can save time by making one big lasagna-like casserole instead of rolling and stuffing each tortilla: In a large baking pan, layer half the sauce, half the tortillas (trim the tortillas to fit, layering in the trimmings too), all the filling, the remaining tortillas and sauce, and finally the cheese. This version will bake in the same time. Cut and serve like lasagna.

MOLE VERDE

¼ cup extra-virgin olive oil

1 cup pumpkin seeds

1 cup finely chopped onion

Sea salt or kosher salt

1 cup vegetable stock or water

1 cup coarsely chopped tomatillos (about 8 ounces; discard the papery skins and rinse before chopping)

2 poblano chilies, roasted (see page 160), peeled, seeded, and chopped

1 large jalapeño, roasted, peeled, seeded, and chopped

6 cups sliced romaine or green leaf lettuce

4 cups packed sliced Swiss chard or spinach leaves (about 5 ounces)

FILLING

3 tablespoons extra-virgin olive oil

2 cups finely chopped onions

1 cup chopped peeled carrots

1 cup chopped celery

1½ tablespoons ground cumin, preferably toasted and freshly ground (page 12)

3 garlic cloves, finely chopped

2 tablespoons tomato paste

½ teaspoon sweet Spanish smoked paprika (optional)

3 cups cooked black beans (8 ounces dried; see page 9), with 1 cup of the cooking liquid, or two 14-ounce cans black beans, rinsed and drained

Sea salt or kosher salt and freshly ground black pepper

6 ounces smoked chicken breast, shredded

6 ounces smoked tofu, chopped

8 8-inch flour tortillas

1½–2 cups coarsely shredded smoked cheddar cheese (about 5 ounces)

FOR THE MOLE: In a wide heavy skillet, heat the oil over medium heat. Add the pumpkin seeds and cook, stirring, until they darken and pop, 3 to 4 minutes. Add the onion and ½ teaspoon salt and cook, stirring, until the onion softens, 3 to 4 minutes. Remove from the heat and let cool slightly.

Transfer the onion mixture to a blender (you can leave the pan on the stove to use for the filling). Add ½ cup of the stock or water and puree. Add the tomatillos, poblanos, and jalapeño and puree until smooth. Add the lettuce and chard or spinach, a handful at a time, blending to a smooth puree.

Where There's Smoke . . .

. . . there's flavor. When you harness smoke, its primal, meaty flavor deepens the whole dish. And you can smoke just about anything, from a chunk of bacon to a chicken breast to a cube of pressed tofu.

Smoked tofu is just what it sounds like, a convenient packaged food with a firm, smooth, chewy texture and a pleasantly smoky flavor. Look for it in natural food stores and in Chinese markets, but be sure to read the ingredients and avoid any that are seasoned with MSG. Other meatless ingredients with a smoky flavor include roasted peppers, smoked cheeses such as cheddar or Gouda, chipotle peppers in adobo sauce, Spanish smoked paprika, and even smoked salt. Smoked paprika and smoked sea salt are available in gourmet markets and online at www.zingermans.com. Several varieties of smoked sea salt are available from www.maineseasalt.com.

Transfer the mole to a wide deep saucepan and bring to a boil over medium heat. Reduce the heat and simmer, uncovered, stirring in the remaining ½ cup stock or water as the sauce thickens, until the mole turns from bright green to drab olive, about 20 minutes. You will have about 5 cups of thick but pourable sauce; thin with a little water if necessary. Taste and adjust the salt. Remove from the heat.

FOR THE FILLING: In a wide heavy skillet (use the pan you started the mole in), heat the oil over medium heat. Add the onions, carrots, celery, and cumin and cook, stirring, until the vegetables begin to soften, 3 to 4 minutes. Add the garlic, tomato paste, and paprika, if using, and cook, stirring, for 2 minutes.

Add the beans and the 1 cup cooking liquid (or 1 cup water if using canned beans) and bring to a boil. Reduce the heat to low, cover, and simmer gently until the vegetables are tender, 10 to 15 minutes. Uncover the pan, raise the heat, and simmer, stirring, until the mixture thickens and all the liquid has been absorbed, about 2 more minutes.

Divide the filling mixture between two bowls, and stir the chicken into one and the tofu into the other. Let cool slightly, then season with salt and pepper.

Set a rack in the middle of the oven and preheat the oven to 350 degrees.

To assemble the enchiladas, spread 1 cup mole over the bottom of a 10-by-15-inch baking dish. Lay a tortilla on your work surface and spread a tablespoon of mole over its center, leaving a 1-inch border all around. Mound ¾ cup of filling in the center of the tortilla. Fold the sides of the tortilla in over the filling, then fold up the bottom over the filling and roll up the tortilla. Place the enchilada seam side down in the baking dish. Fill the remaining tortillas, making a total of 4 chicken and 4 tofu enchiladas, and mark one variety with toothpicks to distinguish it. Pour the remaining mole over the enchiladas and sprinkle with the cheese.

Bake until the enchiladas are heated through and the cheese is bubbling and golden brown, 30 to 35 minutes. Serve.

Avocado, Cucumber, and Hiziki Salsa

Hiziki, an ink-black twiglike sea vegetable, is an unusual addition, but if you don't have any on hand, the salsa will be delicious without it as well. Soak the hiziki in warm water for at least 20 minutes before using, so it will become pliable and pleasantly chewy.

- 2 tablespoons fresh lemon juice
- 1 tablespoon rice vinegar
- ½ teaspoon sea salt or kosher salt
- ½ teaspoon sugar
- 3 tablespoons finely chopped red onion
- 1 tablespoon finely chopped seeded jalapeño
- 2 tablespoons dried hiziki (see page 87), soaked in warm water for at least 20 minutes
- 8 ounces cucumbers, peeled, seeded (see Tip, page 22), and cut into ½-inch cubes (about 2 cups)
- 1 large ripe avocado, pitted, peeled, and cut into ½-inch cubes
- 2–3 tablespoons chopped fresh cilantro

In a small bowl, combine the lemon juice, rice vinegar, salt, and sugar and stir to dissolve. Stir in the red onion and jalapeño. Let stand for 15 minutes (this will mellow the heat of the onion and ignite the spice of the jalapeño).

Drain the soaked hiziki, rinse well, and drain again. In a bowl, toss together the hiziki, cucumbers, and avocado. Add the onion mixture and the cilantro, toss well, and serve.

Don't Call Them Seaweeds

My professional culinary roots are grounded in a macrobiotic approach, so I've been a fan of sea vegetables for years. As my cooking evolves, I continue to value sea vegetables for the essential minerals and flavor compounds they offer—they are truly one of the world's great nutritional powerhouses. They're also incredibly versatile, and once dried, they keep forever. Stock up on wakame, arame, hiziki, dulse, kombu, and nori sheets when you see them in Asian markets or natural food stores. Then try them in soups, beans, or salads, crumbled over rice, or simply toasted as a snack.

Chive Sour Cream

MAKES 1 CUP

This simple, flavorful topping is great on tacos, burritos, and baked potatoes or dolloped into hot or cold soups.

1 cup sour cream

2 tablespoons finely chopped fresh chives

Sea salt or kosher salt and freshly ground black pepper

In a bowl, stir together the sour cream and chives. Season with salt and pepper and serve. Leftovers can be covered and refrigerated for up to 2 days.

MENU 3

SERVES 6

Roasted Squash Potage with Spiced Crème Fraîche

Baked Fish/Ricotta Dumplings over French Lentils

Sautéed Escarole with Red Pepper and Garlic

When the delicate greens of summer subside, revealing a palette of deeper colors beneath, roots and low-growing hard squash and pumpkins are ready to be harvested. This earthy menu features a creamy, warming soup to start, followed by a hearty lentil casserole studded with plump, tender ricotta dumplings or fillets of firm white fish. The casserole is rounded out by a sauté of escarole, a mild succulent green that deserves to be eaten more often.

THE PLAN
1. Soak the lentils.
2. Prepare the soup.
3. While the soup simmers, cook the lentils.
4. Assemble and bake the lentil dish.
5. Meanwhile, make the spiced crème fraîche.
6. Sauté the escarole.

Roasted Squash Potage
with Spiced Crème Fraîche

SERVES 6

This is the quintessential autumn soup (a potage is a thick soup). Roasting the squash concentrates its natural sugars and gives it a caramelized depth of flavor. Kabocha is my favorite squash for soup because its dense flesh yields an intense, bright orange puree. If Kabocha is not available, any winter squash will do. The spiced crème fraîche enriches any naturally sweet root vegetable puree.

SOUP

- 3 pounds winter squash (Kabocha, acorn, or butternut), peeled, seeded, and cut into 2-inch chunks
- 2 tablespoons extra-virgin olive oil
- Sea salt or kosher salt
- 2 tablespoons unsalted butter
- 2 cups chopped onions
- 1 tablespoon minced peeled fresh ginger
- 3 garlic cloves, peeled
- 4 cups vegetable stock or water
- ½ cup apple cider or apple juice
- Freshly ground black pepper

BOUQUET GARNI

- A small handful of celery leaves
- 3–4 fresh sage leaves
- 1 2-inch piece cinnamon stick
- 3 whole cloves

Stop and Take Stock

Making a vegetable soup? Take stock of the trimmings and the other vegetables you have on hand, and consider simmering them into a flavorful broth to enhance the taste and nutrient content of the soup. In a stockpot, combine 6 cups of any of the following: squash and ginger peels; mushroom stems; cabbage cores; parsley stems; chopped carrots, celery, onions, mushrooms, leeks, parsnips, and/or fennel; and garlic (cut a whole head crosswise in half, and leave the skin on). Add a couple of bay leaves and some fresh thyme or sage sprigs, cover with water, and bring to a simmer. Skim off any foam that rises, then simmer gently, uncovered, for 1 hour. Strain and use right away, or let cool and refrigerate for up to 2 days.

SPICED CRÈME FRAÎCHE

½ cup crème fraîche or sour cream

Freshly grated nutmeg

Freshly ground black pepper

Sea salt or kosher salt

Cinnamon, preferably freshly ground, for sprinkling

Chopped fresh parsley, for garnish

Preheat the oven to 400 degrees.

FOR THE SOUP: On a rimmed baking sheet, toss the squash with the oil and season lightly with salt. Spread the squash out and roast, turning several times, until tender and lightly caramelized, 25 to 30 minutes.

While the squash is roasting, in a 4- to 5-quart Dutch oven or other heavy pot, melt the butter over medium heat. Add the onions and ½ teaspoon salt and cook, stirring, for a minute or two. Stir in the ginger and garlic, cover, reduce the heat to medium-low, and cook gently for 15 minutes, stirring once or twice and lowering the heat if necessary to keep the vegetables from browning, until the onions are soft. Remove from the heat if the squash isn't done.

FOR THE BOUQUET GARNI: Bundle the ingredients in a square of cheesecloth and tie it with kitchen twine.

Add the stock or water, apple cider or juice, and roasted squash to the soup, stirring well. Add the bouquet garni and raise the heat to bring the soup to a boil, then reduce the heat to low, cover, and simmer for 20 minutes.

MEANWHILE, FOR THE CRÈME FRAÎCHE: In a small bowl, combine the crème fraîche or sour cream with 5 or 6 gratings of nutmeg, several grinds of black pepper, and a pinch of salt.

Discard the bouquet garni. Pass the soup through the fine holes of a food mill or puree using an immersion blender or, working in batches, in a regular blender. Season with salt and pepper. Reheat the soup if necessary.

Garnish each bowl of soup with a dollop of spiced crème fraîche, a dash of cinnamon, and a sprinkling of parsley.

Baked Fish /Ricotta Dumplings over French Lentils

SERVES 6: 3 SERVINGS FISH, 3 SERVINGS DUMPLINGS

This casserole is based on an all-purpose lentil recipe—when cooked until just tender, the lentils can be drained and dressed for a warm salad; when made with more broth, the recipe becomes a satisfying soup. Here the lentils form a saucy setting in which to nestle portions of fish or ricotta dumplings.

Seasoned with nutmeg and Parmesan and made toothsome with bread crumbs, the dumplings are hearty and flavorful. They're a great vehicle for good ricotta cheese—if you can go beyond the supermarket for this recipe, go to an Italian store that makes creamy ricotta fresh every day, or look for ricotta produced from grass-fed cows.

Halibut is my first choice here, but any firm white fish, such as fluke, flounder, hake, striped bass, cod, or scrod, will be great or a small whole fish. Ask your fishmonger for whatever's best. If using thin fillets such as sole, season them with salt and pepper, then roll them up, skinned side in, before placing them atop the lentils. Watch the fish carefully, and take the casserole out of the oven the moment the fish is cooked through.

Note: You can, of course, double the recipe for ricotta dumplings or the ingredients for the fish to make just one version of the dish. In that case, use a 3- to 4-quart baking dish for the casserole.

If I'm making this dish with just fish, and everyone eats meat, I sometimes dice 2 strips of bacon and add them to the lentils with the onions.

LENTILS

¼ cup extra-virgin olive oil

2 medium onions, finely chopped

1 large celery stalk, finely chopped

2 carrots, peeled and finely chopped

5–6 garlic cloves, coarsely chopped

2 teaspoons finely chopped peeled fresh ginger

2 cups French lentils, soaked for 2 hours (or overnight in the refrigerator) and drained

6 sprigs fresh thyme

4–6 fresh sage leaves

2 bay leaves

3 cups water

2 tablespoons fresh lemon juice

2 teaspoons sea salt or kosher salt

Freshly ground black pepper

FISH

1½ pounds firm white fish fillets or one 2½- to 3-pound whole fish, cleaned

Sea salt or kosher salt and freshly ground black pepper

4 thin lemon slices

2 tablespoons extra-virgin olive oil

2 tablespoons chopped fresh flat-leaf parsley, for serving

DUMPLINGS

1 cup firmly packed fresh sourdough bread crumbs (from 2–3 slices; see page 263)

¾ cup whole-milk ricotta cheese

1 large egg

1 large egg yolk

½ cup packed freshly grated Parmesan cheese (about 2 ounces)

Freshly grated nutmeg

¼ teaspoon sea salt or kosher salt, or to taste

Freshly ground black pepper

2 tablespoons extra-virgin olive oil

Chopped red bell pepper and lemon zest for garnish (optional)

FOR THE LENTILS: In a large heavy saucepan or small Dutch oven, heat the olive oil over medium heat. Add the onions and cook, stirring, until softened, about 5 minutes. Add the celery, carrots, garlic, and ginger and cook, stirring, for 2 minutes.

Stir in the lentils, thyme, sage, bay leaves, and water. Bring to a boil, then reduce the heat, cover, and simmer until the lentils are tender, about 25 minutes. There should be about ½ inch of broth remaining above the level of the lentils; if not, add a little water. Discard the bay leaves and thyme sprigs.

Set a rack in the upper third of the oven and preheat the oven to 375 degrees.

Season the lentils with the lemon juice, salt, and 3 or 4 grinds of black pepper, and divide them between two 1½-quart baking dishes.

FOR THE FISH: Season the fish with salt and pepper. Arrange the fish over one dish of lentils and place lemon slices on top of the fish. If using whole fish, slit the fish on one side in 4 pieces and insert the lemon slices into the slits. Drizzle the olive oil over the top. Bake until the fish is just cooked through, about 15 minutes for fillets or up to 30 minutes for a whole fish.

FOR THE DUMPLINGS: In a large bowl, combine the bread crumbs, ricotta, egg, egg yolk, and Parmesan. Season with 10 gratings (or a healthy pinch) nutmeg, the salt, and 8 grinds black pepper and mix well.

Moisten your hands and gently form the ricotta mixture into 6 dumplings. Arrange the dumplings over the other dish of lentils. Drizzle the olive oil over the top. Bake until the dumplings are lightly browned and cooked through, about 20 minutes.

Scatter the parsley over the fish and the red pepper and zest, if using, over the dumpling and serve.

Don't Flake Out

The advice to cook fish until it flakes is outdated, useful only if you want to re-create the texture of canned fish at home. Briefer cooking will yield more succulent and flavorful results. The leaner the fish, the faster it can go from done to overdone. To test for doneness, pierce a thick piece of a fillet (or a place near the spine for a whole fish) with a thin-bladed knife and part the flesh slightly. The flesh should just be opaque (for whole fish, it should come freely away from the bones at the spine). If you have one, insert an instant-read thermometer into the center of the fish: it should register 120 degrees for medium-rare, 130 degrees for medium.

Sautéed Escarole with Red Pepper and Garlic

SERVES 6

A juicy, tender green with a delicate flavor and pale color, escarole can be found in shops catering to Italian cooks throughout the year and in many supermarkets and produce markets and is never expensive. Unlike the other members of the endive family, escarole is not bitter, making it an especially supportive partner for mild-flavored fish and legumes.

> Sea salt or kosher salt
> 3 pounds escarole (3 medium heads), cored and coarsely chopped
> 3 tablespoons extra-virgin olive oil
> 2 garlic cloves, smashed and peeled
> ¼ teaspoon red pepper flakes
> Freshly ground black pepper

Bring a large pot of salted water to a boil. Add the escarole and boil, uncovered, until the escarole has wilted but still retains its color, 5 to 6 minutes. Drain well.

In a large skillet, heat the olive oil over medium heat. Add the garlic and pepper flakes and cook, stirring, until the garlic is pale gold, 1 to 2 minutes. Add the escarole and toss to coat with the flavored oil. Cook, stirring, for 3 to 4 minutes, or until the escarole is tender. Season with salt and black pepper and serve.

Fall

MENU 4
SERVES 4 TO 6

Lemon-Thyme Roast Chicken

Lemon-Thyme Tofu

Spicy Roasted Winter Squash

Toasted Millet Pilaf

Kale with Cremini Mushrooms

Add cranberry sauce to this menu and you've got yourself a Thanksgiving-worthy meal that you can make more than once a year. The chicken, tofu, and squash can all be roasted at the same time. Cooking the kale with mushrooms, onions, garlic, and thyme makes a wonderful, savory jus that balances the sweetness of the squash and moistens the millet. To simplify things, you could substitute a quick sauté of kale with sliced garlic for this slightly more involved kale dish.

Note: Double either tofu or chicken if you prefer to serve just one.

THE PLAN

1. At least 12 hours (or up to 2 days) ahead, salt the chicken and refrigerate.
2. Weight and drain the tofu.
3. Prepare the ingredients for the squash.
4. Toast the pumpkin seeds.
5. Roast the chicken, squash, and tofu.
6. Meanwhile, cook the millet.
7. Make the kale.

Lemon-Thyme Roast Chicken

SERVES 4

This recipe is my homage to three great cooks and a culmination of their chicken-roasting wisdom. The fine American chef Thomas Keller insists that roasting a chicken without any additional fat is the best technique, and I agree. It's the simplest and most convenient way to produce a succulent bird with a crisp skin. I add a whole lemon, à la great Italian cookbook writer Marcella Hazan, and I presalt the chicken, a technique espoused by Judy Rodgers of Zuni Café in San Francisco. If you can get Meyer lemons, use one instead of a regular lemon—its floral, almost herbaceous aroma and milder juice will really blossom as the chicken cooks. Salt the chicken at least 12 hours (or up to 2 days) in advance.

When it comes out of the oven, I sprinkle the chicken with fresh thyme, which sputters as it hits the hot bird, releasing a gust of perfume. When you carve the chicken, you'll marvel at the sparkling, golden brown, crackling-crisp skin and the heady fragrance.

> 1 3- to 4-pound chicken, preferably organic
> Kosher salt
> 1 lemon, preferably organic, punctured all over with a fork
> 1 tablespoon coarsely chopped fresh thyme
> Freshly ground black pepper
> 1–2 tablespoons unsalted butter, softened

AT LEAST 12 HOURS BEFORE ROASTING IT, SALT THE CHICKEN: Using ¾ teaspoon salt per pound of chicken, rub the chicken inside and out with salt. Stuff the lemon into the cavity. Tuck the wing tips under and tie the legs together with kitchen twine. Place the chicken on a plate and refrigerate, uncovered, for at least 12 hours, or up to 2 days.

Set a rack in the middle of the oven and preheat the oven to 450 degrees.

Thirty minutes before roasting, take the chicken out of the refrigerator and pat it dry (it will have released some liquid).

Place the chicken breast side up in a shallow flameproof roasting pan or heavy ovenproof skillet. Set the pan over high heat for 2 to 3 minutes, until the chicken begins to sizzle. Transfer the pan to the oven and roast undisturbed for 55 minutes, or until the skin is crisp and well browned and the juices run clear when the thigh is poked.

Sprinkle the chicken all over with the thyme, season generously with black pepper, and baste with the pan juices. Tip the chicken up and let the juices flow from the cavity into the roasting pan. Remove the lemon from the cavity (it will be very hot), and reserve. Transfer the chicken to a cutting board (set the roasting pan aside) and let rest for 15 minutes.

Cut the lemon in half, transfer the halves to a strainer, and squeeze the juice into the roasting pan. Set the pan over medium-high heat and bring the liquid to a simmer, scraping up all the caramelized bits from the bottom of the pan. Pour the pan juices into a glass measuring cup and let stand for a minute or so, then skim the clear fat off the top (or use a gravy separator).

Untie the chicken and sever the legs and thighs from the body. Cut the legs from the thighs and cut off the wings at the second joint. Cut the chicken in half lengthwise through the breast, and down either side of the spine. Quarter the breast halves crosswise through the bone. Arrange the chicken pieces on a platter and rub the butter over all. Serve drizzled with the pan juices.

Lemon-Thyme Tofu

SERVES 3 TO 4

This recipe is derived from one I developed for Angelica Kitchen in the early nineties. It's a great all-purpose vegetarian protein that you can whip up if a vegetarian friend drops in, and it's scrumptious on salads and in sandwiches. I like to serve the tofu over a sauce of roasted cherry tomatoes with a side of sautéed spinach for a quick vegetarian "square" meal.

- 1½ **pounds extra-firm tofu**
- 3 **tablespoons fresh lemon juice**
- 3 **tablespoons balsamic vinegar**
- 3 **tablespoons soy sauce, preferably naturally brewed**
- 3 **tablespoons extra-virgin olive oil**
- 1½ **teaspoons finely chopped fresh thyme or rosemary**
- ¼ **teaspoon cayenne pepper**
- 1 **lemon, sliced into thin rounds**

Set a rack in the middle of the oven and preheat the oven to 450 degrees.

Wrap the tofu in a clean kitchen towel and sandwich it between two plates. Set a weight on the top plate (such as a large can of tomatoes or a skillet) and let the tofu drain for 20 minutes.

Unwrap the tofu and slice it into ½-inch-thick triangles.

In a baking dish large enough to hold the tofu in a single snug layer, whisk together the remaining ingredients. Lay the slabs of tofu in the dish and turn to coat.

Roast for 20 minutes. Turn the tofu over, lay the lemon slices on top, and baste with the marinade in the pan. Roast until the tofu is well browned and most of the marinade has been absorbed, 15 to 20 minutes more. Serve.

Spicy Roasted Winter Squash

A squash with a tender skin is best here, since the chunks of squash are roasted unpeeled, which helps keep them from falling apart. If you do use a tougher-skinned squash, such as a butternut, peel it first. Bear in mind that the cooking times will vary, so start checking at 35 minutes and be prepared to roast the squash for up to 1 hour. A mixture of smoky chipotle chilies and maple syrup forms a sweet-and-spicy glaze that both accentuates the sweetness of the squash and gives it a gorgeous shine.

> 3 tablespoons maple syrup
>
> 2 tablespoons extra-virgin olive oil
>
> ¾ teaspoon chipotle powder or hot Spanish smoked paprika or ¼ teaspoon cayenne pepper, or to taste
>
> 1 medium squash (3–4 pounds), such as Buttercup, Kabocha, or Delicata, halved, seeded, and cut into slices
>
> ½ teaspoon sea salt or kosher salt

Preheat the oven to 450 degrees.

In a small bowl, mix the maple syrup, olive oil, chipotle, paprika or cayenne, and salt.

In a large bowl, toss the squash with the maple syrup mixture. Transfer to a baking dish large enough to hold the squash comfortably in a single layer.

Roast, stirring every 10 minutes for even browning, until the squash is tender, 40 to 50 minutes. Add a tablespoon or two of water to the baking dish as the squash roasts if it seems to be drying out. Serve.

Toasted Millet Pilaf

Toasting millet in a dry pan before simmering it gives its tiny yellow grains a nutty flavor and shortens the cooking time. Orange, rosemary, cayenne, and ginger spike the pilaf and brighten the rest of the meal.

1¼ cups millet

1 tablespoon unsalted butter

1 tablespoon extra-virgin olive oil

1 cup finely diced onion

1 teaspoon finely chopped fresh rosemary

1 teaspoon sea salt or kosher salt

1 cup coarsely grated peeled carrots

Finely grated zest of 1 orange

1 teaspoon finely chopped peeled fresh ginger

⅛ teaspoon cayenne pepper

¼ cup fresh orange juice

2⅓ cups water

⅓ cup Toasted Pumpkin Seeds (page 202)

In a large dry skillet, toast the millet over medium heat for 5 minutes or until fragrant, stirring and shaking the pan for even toasting. Transfer to a bowl.

In a medium heavy saucepan, heat the butter and oil over medium heat. Add the onion, rosemary, and salt and cook, stirring occasionally, for 5 minutes. Add the carrots, orange zest, ginger, and cayenne and cook, stirring, for 2 minutes.

Stir in the millet, orange juice, and water. Bring to a boil, then reduce the heat, cover, and simmer for 25 minutes until the millet is tender. Turn off the heat and let stand, covered, for 5 minutes.

Fluff the millet with a fork and serve sprinkled with the toasted pumpkin seeds.

Toasted Pumpkin Seeds

MAKES 1 CUP

You can purchase shelled green pumpkin seeds at natural food stores or Latin American markets (where they are called pepitas). Roasted with a little oil and seasonings, they make an addictive snack. If you like, add ½ teaspoon cayenne pepper along with the salt.

> **1 cup shelled pumpkin seeds**
> **1 teaspoon extra-virgin olive oil**
> **½ teaspoon sea salt or kosher salt**

Preheat the oven to 375 degrees.

In a small bowl, toss the seeds with the oil and salt. Spread on a small rimmed baking sheet and toast in the oven for 15 minutes, tossing every 5 minutes.

Transfer the seeds to a bowl to cool. The seeds can be stored in an airtight container for up to 1 week.

After the Frost

I remember, as a child, going out into my mother's garden after a big snowfall and seeing parsley, green and thriving, peeping out of the snow. I picked and tasted some. That moment was revelatory. While watery summer fruits and vegetables require the heat of the sun to ripen and can't tolerate the crisp days of fall, hardy kale, parsley, cabbage, cauliflower, pumpkins, and squash mature and develop character and sweetness as the weather gets colder.

Kale with Cremini Mushrooms

Kale is a hearty cold-weather green that improves if not harvested until after the first frost. The tighter the curls of the leaves are, the sweeter and more tender the kale will be. Here the earthy, meaty flavors of mushrooms and soy sauce combine with the juices from the kale to create a meatless jus. In addition to sweet, sour, salty, and bitter, the Japanese refer to a fifth "meaty" taste sensation, known as *umami*. You can taste it in the soy sauce and mushrooms, which give this dish an extremely satisfying depth of flavor.

Tip: To trim kale, start at the base of each leaf and pull the curled leaf away from the tough stem with your hands.

Sea salt or kosher salt

2 bunches kale (about 1½ pounds), thick stems removed

3 tablespoons extra-virgin olive oil

1½ cups thinly sliced onions

12 ounces cremini mushrooms, trimmed and sliced

3 garlic cloves, thinly sliced

2 teaspoons finely chopped peeled fresh ginger

1 teaspoon finely chopped fresh thyme

1 tablespoon soy sauce, preferably naturally brewed

Freshly ground black pepper

Bring a large pot of water to a boil and salt it well. Add the kale and cook, uncovered, until it is bright emerald green, about 3 minutes. Drain and let cool slightly, then coarsely chop and transfer to a bowl.

In a large skillet, heat the oil over high heat. Add the onions and cook, stirring occasionally, until they soften and begin to brown at the edges, 3 to 4 minutes. Add the mushrooms and ½ teaspoon salt and continue to cook over high heat, stirring, until the mushrooms give up their juices, 2 to 3 minutes. Add the garlic, ginger, and thyme and cook, stirring, for 1 minute more.

Add the kale to the pan, along with any juices that have collected in the bowl. Stir in the soy sauce and season with black pepper. Cover, reduce the heat to medium-low, and simmer until the kale is very tender, 5 to 7 minutes. Serve.

Fall

MENU 5
SERVES 4

Chestnut Apple Soup

Penne with Beets, Beet Greens,
Goat Cheese, and Walnuts

This nutritious, meatless meal is everything a fall supper should be: comforting, hearty, and complete. The classic bistro combination of beets, goat cheese, greens, and walnuts is mixed with penne for a vibrant main-course pasta, while the soup is soothing and subtle. Look for fresh chestnuts and walnuts in the shell during autumn—they're sweet and moist, and they stay fresh longer in the shell. I prefer Italian chestnuts, which are usually available in stores in the fall.

THE PLAN
1. Prepare the chestnuts in their shells, if using.
2. Roast the beets.
3. Make the soup.
4. Just before serving, finish the pasta.

Chestnut Apple Soup

SERVES 6

This rich, smooth soup will not suffer from omitting the half-and-half or cream, if you prefer not to use it, but the addition is a luxury that gives the texture a lovely satin finish. Browning the butter used to cook the vegetables enhances the nutty richness of the chestnuts.

Tip: To score chestnuts, hold each one against your work surface and draw a very sharp knife over the flattest side, slicing an X into the shell. Soaking the chestnuts for 30 minutes before roasting softens their shells.

1 pound chestnuts in the shell (3 cups), scored and soaked in warm water for 30 minutes, or 2 cups (10 ounces) vacuum-packed shelled peeled chestnuts (available in specialty markets)

4 tablespoons (½ stick) unsalted butter

2 cups finely chopped onions

2 teaspoons chopped fresh sage

2 teaspoons chopped peeled fresh ginger

Sea salt or kosher salt

2 medium Yukon Gold potatoes (8 ounces), peeled and chopped

2 medium parsnips (8 ounces), peeled and chopped

1 large (8–10 ounce) apple, such as Mutsu, Winesap, Gala, or Golden Delicious, peeled, cored, and chopped

4½–5 cups vegetable stock or water

⅔ cup half-and-half or heavy cream (optional)

Freshly ground black pepper

Maple syrup, for serving

If using chestnuts in the shell, preheat the oven to 350 degrees.

Spread the soaked chestnuts on a rimmed baking sheet. Roast until the shells crack open and you can peel the brown skins away easily, 45 minutes to an hour. Wrap the chestnuts in a clean cotton towel and let steam until just cool enough to handle, 5 to 10 minutes.

Pull away the shells, then the skins from the chestnuts; briefly return any to the oven that are difficult to peel.

In a 4- to 5-quart Dutch oven or other heavy pot, melt the butter over medium heat and let it cook until it has turned golden and ceased to sputter, about 5 minutes. Add the onions, sage, ginger, and ½ teaspoon salt, cover, and cook, stirring frequently and adjusting the heat as necessary to keep the onions from browning, until the onions are golden and meltingly tender, about 15 minutes.

Add the potatoes, parsnips, apple, chestnuts, and enough stock or water to cover the vegetables (about 4½ cups). Bring to a boil, then cover, reduce the heat, and simmer until the vegetables are tender enough to crush against the side of the pot, 25 to 30 minutes.

Using an immersion blender, or working in batches in a regular blender, puree the soup until smooth. Blend in the half-and-half or cream, if using, and thin with more stock or water if desired. Transfer to a saucepan and reheat, season with salt and pepper, and serve, drizzling each bowl with a little maple syrup.

Penne with Beets, Beet Greens, Goat Cheese, and Walnuts

SERVES 4

Look for beets with healthy greens (limp, torn leaves won't make for good eating). If nice beet greens are not available, use 12 ounces of Swiss chard or spinach in their place. Pecans can be substituted for the walnuts.

- 2 bunches beets with greens (about 2 pounds), trimmed, greens reserved, and beets scrubbed
- Sea salt or kosher salt
- 8 ounces whole wheat penne
- ¼ cup extra-virgin olive oil
- 4 garlic cloves, thinly sliced
- 1 tablespoon chopped fresh tarragon
- ¼–½ teaspoon red pepper flakes
- 4 ounces fresh goat cheese, crumbled (about ½ cup)
- ¼ cup heavy cream or crème fraîche
- Freshly ground black pepper
- ¾ cup walnuts, toasted (see page 208) and coarsely chopped

Preheat the oven to 400 degrees.

Wrap the beets in foil (or place them in a tightly covered ovenproof skillet with ½ cup water), place on a baking sheet, and roast until they can be pierced easily with the tip of a knife, about 45 minutes.

Wash and drain the beet greens. Cut into ½-inch-wide ribbons and set aside.

Unwrap the beets, transfer to a colander, and cool under cold running water. Slip off the skins and discard. Trim the ends of the beets and slice them vertically ½ inch thick. Stack the slices and cut into ½-inch-wide sticks.

Bring a large pot of salted water to a boil. Add the penne and cook until al dente, about 8 minutes.

Meanwhile, in a large skillet, heat the oil over medium heat until it shimmers. Add the garlic, tarragon, and pepper flakes and cook, stirring, until the garlic is lightly colored, 1 to 2 minutes. Add the beets and greens and cook, stirring, until the greens have wilted, 1 to 2 minutes.

Drain the pasta and add it to the pan. Stir in the goat cheese and cream or crème fraîche and bring to a simmer. Season with salt and pepper.

Serve immediately, sprinkled with the walnuts.

Fall

MENU 6
SERVES 6

**White Beans/Shrimp with Brown Butter
and Tons of Herbs**

Soft Polenta

Roasted Broccoli with Parmesan

In my family, polenta, beans, and broccoli are comfort foods. Adding shrimp is a treat. This menu requires no unusual ingredients or labor-intensive techniques, but it is far more than a sum of its parts, primarily because of the sumptuous brown butter sauce. The butter is cooked until its milk solids turn nut brown and take on a deliciously toasted flavor, then poured over fresh herbs, chilies, and garlic. Its heat instantly brings their flavors together in a lively, delectable sauce for the white beans or shrimp.

THE PLAN
1. Soak the beans.
2. Simmer the beans.
3. Roast the broccoli.
4. Meanwhile, cook the polenta and keep warm in a double boiler.
5. Make the brown butter sauce.
6. Finish the beans.
7. Cook the shrimp.

White Beans/**Shrimp**
with Brown Butter and Tons of Herbs

SERVES 6: 3 SERVINGS BEANS, 3 SERVINGS SHRIMP

Gently simmered white beans and cooked shrimp turn luxurious when tossed in warm brown butter with aromatic herbs, garlic, and crushed chili. You can vary the herbs, using any fresh, tender leaves, such as sage, oregano, or even mint, but do use the full amount of parsley, which contributes a lovely freshness. When you pour the piping hot brown butter over the herbs, it will foam up, so choose a deep bowl.

Buy the shrimp the day you'll use them and cook them briefly, undisturbed, so they can brown slightly, their juices caramelizing in the pan. They'll be sweet and firm.

The technique of soaking, blanching, draining, and then simmering the beans very gently in minimal water ensures that they will be fully cooked and easy to digest, without turning to mush.

Tip: This recipe yields more beans than you'll sauce and serve, because I always like to cook extra. They're great in soups, salads, or pasta dishes. If you prefer to wind up with the exact amount of beans needed here, use 1 cup dried beans to yield 3 servings. Start soaking the beans 12 hours ahead (or use the quick-soak method on page 9) and count on simmering them for up to 1½ hours.

Note: If you prefer all beans or all shrimp, double one and leave off the other, making the brown butter in any event.

BEANS

2 cups great northern beans, soaked (see page 9)

1 carrot, peeled and quartered lengthwise

1 small onion, peeled and halved lengthwise

2–3 garlic cloves, peeled

1 small celery stalk with leaves

2–3 sprigs fresh herbs, such as thyme, rosemary, or sage

Sea salt or kosher salt and freshly ground black pepper

Juice of ½ lemon, or to taste

BROWN BUTTER SAUCE

2 tablespoons finely chopped fresh flat-leaf parsley

1 tablespoon finely chopped fresh tarragon

1 tablespoon finely chopped fresh thyme

1 garlic clove, very finely chopped

  Pinch of red pepper flakes

8 tablespoons (1 stick) unsalted butter

SHRIMP

1 tablespoon extra-virgin olive oil

1 pound large shrimp, peeled and deveined

  Juice of ½ lemon

  Sea salt or kosher salt and freshly ground black pepper

  Lemon wedges, for serving

FOR THE BEANS: Drain the beans and transfer to a pot. Cover with a few inches of water, bring to a boil over high heat, and boil until foam rises, 2 to 3 minutes. Drain the beans and rinse. Wash out any scum clinging to the sides of the pot, and return the beans to the pot. Add the carrot, onion, garlic, celery, herbs, and enough cold water to cover the beans by ½ inch. Bring to a boil over medium-high heat. Cover, reduce the heat, and simmer gently until the beans are nearly tender, about 40 minutes. Add ½ teaspoon salt and a generous grind of pepper, cover, and simmer until the beans are cooked through, 30 to 45 minutes more. Remove from the heat.

FOR THE BROWN BUTTER SAUCE: Place the herbs, garlic, and pepper flakes in a 4-cup glass measuring cup or a deep bowl.

In a small saucepan, melt the butter over medium heat. Let the butter cook, swirling the pan occasionally, until the white milk solids fall to the bottom of the pan and the butter has turned amber brown, about 4 minutes. Immediately pour the butter over the herbs (take care, as the hot butter may sputter).

Remove the vegetables from the beans and discard (or chop and add them to the beans before serving). Drain the beans, and transfer half of them to a serving bowl; discard the herb sprigs. Reserve the remaining beans for another use. Toss the beans with ¼ cup of the brown butter sauce. Season with salt to taste and finish with the lemon juice. Keep warm.

FOR THE SHRIMP: In a large skillet, heat the olive oil over medium heat. Add the shrimp and cook, undisturbed, until lightly browned on the first side, about 2 minutes. Turn and cook until cooked through, 1 to 2 minutes. Add the remaining ¼ cup brown butter sauce and the lemon juice and stir, scraping the bottom of the pan to release any browned bits. Season with salt and pepper.

Serve the beans and the shrimp spooned over the polenta with lemon wedges.

Butter Made Better

Next time you're hungry and short on groceries, check the butter dish: a stick of butter, browned and tossed with some aromatics, is an instant sauce. When you brown butter, you're evaporating the water in it and caramelizing the milk solids, which creates a nutty aroma and super-buttery flavor that will turn 12 ounces of pasta into a rich meal. Brown butter gives even the plainest vegetable the savor of a well-seared steak: beans, potatoes, steamed carrots, all rise to new heights tossed with a little brown butter. Or drizzle some over grilled or pan-seared fish fillets. Plain brown butter can be chilled and kept on hand in the refrigerator or freezer; it has a longer shelf life than fresh butter. Try it in a cookie or cake recipe, or spread some on warm toast.

To brown butter, cook it in a saucepan over medium heat until it has stopped popping and spitting (that is the sound of the moisture in the butter boiling off). Then reduce the heat and cook, swirling the pan a few times, until the milk solids have begun to take on a nut-brown color and a toasty fragrance. Immediately transfer the butter to a bowl to stop the cooking.

Once the butter is browned, it can be flavored by adding fresh herbs, minced garlic, chopped nuts, fresh citrus juice, vinegar, or, for a dessert sauce, honey and hazelnuts. Be sure to use a deep bowl when tossing the hot butter with anything moist or cold, as it will foam up remarkably. These additions arrest the cooking before the butter begins to burn, and the warm butter draws out all their flavors.

Soft Polenta

Coarse polenta or corn grits are a convenient staple to keep in your pantry to round out a meal whenever you're tired or short on time. I often enrich my polenta with butter, olive oil, and/or grated cheese. However, because of the brown butter sauce, this menu calls for a leaner version.

Tip: Pour any leftover polenta into a baking dish and refrigerate until firm. Then slice and grill, broil, or panfry the firm polenta squares. Serve topped with your favorite sauce, a juicy vegetable sauté, or melted cheese.

> **4 cups water**
> **1½ cups coarse polenta or medium corn grits**
> **1 teaspoon sea salt or kosher salt**

Bring the water to a boil in a medium heavy saucepan. Whisk in the polenta or grits and salt and stir until the mixture begins to thicken. Lower the heat so the polenta sputters gently and continue to cook, uncovered, stirring occasionally, until the polenta is thick and smooth, 5 to 7 minutes. Serve.

Roasted Broccoli with Parmesan

Broccoli isn't commonly roasted, but the crispy browned florets and slightly crunchy stems are very good. The best way to trim the broccoli for this dish is to cut the bottom ½ inch off each stalk, then peel the stalks completely and cut down the whole length of each one to divide the broccoli into medium-sized florets attached to long, thin stems (they will resemble the slender stalks of broccolini).

> 3 pounds broccoli, bottoms trimmed, stems peeled, and cut into long-stemmed florets (see headnote above)
>
> 6 tablespoons extra-virgin olive oil
>
> ¾ teaspoon red pepper flakes
>
> Sea salt or kosher salt and freshly ground black pepper
>
> ¾ cup freshly grated Parmesan cheese (about 3 ounces)
>
> ⅓ cup white wine vinegar

Place a 10- to 12-inch cast-iron pan, a heavy rimmed baking sheet, or a roasting pan on the middle rack of the oven and preheat the oven to 450 degrees.

In a large bowl, toss the broccoli with 5 tablespoons of the oil, the pepper flakes, and salt and pepper to taste.

Carefully transfer the hot pan to the stovetop and add the broccoli. Sprinkle the cheese evenly over the broccoli and drizzle with the remaining 1 tablespoon oil.

Return the pan to the oven and roast until the broccoli is crispy and browning on the edges and the stems have begun to soften, about 25 minutes.

Transfer the broccoli to a serving platter. Add the vinegar to the hot pan and stir, scraping up the caramelized bits cooked onto the bottom. Pour the pan juices over the broccoli and serve.

Fall

MENU 7
SERVES 4 TO 6

Autumn Stew with Miso and Duck/Tofu

Napa Cabbage Salad with Sweet Peppers and Sesame Vinaigrette

Sweet Brown Rice

Aged miso enhances just about any soup or stew with its earthy, complex flavors. This soulful, hearty stew goes wonderfully with duck and is just as stick-to-your-ribs when served with fried tofu. The sweet brown rice is a great cold-weather dish on its own; add the crisp cabbage salad to the menu if time and inclination allow. The salad can be made ahead and chilled while the stew simmers.

THE PLAN
1. Soak the rice.
2. Make the cabbage salad and refrigerate.
3. Cook the stew.
4. Meanwhile, cook the rice.
5. Roast the duck.
6. Fry the tofu.
7. Finish the stew.

Autumn Stew with Miso and Duck/Tofu

SERVES 4 TO 6: 2 TO 3 SERVINGS DUCK, 2 TO 3 SERVINGS TOFU

To "confit" something is to preserve it by slowly heating it in either fat or a sugar syrup (as in confit fruits). Duck confit is a convenient delicacy with depth of flavor, and because it's rich, a little goes a long way. It has a long shelf life too, so it's a good thing to keep on hand in your fridge for dressing up everything from stews and soups to pasta, sandwiches, and salads. Duck confit is sold at specialty butchers and gourmet food shops.

Tofu is felt to have an energy that cools the body down, and the Japanese believe that the warmth and energy that comes from deep-frying balances this cooling energy. The crisp, warm tofu replicates the richness of the duck and offers a delicate textural contrast to the stew. On a cold night, give this stew a little kick by adding a pinch of chili pepper flakes along with the carrots, or pass your favorite bottled hot sauce at the table.

Note: Double the tofu or duck and serve with the stew if you want.

STEW

- 1 tablespoon extra-virgin olive oil
- 1 tablespoon unsalted butter
- 2 medium onions, cut into 1-inch chunks (about 3 cups)
- 1 large burdock root (about 8 ounces; see page 256), scrubbed and cut on the diagonal into ⅓-inch-thick slices
- 8 ounces cremini mushrooms, trimmed, halved if large (about 2½ cups)
- 12 thin slices peeled fresh ginger
- 3 garlic cloves, thinly sliced
- 1 large sprig fresh thyme
- 1¼ pounds winter squash, such as Kabocha, butternut, Buttercup, or Red Kuri, peeled, seeded, and cut into large chunks (about 4 cups)
- 2 large carrots (about 8 ounces), peeled and cut on the diagonal into ⅓-inch-thick slices
- 2 large celery stalks, cut on the diagonal into ⅓-inch-thick slices
- ⅓ cup *mugi* (dark, barley) miso
- 1 tablespoon arrowroot or cornstarch
- 2 tablespoons cold water

DUCK

2 duck confit legs

TOFU

Vegetable oil, for deep-frying

½ cup arrowroot or cornstarch, for dredging

1 pound extra-firm tofu, cut into four ¾-inch-thick slabs

2 tablespoons sesame seeds, toasted (see page 11), for garnish

Chopped fresh flat-leaf parsley, for garnish

FOR THE STEW: In a 4- to 5-quart Dutch oven or a large heavy saucepan, heat the olive oil and butter over medium heat. Add the onions and cook, stirring, until lightly browned, about 10 minutes. Add the burdock and mushrooms and cook, stirring, until both are well browned, about 6 minutes more.

Add the ginger, garlic, and thyme and cook, stirring, for 2 minutes. Add the squash, carrots, celery, and enough water to barely cover the vegetables (about 4 cups). Bring to a boil, then partially cover, reduce the heat, and simmer, stirring occasionally, until the vegetables are tender, about 35 minutes. Discard the thyme. Adjust the heat if necessary to keep the vegetables from scorching on the bottom.

MEANWHILE, FOR THE DUCK: Preheat the oven to 350 degrees.

Place the duck legs in a cast-iron skillet, skin side up, and heat over high heat until they start to sizzle, about 3 minutes. Transfer the pan to the oven and roast until the duck has rendered much of its fat and the skin is browned and crisp, 25 to 30 minutes.

Transfer the legs to a board. As soon as they are cool enough to handle, pull the meat off the bones. Cut or shred the duck meat and skin. (Save the bones for stock, if you like.) Keep the meat warm.

FOR THE TOFU: Fill a small deep pot with at least 2 inches of oil and clip a deep-frying thermometer to the side of the pot (be sure it is not touching the bottom of the pot). Heat the oil over high heat until it reaches 375 degrees. While the oil heats, place the arrowroot or cornstarch in a shallow bowl and line a plate with paper towels. Pat the tofu dry and dredge it in the arrowroot or cornstarch, then carefully slip the pieces into the hot oil and fry, turning occasionally and adjusting the heat as necessary to keep the oil at 350 degrees,

until golden and crisp, 4 to 5 minutes. Use a slotted spoon or a wire skimmer to transfer the tofu to the paper-towel-lined plate.

TO FINISH THE STEW: Ladle some of the liquid from the stew into a bowl and add the miso. Stir until the miso is dissolved, then stir some or all of the miso mixture into the stew, adding it little by little and tasting as you go. Misos vary in salt content—the stew should taste savory but not briny.

In a small bowl, combine the 1 tablespoon arrowroot or cornstarch with the cold water and stir well. Stir about half of this mixture into the stew and simmer for 1 minute, then add more if the stew is not as thick as you'd like and simmer for 1 more minute.

Ladle the stew into bowls and top half the bowls with the shredded duck meat and crispy skin and the other half with the tofu. Sprinkle with the sesame seeds and parsley. Serve.

Body by Miso

Like yogurt, miso is a "live food" beneficial to digestion. A concentrated paste of fermented soybeans preserved with a significant amount of sea salt, it's an essential element of Japanese cooking, best known for its role in miso soup, where it is thinned with a little of the clear dashi (Japanese broth), then stirred into the larger pot of broth. The salty paste can also be added to stews and sauces, blended into salad dressings, or thinned and used as a glaze for grilling or as a marinade. It's a potent flavor base, one that I turn to, where some chefs would use a reduced meat stock, to add body and depth.

Misos vary in color and flavor. The lighter varieties, such as white miso (actually a golden color, also called mellow or sweet miso), are sweeter and milder than the darker ones, such as amber-colored *mugi* (barley) miso. Lighter misos are more appropriate for delicate warm-weather dishes, darker ones for heartier cold-weather ones. Look for unpasteurized miso in the refrigerator case of natural food stores or Japanese markets. Once you add miso to a soup or stew, keep it below a boil to avoid killing the health-supporting cultures.

Napa Cabbage Salad with Sweet Peppers and Sesame Vinaigrette

SERVES 4

This colorful, slawlike Asian salad gets its refreshing crispness from napa, or Chinese, cabbage, a softer, more watery variety with a sweeter, milder flavor than regular green cabbage. Choose tight, pale, elongated heads that are heavy for their size, with firm, unblemished white stems. If you end up with a larger cabbage than needed here, slice the rest into a stir-fry or into miso broth for a quick soup.

VINAIGRETTE

- 3 tablespoons rice vinegar
- 3 tablespoons fresh lemon juice
- 1½ tablespoons soy sauce, preferably naturally brewed
- 1 tablespoon sugar
- ¾ teaspoon sea salt or kosher salt
- 1½ tablespoons extra-virgin olive oil
- 1 tablespoon toasted sesame oil
- 2 serrano peppers or 1 large jalapeño, finely chopped (seeds and veins discarded for a milder dressing)

SALAD

- 1 1-pound napa cabbage, trimmed and leaves cut crosswise into thin strips (about 6 cups)
- 1 red bell pepper, peeled if desired (see page 131) and thinly sliced
- 1 large yellow pepper, peeled if desired and thinly sliced
- 3 scallions, green parts only, thinly sliced (reserve the whites for another use)
- 1 tablespoon sesame seeds, lightly toasted (see page 11)
- Sea salt or kosher salt and freshly ground black pepper

FOR THE VINAIGRETTE: In a large serving bowl, whisk together the vinegar, lemon juice, soy sauce, sugar, and salt until dissolved. Whisk in the olive and sesame oils and the chili pepper.

FOR THE SALAD: Add the cabbage, bell peppers, scallions, and sesame seeds to the bowl and toss well. Cover and refrigerate for 15 minutes to allow the cabbage to absorb the seasonings. (You can make the salad up to 4 hours ahead and refrigerate, covered.)

Taste the salad, season with salt and pepper, and serve.

Sweet Brown Rice

Also called glutinous brown rice, this short-grain rice is chewy, with a wholesome texture that I especially appreciate during the colder months.

Tip: Brown rice should usually be soaked for 6 hours before it is cooked, to soften its outer hull. However, I've discovered that a technique much like the "quick-soak" method used for beans works beautifully. For this recipe, you can either soak the rice in cold water to cover for at least 6 hours, then drain and rinse it, or place the rice in a saucepan with cold water to cover by 2 inches, bring to a boil, and simmer for 1 minute. Turn off the heat and let sit, uncovered, for 1 hour, then drain and rinse before cooking.

1½ **cups sweet brown rice, soaked and drained**
2 **cups water**
¾ **teaspoon sea salt or kosher salt**

In a medium saucepan, combine the rice with the water and salt and bring to a simmer. Reduce the heat to low and simmer, covered, until the rice is tender and the water is absorbed, about 40 minutes. Serve.

Fall

MENU 8
SERVES 6

Lasagna with Fall Vegetables, Gruyère, and Sage Béchamel

Roasted Brussels Sprouts with Fennel Seeds and Balsamic

Ordinary vegetarian lasagnas feature canned tomatoes and eggplant or zucchini layered with plain noodles and ricotta. This one is made with golden egg noodles, Gruyère cheese, butternut squash, mushrooms, and hearty greens, bound by a smooth sage béchamel. It's so satisfying that it may win over even committed carnivores at Thanksgiving. Since the lasagna can be assembled a day in advance (and the Brussels sprouts blanched ahead as well), this is a great menu for entertaining.

THE PLAN

1. Make the pasta dough and let it rest (or make it up to 3 days ahead and refrigerate; bring to room temperature before proceeding).
2. Cook the lasagna filling and the spinach.
3. Infuse the milk for the béchamel.
4. Meanwhile, roll, cut, and cook the pasta.
5. Make the béchamel.
6. Assemble and bake the lasagna.
7. Meanwhile, roast the Brussels sprouts.

Lasagna with Fall Vegetables, Gruyère, and Sage Béchamel

SERVES 6

Making lasagna with homemade noodles is a labor of love, but these exquisite noodles are more than worth the trouble. If you won't have a stretch of uninterrupted time for cooking, spread out the work. You can make the pasta dough, béchamel, and filling ahead. Alternatively, you can assemble the unbaked lasagna a day ahead (take the pan out of the fridge an hour or two before baking to lose the chill).

Tip: There's no need to preboil the fresh noodles; they will absorb the sauce and fully cook in the time it takes to bake the lasagna.

NOODLES

6 large egg yolks

1 large egg

1½ tablespoons extra-virgin olive oil

2 tablespoons whole milk

2 cups unbleached all-purpose flour, plus additional for kneading

Sea salt or kosher salt

VEGETABLE FILLING

3 pounds butternut squash, peeled, seeded, and cut into ½-inch cubes

1½ pounds portobello mushroom caps or cremini mushrooms, trimmed if necessary and cut into ½-inch cubes

3 tablespoons extra-virgin olive oil

Sea salt or kosher salt and freshly ground black pepper

2 dried ancho chilies

2 tablespoons unsalted butter

1 very large or 2 medium onions, diced (2½ to 3 cups)

2 garlic cloves, finely chopped

2 pounds spinach (2–3 bunches), washed and tough stems discarded

Freshly grated nutmeg

SAGE BÉCHAMEL

    4 cups whole milk

    ½ cup finely chopped onion

    1 large or 2 small shallots, finely chopped

    ¼ cup coarsely chopped fresh sage

    1 bay leaf

    6 tablespoons (¾ stick) unsalted butter

    6 tablespoons all-purpose flour

    8 ounces Gruyère cheese, coarsely grated (about 2¼ cups)

    4 ounces Parmesan cheese, finely grated (about 1 cup)

FOR THE NOODLES: In a medium bowl, stir together the egg yolks, egg, olive oil, and milk.

Place the flour and ½ teaspoon salt in a food processor. Add the egg mixture and pulse until the dough comes together in a mass. Transfer the dough to a lightly floured surface and knead until the dough is smooth and satiny, 2 to 3 minutes. Test the dough by inserting a clean fingertip: if the dough sticks to your finger, add a bit more flour and knead until smooth. Dribble on a few drops of milk if the dough is too dry.

Wrap the dough in plastic and set aside for 30 minutes at room temperature (the dough can be refrigerated for up to 3 days—bring it to room temperature before proceeding).

Divide the dough into 4 equal pieces. Work with one piece of dough at a time, keeping the remainder wrapped in plastic wrap. Adjust the rollers on your pasta machine to the widest setting. Flatten the first piece of dough and run it through the machine. Fold the dough into thirds, insert a narrower end into the machine, and roll it through again. Lay the rolled dough flat on a towel. Repeat the process until all 4 pieces of dough have been rolled twice. Make sure the pieces do not touch each other when you lay them on the towel or they may stick together.

Bring the rollers of the pasta machine one notch closer together. Insert a narrower end of the first piece of dough into the machine and roll it through. Repeat with the remaining pieces, always rolling them in the same order to prevent uneven drying and to ensure consistent texture and color in the finished pasta. Continue rolling, narrowing the rollers one notch at a time, until you have passed all the sheets of dough through the next-to-the-last setting.

Cut the sheets of dough into pieces to fit the length of your lasagna pan. Lay the pieces on a sheet of floured wax or parchment paper, without touching each other. When the sheet is filled, top it with another lightly floured piece and set the lasagna noodles on top. Repeat until all the noodles are cut to size. Cover the noodles with plastic and set aside.

Preheat the oven to 450 degrees.

FOR THE FILLING: In a large bowl, toss the squash and mushrooms with 2 tablespoons of the olive oil, 1 teaspoon salt, and plenty of pepper. Spread the mixture on a rimmed baking sheet, setting aside the bowl (you'll use it again). Roast the vegetables, stirring every 10 minutes, until tender, 25 to 30 minutes.

Meanwhile, cut open the chilies with kitchen shears and discard the seeds and stem. Place the chilies in a small bowl and cover them with boiling water. Let sit until soft, 8 to 10 minutes. Drain and finely chop.

In a medium skillet, melt the butter and the remaining 1 tablespoon oil over medium heat.

Add the onions and ½ teaspoon salt and cook, stirring, until the onions are softened, 5 to 7 minutes. Stir in the chilies and garlic and cook, stirring, for another 3 to 4 minutes. Remove from the heat.

Return the roasted vegetables to the bowl and stir in the onion mixture. Season with salt and pepper. (The filling can be made up to 2 days ahead, covered, and refrigerated.)

Place the spinach, with some water still clinging to its leaves, in a large pot and cook, covered, over high heat until wilted, 1 to 2 minutes. Drain and rinse under cold running water until cool, then squeeze dry and coarsely chop.

Transfer the spinach to a bowl and season with salt, pepper, and a little nutmeg. (The spinach can be cooked up to 2 days ahead and refrigerated.)

FOR THE BÉCHAMEL: Pour the milk into a large saucepan and bring to a boil. Immediately take the pan off the heat. Stir in the onion, shallots, sage, and bay leaf, cover, and let sit for 30 minutes. Strain the milk and discard the solids.

In a medium skillet, melt the butter over medium heat. Add the flour and cook, stirring constantly, until the roux is fragrant and a shade darker, about 3 minutes. Slowly whisk in the milk until smooth. Bring to a simmer, then reduce the heat and cook gently, stirring occasionally, until thick, about 20 minutes. (The béchamel can be made up to 2 days ahead. Allow the sauce to cool, then press plastic wrap directly onto the surface before refrigerating.)

In a bowl, toss together the Gruyère and Parmesan.

Preheat the oven to 400 degrees.

TO ASSEMBLE THE LASAGNA: Spread a quarter of the béchamel on the bottom of a 9-by-13-inch lasagna pan or gratin dish. Make one layer of noodles, slightly overlapping. Spread half of the roasted vegetables over the noodles and sprinkle with a quarter of the cheese mixture. Make a second layer of pasta and top with another quarter of the sauce, then all of the chopped spinach, and another quarter of the cheese mixture. Make a third layer of noodles and spread with half of the remaining béchamel, the remaining roasted vegetables, and half of the remaining cheese mixture. Make a fourth layer of noodles, spread with the remaining sauce, and sprinkle with the remaining cheese.

Butter a piece of parchment paper and lay it buttered side down over the lasagna. Cover the pan loosely with foil and bake for 40 minutes.

Remove the foil and parchment and bake until the lasagna is golden brown and bubbling, 10 to 15 minutes more. Let rest for 10 minutes before cutting and serving.

Roasted Brussels Sprouts with Fennel Seeds and Balsamic

SERVES 6

My teenage daughter, Emma, is addicted to this dish. Even the Brussels sprout–leery will want to try these tender sprouts with their crisped brown exterior and creamy centers. They're also scrumptious cold, and Emma insists they be in the fridge all fall to snack on, so I always make extra.

Tips: Fennel seeds are not especially hard, but they do roll when you try to crush them. To lightly crush them to release their anise scent, mound them on a large cutting board and press down hard on them with the bottom of a heavy pan, or place them in a mortar and pound with the pestle until coarsely crushed.

Scoring an X in the stem of each Brussels sprout allows the boiling water to reach the dense, crunchy centers, helping them cook more evenly.

>   Sea salt or kosher salt
>   3 pounds Brussels sprouts, trimmed and stems scored with an X
>   ⅓ cup balsamic vinegar
>   3 tablespoons extra-virgin olive oil
>   ¾ teaspoon lightly crushed fennel seeds
>   Freshly ground black pepper

Preheat the oven to 400 degrees.

Bring a large pot of salted water to a boil. Add the sprouts and boil, uncovered, until crisp-tender, 4 to 5 minutes. Drain well and transfer to an 11-by-17-inch baking pan or other baking dish in which they will fit in a single layer (or use two smaller pans).

Drizzle the sprouts with the vinegar and oil, sprinkle with the fennel seeds, and season lightly with salt and pepper. Roast, stirring occasionally, until the outer leaves are crisp and burnished, 35 to 40 minutes. Sprinkle with salt before serving.

Fall

MENU 9

SERVES 4 TO 6

**Pan-Seared Seitan
with Thyme, Lemon, and Mustard**

**Pan-Seared Lamb Steak with
Thyme, Lemon, and Mustard**

Carrots with Black Olives and Mint

Spicy Lentils with Pumpkin and Greens over Couscous

In this Mediterranean-style menu, your guests can choose between seared seitan and seared lamb. These recipes show how easily a meal can be customized to vegetarians or omnivores without compromising flavor or elegance. Of course, you can serve just one of these dishes, doubling the recipe. For a much simpler but still complete meal, you could leave out the seitan and lamb—the lentil stew, served over couscous, makes a great supper on its own.

THE PLAN

1. Soak the lentils.
2. Marinate the lamb.
3. Cook the lentils and kale.
4. Meanwhile, cook the carrots (serve warm or chilled).
5. Sear the seitan and lamb.

Pan-Seared Seitan with Thyme, Lemon, and Mustard

SERVES 3 TO 4

You can use store-bought or homemade seitan for this gorgeous "wheat-meat" dish. Homemade seitan has the advantage of not falling apart as you slice it, but in either case you should be able to create ½-inch-thick slices for searing. The surface of the seitan becomes richly browned as it cooks, while the interior remains succulent, redolent of garlic, mustard, and herbs.

Seitan absorbs flavorings readily and is tender to begin with, so a mere 15 minutes is all it needs in the marinade. The soy and mirin in the marinade both create a delicious complexity of flavor and encourage browning. Squeezing out the excess liquid from the spongy seitan first will give you a better sear and a more flavorful finished dish, as will preheating your pan well. Cast-iron results in the best sear, but any heavy skillet will do.

MARINADE

6 tablespoons extra-virgin olive oil

3 tablespoons soy sauce, preferably naturally brewed

3 tablespoons mirin (see Tip, page 85)

1½ tablespoons Dijon mustard

1 tablespoon finely chopped fresh thyme

3 garlic cloves, crushed through a garlic press or finely grated

Finely grated zest of 1½ lemons

¾ teaspoon sea salt or kosher salt

Freshly ground black pepper to taste

1 pound seitan, gently squeezed to remove excess liquid and sliced ½ inch thick

Juice of 1½ lemons, combined with 2 tablespoons water

FOR THE MARINADE: In a medium bowl, combine all the ingredients. Add the seitan and toss until well combined. Let marinate for 15 minutes.

TO PREPARE THE SEITAN: Heat a cast-iron or other heavy 8- to 10-inch skillet over high heat until very hot. Pour the seitan and all of its marinade into the pan, reduce the heat to medium, and cook undisturbed until the seitan is nicely browned on the bottom, about 2 minutes. Flip the seitan pieces and cook until browned on the second side, about 2 minutes more. Turn off the heat.

Transfer the seitan to a platter. Pour the lemon juice mixture into the pan, scraping up all the caramelized bits from the bottom of the pan with a wooden spoon. Pour this pan sauce over the seitan and serve.

Pan-Seared Lamb Steak with Thyme, Lemon, and Mustard

SERVES 3 TO 4

Lamb is lean and tasty when cooked briefly (overcooking will dry it out), and slices of seared lamb steak make for an elegant presentation. Marinating the meat for at least 2 hours gives it a wonderful flavor. If lamb steaks cut from the leg prove hard to find, you can substitute 4 medium rib or loin chops.

MARINADE

1 tablespoon Dijon mustard

1 tablespoon finely chopped fresh thyme

Finely grated zest of 1 lemon

2 garlic cloves, crushed through a garlic press or finely grated

1 teaspoon sea salt or kosher salt

2 lamb steaks (cut from the leg; about 12 ounces each), rinsed and patted dry

1 teaspoon extra-virgin olive oil, plus additional for drizzling

Freshly ground black pepper

Juice of ½ lemon

FOR THE MARINADE: In a small bowl, combine the mustard, thyme, lemon zest, garlic, and salt. Smear this mixture all over the lamb, wrap the meat well, and refrigerate for at least 2 hours, or overnight.

TO PREPARE THE LAMB: Heat a cast-iron skillet or ridged grill pan over medium-high heat until hot. Brush the hot pan with the olive oil and add the steaks. Cook, turning once, for 3 to 4 minutes per side for medium-rare. Transfer the steaks to a cutting board, cover loosely with foil, and let rest for 3 to 4 minutes.

Slice the steaks against the grain into thin strips and transfer to a warm serving plate. Season with black pepper, then drizzle the lemon juice and olive oil over the meat, and serve.

Carrots with Black Olives and Mint

SERVES 4 TO 6

Moroccan seasonings create a backdrop for these carrots that is at once sweet, spicy, briny, and fresh. Leftovers are great cold.

3 pounds carrots, peeled, quartered lengthwise, and cut into 1-inch lengths

2 tablespoons honey

1½ tablespoons fresh lemon juice

1 large garlic clove, minced

1 2-inch piece cinnamon stick

¾ teaspoon coriander seeds

¾ teaspoon red pepper flakes

2 large sprigs fresh mint, plus 1 tablespoon chopped fresh mint

1½ tablespoons extra-virgin olive oil

1½ teaspoons white wine vinegar, or to taste

½ cup pitted oil-cured black olives

Sea salt or kosher salt and freshly ground black pepper

In a large saucepan, combine the carrots, honey, lemon juice, garlic, cinnamon stick, coriander, pepper flakes, and mint sprigs. Add water to cover and bring to a boil over high heat. Reduce the heat, cover, and simmer until the carrots are tender, about 15 minutes. Discard the mint sprigs and cinnamon stick.

Use a slotted spoon to transfer the carrots to a serving dish. Pour any cooking liquid that accumulates in the bowl back into the pan, set the pan over high heat, and boil until the liquid is reduced to 2 tablespoons, 1 to 2 minutes. Stir in the olive oil and vinegar.

Toss the carrots with the reduced cooking liquid. Stir in the olives and season with salt and pepper. Serve warm or chilled, sprinkled with the chopped mint.

Spicy Lentils with Pumpkin and Greens over Couscous

SERVES 4 TO 6

Because of their resemblance to coins, lentils are considered lucky in the Mediterranean. Here this lucky Old World food is paired with Mediterranean kale and a host of bright flavors from the New World: chilies, tomatoes, and pumpkin. The resulting stew is colorful and highly nutritious.

This recipe provides a great opportunity to use up all the odd amounts of dried lentils that inevitably linger in the cupboard. Varieties, like French green, beluga, or brown lentils or a mix of these varieties will work well too.

Lacinato kale has multiple names, including Tuscan, dinosaur, and black kale, or *cavolo nero*. What you're looking for is a kale with very dark green, long, dimpled leaves, rather than the paler, sometimes purple-touched, curly leaves of regular kale. I find that lacinato kale is both sweeter and more tender. Feel free to substitute mustard or collard greens or the more common curly kale here.

3 tablespoons extra-virgin olive oil

2 medium onions, diced

2 tablespoons hot or sweet Spanish smoked paprika

2 teaspoons ground cumin, preferably toasted and freshly ground (see page 12)

2 teaspoons ground coriander, preferably toasted and freshly ground

¼ teaspoon red pepper flakes, or to taste

1 cup French green lentils, soaked for at least 2 hours (or up to 24 hours) in the refrigerator

1 28-ounce can whole peeled tomatoes, with their juice

2 pounds pumpkin or winter squash, peeled, seeded, and cut into 1-inch cubes

Sea salt or kosher salt

1 pound lacinato kale, tough stems discarded

Freshly ground black pepper

1½ cups quick-cooking couscous (regular or whole wheat), prepared according to package directions

In a large saucepan, heat the olive oil over medium heat. Add the onions and cook, stirring occasionally, until softened, about 10 minutes. Add the paprika, cumin, coriander, and red pepper flakes and cook, stirring, for 2 more minutes.

Drain the lentils and add them to the onions, along with the tomatoes and their juice. Add enough cold water to just cover and bring to a boil over high heat. Reduce the heat, cover, and simmer for 20 minutes.

Add the pumpkin or squash, cover, and simmer, stirring a few times, until tender, about 20 minutes.

Meanwhile, bring a medium pot of lightly salted water to a boil. Add the kale and boil for 2 minutes, until wilted. Drain and coarsely chop.

Add the kale to the lentils and season with salt and pepper. Simmer for another 3 minutes, and serve over the couscous.

Fall

MENU 10
SERVES 6

Stuffed Dumpling Squash/Poussin with Quinoa, Dried Fruit, and Pumpkin Seeds

Pinto Beans with Chipotle and Melted Garlic

Mustard Greens with Shallots and Vinegar

This menu requires a little more work than most of us plan for on a nightly basis—consider it for a dinner party (or even a nontraditional Thanksgiving). My vegetarian daughter, Kayla, and I created the quinoa stuffing to take to her aunt's house for Thanksgiving. I've made it a few times since, stuffing poussin as well as squash to please my other daughter, Emma. The stuffing is equally delicious with squash or fowl. Add the greens and beans, and you've got a memorable menu.

THE PLAN
1. Soak the beans.
2. Prepare the quinoa stuffing.
3. Cook the beans.
4. Meanwhile, marinate the shallots for the greens.
5. Roast the squash and poussins.
6. Cook the mustard greens.

Stuffed Dumpling Squash/Poussin with Quinoa, Dried Fruit, and Pumpkin Seeds

SERVES 6: 3 SERVINGS SQUASH, 3 SERVINGS POUSSIN

Poussins are young chickens. Sweet and tender, each bird is a perfect single serving, making for a great presentation, and they're fast-cooking, which makes them an appealing alternative to larger stuffed birds. After roasting the poussins, I like to pass them under the broiler to crisp and color their skin. If poussins are unavailable, you can substitute Cornish game hens, cooking them a little longer if they are much bigger. You could also use my roast chicken recipe (page 197), stuffing the chicken with the quinoa mixture instead of using lemon and thyme.

Note: You can use double the poussin or squash with this stuffing if you prefer an all-meat or all-vegetarian meal.

If dumpling squash is unavailable, you can substitute 2 small acorn squash. Halve them, scoop out the seeds and membranes, and roast them cut side down until softened. Then stuff them and continue to roast as directed.

QUINOA STUFFING

2 cups quinoa, preferably red quinoa

4 cups water

4 tablespoons (½ stick) unsalted butter

1½ cups chopped onions

Sea salt or kosher salt

½ cup diced peeled carrots

½ cup diced celery

1 tablespoon minced peeled fresh ginger

1 tablespoon chopped fresh sage

½ cup dried cranberries

⅓ cup dried apricots, chopped into pieces the size of raisins

¼ cup dried currants

⅓ cup pumpkin seeds, toasted (see page 202)

½ teaspoon freshly grated nutmeg

¼ teaspoon ground cinnamon

Freshly ground black pepper

SQUASH

3 small dumpling squash

Extra-virgin olive oil, for brushing

POUSSIN

3 poussins

1½ teaspoons sea salt or kosher salt

Freshly ground black pepper

2 tablespoons unsalted butter, softened

Set a rack in the middle of the oven and preheat the oven to 350 degrees.

FOR THE STUFFING: In a medium saucepan, combine the quinoa with the water and bring just to a boil. Reduce the heat and simmer until the quinoa is fluffy, 15 to 20 minutes. Remove from the heat.

Meanwhile, in a large saucepan, melt the butter over medium heat. Add the onions and ½ teaspoon salt and cook, stirring, until the onions are softened, 3 to 4 minutes. Stir in the carrots, celery, ginger, and sage, cover, and cook until the vegetables are tender, 5 to 7 minutes (add a tablespoon of water if necessary to prevent scorching). Remove from the heat.

In a large bowl, toss together the quinoa and vegetables. Stir in the dried fruit, pumpkin seeds, nutmeg, and cinnamon. Season with salt and pepper.

FOR THE SQUASH: Slice off the squash tops to expose the inside. Scoop out the seeds and membranes. Brush the skin of the squash lightly with oil. Place the squash cut side down in a baking pan large enough to hold them in a snug single layer, and pour ½ inch boiling water into the pan.

Bake the squash for 20 minutes, or until it has softened slightly. Transfer to a plate and let rest until cool enough to handle. Discard the water in the baking pan.

Stuff the squash with half the quinoa mixture. Return them (stuffing side up) to the pan and bake until the flesh can be easily pierced with the tip of a paring knife, 20 to 30 minutes more.

MEANWHILE, FOR THE POUSSINS: Season each bird with ½ teaspoon salt and some pepper. Stuff each one with ½ cup of the remaining quinoa mixture. Tuck the wing tips under and tie the legs together with kitchen twine. Smear each bird with 1 teaspoon of the butter and place breast side up in a baking dish.

Roast the poussins, basting several times with the pan juices, until an instant-read thermometer pierced into the thickest part of a thigh registers 175 to 180 degrees, 35 to 40 minutes.

Remove the poussins from the oven and turn on the broiler. Brush each bird with another 1 teaspoon butter and broil, watching carefully, until the skin is a lustrous golden brown, 2 to 3 minutes. Take the birds out of the oven and let rest for 5 to 10 minutes. Serve the squash and the poussins.

Pinto Beans with Chipotle and Melted Garlic

SERVES 6

Throughout the Mediterranean and Asia, cooks have intuitively understood the digestive power and flavor-enhancing properties of chili, cumin, fennel, sage, and bay for thousands of years. Here, these seasonings create a deep-flavored yet humble vegetarian bean dish. If everyone you're cooking for likes meat, simmer a smoked ham hock along with the beans. The longer the beans simmer, the better, as this should be a soft stew.

Canned chipotle chilies in adobo sauce are available in most supermarkets and wherever Mexican products are sold.

1 pound diced pinto beans, soaked (see page 9) and drained
1 large onion, quartered
5–6 garlic cloves, peeled and left whole
3–4 fresh sage leaves
2 bay leaves
1 tablespoon sesame seeds
1 tablespoon cumin seeds
1 teaspoon fennel seeds
2 tablespoons extra-virgin olive oil
Sea salt or kosher salt
1 chipotle chili in adobo sauce, finely chopped, plus 1–2 teaspoons adobo sauce
2 teaspoons red wine vinegar
Freshly ground black pepper

Place the beans in a large saucepan, add cold water to cover by 1 inch, and bring to a boil over high heat. Boil until foam rises to the surface, 1 to 2 minutes. Drain the beans and rinse out the pan. Return the beans to the pan, add the onion, garlic, sage, bay leaves, and water to cover by 1 inch, and bring to a boil. Reduce the heat to low, cover, and simmer for 1 hour.

Meanwhile, heat a small skillet over medium heat until hot. Add the sesame seeds, cumin, and fennel and toast, tossing constantly, until fragrant, 1 to 2 minutes. Transfer the seeds to a plate and let cool, then grind the seeds to a powder in a clean electric coffee grinder or spice mill (or use a mortar and pestle).

When the beans are tender, remove the pan from the heat and discard the sage and bay leaves. Remove the onion and set it aside until cool enough to handle, then chop and return it to the pan.

Add the ground seed mixture, olive oil, 2 ½ teaspoons salt, chipotle, and adobo sauce to taste to the beans, return to a simmer, and simmer, covered, until the beans are tender, 30 minutes to 1 hour, depending on the age of your beans.

Stir in the vinegar and simmer for 2 to 3 minutes more. Season with additional salt and black pepper and serve.

Mustard Greens with Shallots and Vinegar

With honey, cider vinegar, garlic, cayenne, and dark leafy greens, this dish is not only delicious, it will cure what ails you. When you remove the cooked greens from the pot, what's left behind is the "pot liquor" that you can pour into a mug and sip—it's especially great for a cold.

Tip: Cooking bacon in the oven minimizes smoke and mess.

1½	cups cider vinegar
4	large shallots, halved and very thinly sliced
2	teaspoons honey
2	garlic cloves, finely chopped
¼	teaspoon cayenne pepper
	Sea salt or kosher salt
10–12	slices bacon (optional)
6	tablespoons extra-virgin olive oil
6	bunches mustard greens (5–6 pounds), rinsed well, trimmed, and coarsely chopped

If using bacon, preheat the oven to 400 degrees.

In a small bowl, combine the vinegar, shallots, honey, garlic, cayenne, and a pinch of salt. Let sit at room temperature for 30 minutes (or cover and keep on the counter for up to 2 days).

Meanwhile, if using bacon, lay the slices on a rimmed baking sheet and bake, turning once, until crisp, 15 to 20 minutes (depending how thick your bacon is and how crisp you like it). Transfer to a paper-towel-lined plate.

In a large pot, heat the olive oil over high heat. Add the mustard greens, with some water still clinging to the leaves, and 2 teaspoons salt, cover, and cook until the greens are wilted and tender, 10 to 15 minutes.

Uncover the pot and cook, stirring, until some of the liquid cooks off, 4 to 5 more minutes. Use a slotted spoon to transfer the greens to a serving dish.

Season the greens with the shallot mixture to taste, crumble on the bacon, if using, and serve.

Winter

MENU 1 • 253
Pan-Seared Rosemary Duck Breasts/Tofu
Teriyaki-Style Burdock, Carrots, and Leeks
Soba with Garlicky Spinach and Sesame Oil

MENU 2 • 260
Barley Mushroom Soup
Gratin of Winter Vegetables
Shaved Fennel Salad with Olives/Marinated Sardines

MENU 3 • 267
Slow-Cooked Lamb Shanks in White Wine with Escarole
Slow-Cooked Red Beans in White Wine with Escarole
Millet Cauliflower "Polenta" with Crispy Shallots

MENU 4 • 276
Batter-Fried Cod/Tofu with Kimchi
Gingery Rice with Hiziki, Shredded Omelet, and Shiitakes

MENU 5 • 283
Phyllo Pie with Lemon Tofu, Winter Greens, and Mushrooms
Roasted Winter Vegetable Salad with Red Onion Vinaigrette

MENU 6 • 288

Creamy Root Vegetable Soup with Honey-Crisped Walnuts

Braised Duck Legs

Sauerkraut with Fried Tempeh/Smoked Whitefish,
Green Apples, and Onions

MENU 7 • 296

My Favorite Winter Tomato Soup with Goat Cheese Crostini

Spanish-Style Eggs with Kimchi/Chorizo over Farro

Fennel with Lemon and Fennel Salt

MENU 8 • 306

Short Rib Cholent

Seitan Cholent

Shaved Winter Vegetable Salad with Apple and Raisins

MENU 9 • 315

Pizzoccheri Casserole

Seitan/Chicken Liver Schnitzel with Red Wine–Shallot Compote
and Bitter Greens

MENU 10 • 323

Chicken/Tempeh in Mole Negro

Creamy Masa Harina

Pickled Vegetable Salad

Winter

MENU 1
SERVES 4

Pan-Seared Rosemary Duck Breasts/Tofu

Teriyaki-Style Burdock, Carrots, and Leeks

Soba with Garlicky Spinach and Sesame Oil

Crisp duck or tofu served over flavorful vegetables and slippery soba noodles makes for a great meal in the Asian tradition. None of the dishes requires much labor, though the duck and tofu should be marinated for at least 4 hours, or up to 24 hours.

THE PLAN

1. Marinate the duck breasts and tofu.
2. Cook the burdock.
3. Meanwhile, sear the duck and tofu and keep warm.
4. Make the soba.

Pan-Seared Rosemary Duck Breasts/Tofu

SERVES 4 TO 6: 2 TO 3 SERVINGS DUCK, 2 TO 3 SERVINGS TOFU

I use Long Island, or Pekin, duck breasts, which are relatively lean, for this dish. The duck fat must be rendered and poured off (save it for the soba noodles if you like), and some oil is needed to crisp the tofu, but otherwise the techniques I use for the tofu and duck are similar, and they yield equally delightful results.

Note: If you like, double the duck or tofu components and leave out the other.

SEASONING MIXTURE

4 teaspoons finely chopped fresh rosemary

2 teaspoons finely chopped garlic

¼ teaspoon freshly ground black pepper

⅛ teaspoon cayenne pepper

DUCK

2 7- to 8-ounce skin-on boneless Long Island (Pekin) duck breasts

½ teaspoon sea salt or kosher salt

Freshly ground black pepper

Juice of ½ lemon

TOFU

1 14- to 16-ounce package extra-firm tofu, pressed (see page 279) and cut into 4 slabs

¾ teaspoon sea salt or kosher salt

Freshly ground black pepper

2 tablespoons neutral vegetable oil, such as canola or grapeseed

Juice of ½ lemon

Chopped scallions, for serving

Toasted nori, cut into strips, for serving

FOR THE SEASONING MIXTURE: In a small bowl, stir together the rosemary, garlic, black pepper, and cayenne.

TO MARINATE THE DUCK: Rub the duck breasts all over with the salt. Sprinkle half of the seasoning mixture on the flesh sides of the duck breasts. Sandwich them with the flesh sides together (skin sides out) on a plate, cover with plastic wrap, and refrigerate for at least 4 hours, or overnight.

TO MARINATE THE TOFU: Place the tofu on a plate or baking dish that holds the slices in a single layer. Rub the tofu all over with the salt, then rub the remaining seasoning mixture evenly into the tofu. Cover with plastic wrap and refrigerate for at least 4 hours, or overnight.

TO COOK THE DUCK: Take the duck out of the refrigerator and use a paper towel to wick away any moisture (it's fine if some of the garlic and herbs rub off). Season both sides with black pepper.

Heat a large skillet over medium heat until hot. Place the duck breasts skin side down in the skillet and cook undisturbed until most of the fat has been rendered, about 8 minutes. Pour off the fat from the pan (save it for another use if desired). Flip the breasts and cook for 1 minute more. Transfer the duck to a platter and turn off the heat. Add the lemon juice to the pan and scrape up any caramelized bits.

MEANWHILE, COOK THE TOFU: Take the tofu out of the refrigerator and use a paper towel to wick away any moisture (it's fine if some of the garlic and herbs rub off). Season both sides with black pepper.

In a large skillet, heat the oil over medium heat until it shimmers. Add the tofu, raise the heat to medium-high, and cook undisturbed for about 4 minutes. When a golden brown crust forms on the bottom, the tofu will release easily from the pan. Flip the tofu and cook for 4 minutes more. Transfer the tofu to a platter and turn off the heat. Add the lemon juice to the pan and scrape up any caramelized bits. Remove from the heat.

Serve the duck and tofu drizzled with their respective pan juices and garnished with scallions and nori.

The Glory of Nori

Nori seaweed is usually dried and pressed into paper-thin sheets that turn from purple-black to deep green when lightly toasted. Nori is high in protein and vitamin A and makes for a delicious garnish or wrapper for rice and vegetables. It's available from health-food stores and Asian markets.

Teriyaki-Style Burdock, Carrots, and Leeks

SERVES 4

This sweet salty side dish, often part of a Japanese bento box selection, features the earthy flavor of burdock and the nutty crunch of sesame seeds. My version gets a little kick from ginger and lemon.

½ cup honey

⅓ cup soy sauce, preferably naturally brewed

⅓ cup mirin (see Tip, page 85)

2 teaspoons finely grated peeled fresh ginger

½ cup water

2 tablespoons neutral vegetable oil, such as canola or grapeseed

1 pound burdock, scrubbed and cut into matchsticks

1 large or 2 medium leeks, white and tender green parts only, cleaned and cut into matchsticks

Sea salt or kosher salt

8 ounces carrots, peeled and cut into matchsticks

2 tablespoons sesame seeds, lightly toasted (see page 11)

2 scallions, white parts only, thinly sliced

Lemon wedges, for serving

1 bunch watercress, tough stems discarded

A Burdock in the Hand

It looks like a dark brown carrot, with which it's often served, but burdock is actually a root in the daisy family. It has an earthy sweetness and great crunch. For the sweetest, freshest flavor, look for firm roots no more than 1 inch wide at their thickest part. I like to cook burdock unpeeled since it provides a good color contrast and the mineral-rich skin is thin and tender, not at all bitter or tough. To prepare burdock, scrub with a stiff natural-bristle vegetable brush in a basin of cold water, or use a damp kitchen towel to rub off any dirt.

In a small bowl, whisk together the honey, soy sauce, mirin, ginger, and water.

In a large heavy skillet, heat the oil over high heat. Add the burdock and cook, stirring, for 2 minutes. Add the leeks and a pinch of salt and cook and stir until the leeks wilt, about 2 minutes. Pour in the honey mixture and bring to a boil. Reduce the heat, cover, and simmer for 10 minutes.

Stir in the carrots, cover the pan again, and simmer until the vegetables are tender, 15 to 20 minutes longer.

Uncover the pan, raise the heat, and simmer until the juices have reduced to a glaze. Sprinkle the vegetables with the sesame seeds and scallions, and serve with lemon wedges on a bed of watercress.

Soba with Garlicky Spinach and Sesame Oil

SERVES 4

If you are making the duck in this menu, feel free to replace the sesame oil in this tasty recipe with duck fat—or divide the recipe between two pans and make one sesame and one ducky. Duck fat is a splendid, savory addition. Then again, so is sesame oil.

Sea salt or kosher salt

8 ounces soba noodles

2 tablespoons toasted sesame oil or duck fat (see page 254)

2 garlic cloves, finely chopped

1½ pounds spinach (about 3 bunches), trimmed and rinsed

Sesame seeds, toasted (see page 11), for garnish

Soy sauce, preferably naturally brewed, for serving

Bring a large pan of lightly salted water to a boil. Add the soba noodles and cook until al dente, about 6 minutes. Scoop out and reserve 2 cups of the cooking water, then drain the noodles.

Wipe the pan dry and set it over medium heat. Add the oil or duck fat and the garlic and let sizzle until the garlic is lightly colored, about 30 seconds. Add the spinach, raise the heat to high, and cook, stirring, until wilted. Return the noodles and the reserved cooking water to the pan and heat through.

Divide the brothy noodles among four bowls and sprinkle with sesame seeds. Pass soy sauce at the table.

Winter

MENU 2
SERVES 4 TO 6

Barley Mushroom Soup

Gratin of Winter Vegetables

Shaved Fennel Salad with Olives/Marinated Sardines

Bursting with whole grains, mushrooms, root vegetables, cabbage, and cheese, the soup and gratin in this menu reflect the way I like to eat during the winter. The salad, a crisp, sweet, and briny combination of fennel with olives or sardines, is a great foil for the heartier cooked dishes. The gratin and mushroom soup make terrific leftovers.

THE PLAN
1. Marinate the sardines and the onion.
2. Meanwhile, make the soup (reheat before serving).
3. Bake the gratin.
4. Make the salad.

Barley Mushroom Soup

SERVES 4 TO 6

When I first gave up eating meat, I scoured the kosher delis and dairy restaurants of New York's Upper West and Lower East Sides, where generations of Eastern European Jews had settled, in search of satisfying vegetarian versions of this classic soup. Here is my take on the staple of my ancestors. Soy sauce adds an earthy flavor to the broth, standing in for the traditional beef bouillon.

⅔ cup pearl barley

6 cups cold water

1 tablespoon extra-virgin olive oil

1 tablespoon unsalted butter

12 ounces mushrooms, trimmed and thinly sliced (about 3 cups)

1 cup chopped onion

1 cup shredded kale or other dark leafy green

½ cup diced peeled carrots

½ cup diced celery

1 teaspoon sea salt or kosher salt

2 tablespoons chopped fresh dill

2 tablespoons soy sauce, preferably naturally brewed

Freshly ground black pepper

In a 4- to 5-quart Dutch oven or other heavy pot, combine the barley with the water and bring to a boil over high heat. Reduce the heat to low and simmer, partially covered, until the barley is tender, 35 to 45 minutes.

While the barley cooks, heat the oil and butter in a large skillet over medium heat. Add the mushrooms, onion, kale, carrots, celery, and salt and cook, stirring occasionally to prevent browning, for 3 to 5 minutes. Reduce the heat to low, cover, and cook until the vegetables are tender, about 15 minutes.

When the barley is plump and tender, stir in the vegetables. Add the dill and soy sauce and simmer for 3 minutes. Season the soup generously with black pepper and serve.

Gratin of Winter Vegetables

SERVES 6

Baking this gratin in a wide skillet allows you to cover it with a generous blanket of crispy, cheesy bread crumbs so no one will have to fight over the topping. If you don't like rutabaga (sometimes called golden or yellow turnip), use white turnips, celery root, and/or parsnips instead.

Tips: Thinly slicing the root vegetables is easiest using a mandoline or Benriner (set it to slice ⅛ inch thick).

If you want to serve this in a pretty gratin dish instead of the skillet, you can cook the onions in a pan, then transfer them to the baking dish. Bring the stock or water to a boil before adding it to the dish, since you won't be able to heat the whole thing up on the stovetop once assembled.

½ cup extra-virgin olive oil

1 tablespoon unsalted butter

2 cups thinly sliced onions

3 garlic cloves, finely chopped

1 tablespoon caraway seeds

Pinch of red pepper flakes

Sea salt or kosher salt

1 medium rutabaga (12 ounces), peeled and thinly sliced

12 ounces Yukon Gold or baking potatoes, peeled and thinly sliced (about 2½ cups)

Freshly ground black pepper

½ small head green cabbage, halved lengthwise, cored, and sliced crosswise ⅓ inch thick (about 3 cups)

Juice of 1 lemon

1 cup vegetable or chicken stock or water

2 cups firmly packed fresh sourdough bread crumbs (from about 8 slices bread; see opposite)

½ cup freshly grated Parmesan cheese (about 2 ounces)

½ cup coarsely grated Gruyère cheese (about 2 ounces)

Set a rack in the middle of the oven and preheat the oven to 400 degrees.

In a large ovenproof skillet, preferably cast-iron, heat 1 tablespoon of the olive oil and the butter over medium-high heat. Add the onions and cook, stirring occasionally, until lightly browned, 5 to 7 minutes. Add the garlic, caraway seeds, pepper flakes, and ½ teaspoon salt and cook, stirring, for 1 more minute. Transfer the mixture to a medium bowl. Set the skillet aside.

In a large bowl, toss the rutabaga and potatoes with 2 tablespoons of the olive oil. Season with 1 teaspoon salt and a generous grinding of pepper. In a third bowl, toss the cabbage with 1 tablespoon of the olive oil, the lemon juice, and ½ teaspoon salt.

Layer half the potatoes and rutabaga in the bottom of the skillet. Next layer in half the cabbage, then half the onions. Repeat, finishing with onions. Pour in the stock or water.

In a medium bowl, toss the bread crumbs with the remaining ¼ cup olive oil and both cheeses. Season with salt and pepper.

Spread the bread crumb mixture over the vegetables. Place the skillet over medium heat and bring to a simmer.

Transfer to the oven and bake until the vegetables offer no resistance when pierced with a fork and the topping is crisp and golden, about 40 minutes. If the bread crumbs brown too quickly, cover the gratin with aluminum foil (remove the foil and let the top brown for the final 5 minutes of cooking). Let the gratin rest for 5 to 10 minutes before serving.

Shaved Fennel Salad with Olives/**Marinated Sardines**

SERVES 4 TO 6: 2 TO 3 SERVINGS OLIVES, 2 TO 3 SERVINGS SARDINES

Fennel and parsley are a refreshing counterpoint to the assertive flavor of sardines and the brininess of olives. I usually drain the oil from tinned sardines, but you can incorporate some of it into the salad for a stronger sardine flavor if desired. Marinating the sardines (and, separately, the onions) results in a milder, fresher taste. If you have celery leaves on hand, they will add a layer of herbaceous flavor.

Tip: If you have a mandoline or Benriner, it will make short work of the vegetables.

Ode to the Tinned Sardine

I'm a sardine fan. In winter, I use Portuguese canned sardines, which are a convenient source of high-quality protein and omega-3 fatty acids. The bones, which are completely edible, are a nutritional powerhouse. Look for whole sardines packed in extra-virgin olive oil—Bela brand, which are caught off the southern coast of Portugal and packed in extra-virgin olive oil within eight hours of harvest, are my favorite.

I like canned sardines on salad and in spaghetti, and with bread and pickled vegetables—the ultimate fast food. Probably my favorite time for sardines is breakfast. For my breakfast of champions, I stack 2 slices of whole-grain artisanal bread, so they will toast only on the outside, toast them in the toaster oven or oven, and then transfer them to a cutting board, toasted side down. I place as many sardines as will fit on the steamy soft side of one slice of bread. Then I spread the other slice with horseradish or mustard, pile on sauerkraut or kimchi, and drizzle with a little extra-virgin olive oil. Sandwich together, slice, and enjoy. The result is milder than you might expect and will really keep you going.

SARDINES

1 4¼-ounce tin sardines packed in extra-virgin olive oil, drained

2 tablespoons extra-virgin olive oil

2 teaspoons fresh lemon juice

1 teaspoon red wine vinegar

¼ teaspoon coriander seeds, toasted (see page 11) and coarsely crushed

Pinch of red pepper flakes

SALAD

¼ cup shaved or very thinly sliced red onion

¼ cup fresh lemon juice

½ teaspoon sea salt or kosher salt

1 very large or 2 medium fennel bulbs, cored, trimmed, fronds reserved, and bulbs shaved or very thinly sliced

1 cup loosely packed fresh flat-leaf parsley leaves

¼ cup coarsely chopped celery leaves (optional)

2 tablespoons extra-virgin olive oil

Freshly ground black pepper

12 pitted brine-cured green olives, such as Picholine

FOR THE SARDINES: In a small bowl, toss the sardines with the oil, lemon juice, vinegar, coriander, and pepper flakes. Cover and refrigerate for at least 30 minutes, or up to 2 hours.

MEANWHILE, FOR THE SALAD: In another bowl, toss the onion with the lemon juice and ¼ teaspoon of the salt. Cover and refrigerate for 30 minutes.

Chop enough of the reserved fennel fronds to make 2 to 3 tablespoons. In a large bowl, toss the fennel, chopped fennel fronds, parsley, and celery leaves, if using, with the olive oil and the onion and its liquid. Season with the remaining ¼ teaspoon salt and pepper to taste.

Mound the salad in bowls. Top each with sardines and/or olives, and drizzle the sardines with some of their marinade. Serve.

Winter

MENU 3
SERVES 4: 2 SERVINGS LAMB, 2 SERVINGS BEANS

Slow-Cooked Lamb Shanks in White Wine with Escarole

Slow-Cooked Red Beans in White Wine with Escarole

Millet Cauliflower "Polenta" with Crispy Shallots

Both the lamb shanks and the beans cook "low and slow," producing a succulent gravy that's perfect for serving over a starch. In place of plain noodles or potatoes, I make something much more interesting, tossing golden little grains of millet together with cauliflower, cheese, and sweet frizzled shallots.

You'll need to soak the beans and salt the meat at least overnight, so plan ahead.

Note: You can serve either the lamb or the beans as a main dish, doubling them if you wish, but if you make both, the carnivores can enjoy some beans on the side.

THE PLAN
1. At least 12 hours (or up to 2 days) ahead, salt the lamb shanks.
2. Soak the beans.
3. Braise the lamb and cook the beans.
4. Meanwhile, make the "polenta."
5. Fry the shallots.

Slow-Cooked Lamb Shanks in White Wine with Escarole

SERVES 2

These lamb shanks are hearty and falling-off-the-bone tender. I find that a little goes a long way with this flavorful and succulent cut. Like most braises, this one definitely improves after a night's rest in the fridge, and leftovers, if there are any, just get better.

2 1-pound lamb shanks

Sea salt or kosher salt

1 tablespoon vegetable oil

1 tablespoon extra-virgin olive oil

1 head garlic, cloves separated but not peeled

1 small onion, chopped

1 medium carrot, peeled and chopped

1 small celery stalk with leaves, chopped

1 tablespoon tomato paste

¼ teaspoon whole black peppercorns

¼ teaspoon fennel or caraway seeds

2 2-inch strips lemon zest

2 sprigs fresh thyme

1 large sprig fresh rosemary

1 cup dry white wine

1 large head escarole, cored and coarsely chopped

Chopped fresh flat-leaf parsley, for garnish

Rinse and dry the lamb shanks. Season all over with 2 teaspoons salt. Cover and refrigerate for at least 12 hours, or up to 2 days.

Set a rack in the middle of the oven and preheat the oven to 300 degrees.

In a 10-inch skillet with a lid, heat the vegetable oil over medium heat. Add the shanks and sear until golden brown on all sides, 12 to 15 minutes. Lower the heat if the shanks are browning too quickly. Transfer the lamb to a plate and wipe out the pan with a paper towel.

Add the olive oil to the pan and heat over medium heat. Add the garlic cloves, onion, carrot, celery, and tomato paste and cook, stirring, until the oil turns reddish orange and the garlic is fragrant, about 2 minutes. Stir in the peppercorns and fennel or caraway seeds. Arrange the lamb shanks over the vegetables and tuck the lemon zest and herb sprigs in and around the shanks. Pour in the wine and enough cold water to come halfway up the sides of the lamb (½ to ¾ cup) and bring to a boil.

Cover the pan and transfer to the oven. Braise until the meat is fork-tender and practically falling off the bone, 2½ to 3 hours. Discard the lemon zest and herb sprigs. Transfer the lamb to a plate and let rest until cool enough to handle. Set the pan aside for the moment.

Meanwhile, bring a large pot of lightly salted water to a boil. Add the escarole and boil until tender but still bright green, 2 to 3 minutes. Drain well.

Strain the lamb juices through a medium sieve into a clean skillet. Using a wooden spoon or a ladle, press down hard on the solids to push the garlic and vegetable pulp through the sieve into the juices. Boil the juices over high heat until reduced by half, about 10 minutes. Add the escarole and simmer for 2 to 3 minutes more.

Pull the lamb from the bones and add it to the simmering escarole. Simmer until the lamb is hot, 1 to 2 minutes. Sprinkle with chopped parsley and serve.

Slow-Cooked Red Beans in White Wine with Escarole

SERVES 2 TO 4

Cooking beans slowly in a covered casserole in the oven ensures melting tenderness and keeps them from bursting or drying out.

- 1 cup red kidney beans, soaked (see page 9) and drained
- 1 tablespoon extra-virgin olive oil
- 1 head garlic, cloves separated and peeled
- 1 small onion, chopped
- 1 medium carrot, peeled and chopped
- 1 small stalk celery with leaves, chopped
- ¼ teaspoon fennel or caraway seeds
- ¼ teaspoon whole black peppercorns
- 1 tablespoon tomato paste
- 2 sprigs fresh thyme
- 1 large sprig fresh rosemary
- 2 2-inch strips lemon zest
- 1 cup dry white wine
- Sea salt or kosher salt
- 1 large head escarole, cored and coarsely chopped
- 1 tablespoon unsalted butter
- Freshly ground black pepper

Place the beans in a medium pot with cold water to cover by 1 inch, bring to a boil and cook until foam rises to the surface, 2 to 3 minutes. Drain.

Preheat the oven to 300 degrees.

In a 4- to 5-quart Dutch oven or other heavy pot, heat the oil over medium heat. Add the garlic cloves, onion, carrot, celery, fennel or caraway seeds, and black peppercorns, raise the heat to high, and cook, stirring, until the vegetables begin to caramelize, 5 to 7 minutes. Stir in the tomato paste and cook, stirring, until the oil turns reddish orange, 1 to 2 minutes. Lower the heat and add the herb sprigs and lemon zest. Spoon the beans over the vegetables. Pour in the wine and enough water to cover the beans by 1 inch, raise the heat, and bring to a boil.

Cover the casserole and transfer it to the oven. Cook until the beans are tender, 2 to 3 hours. Check occasionally and add a little water if the beans appear dry. They should remain submerged in the cooking liquid throughout the cooking. When the beans are tender, season them with salt and return the pot to the oven while you prepare the escarole.

Bring a large pot of lightly salted water to a boil. Add the escarole and boil until tender but still bright green, 2 to 3 minutes. Drain well.

Place the pot of beans on the stovetop over medium heat. Discard the herb sprigs and lemon zest. Stir in the escarole and simmer, uncovered, for 3 to 5 minutes, or until the liquid has thickened to a rich gravy.

Stir in the butter. Taste and season with additional salt and with pepper. Serve.

Millet Cauliflower "Polenta" with Crispy Shallots

SERVES 4

You might recognize the tiny round grains of millet from birdseed mixes, but this whole grain isn't just for the birds. Millet is quick-cooking, and it can be toasted and steamed to yield fluffy, nutty results or simmered like polenta until creamy. Combined with cauliflower, sweet crispy shallots, and plenty of Parmesan cheese, it makes for a comforting side dish. I make the shallots in my little cast-iron skillet and use them not only here but to dress up everything from rice pilaf, beans, and salads to sandwiches. And the resulting shallot oil is a luxurious flavoring to drizzle over grains or beans, as well as a great base for a vinaigrette.

1 small cauliflower, cored and coarsely chopped (about 3 cups)

1 cup millet, rinsed and drained

4 large garlic cloves, peeled and left whole

¼ teaspoon saffron threads

Sea salt or kosher salt

4 cups water

½ cup vegetable oil, or as needed

½ cup extra-virgin olive oil, or as needed

1 heaping cup sliced shallots

Pinch of red pepper flakes

½ cup freshly grated Parmesan cheese (about 2 ounces), plus additional for serving if desired

1 tablespoon unsalted butter

In a heavy 2- to 3-quart saucepan, combine the cauliflower, millet, garlic, saffron, 1 teaspoon salt, and water and bring to a boil over high heat. Reduce the heat to low, cover, and simmer until the water has been absorbed and the millet is tender, 25 to 30 minutes.

Meanwhile, in a small skillet, heat the vegetable and olive oils over medium heat until hot but not smoking. Add the shallots (if the oil does not cover the shallots, add a little more). Cook slowly, stirring often, until the shallots are a deep golden brown, about 20 minutes; regulate the heat as necessary to prevent burning.

Transfer the shallots to paper towels to drain, reserving the oil. (The oil can be strained and stored in the refrigerator for 1 week.) Sprinkle the shallots with salt and the pepper flakes.

When the millet is cooked, stir in the Parmesan and butter. Serve the millet topped with the crispy shallots and, if desired, additional grated cheese. For extra seasoning, drizzle with some of the shallot oil.

Winter

MENU 4
SERVES 4 TO 6

Batter-Fried Cod/Tofu with Kimchi

Gingery Rice with Hiziki, Shredded Omelet, and Shiitakes

Kimchi, the nutritious fermented cabbage condiment of Korea, is full of warming chilies, garlic, vitamin C, and live cultures, and I'm sure it's what keeps me from getting colds. Here it serves as a bed for crisp tempura-fried fish or tofu, accompanied by a hearty fried rice that is full of chewy seaweed, dried mushrooms, carrots, and Chinese greens. Frying the fish or tofu and the gingery rice should be done at the last minute. This menu is great with a beer.

THE PLAN

1. Soak the shiitake mushrooms. If using brown rice, soak it.
2. Cook the rice.
3. Soak the hiziki.
4. Make the omelet.
5. Prepare the kimchi.
6. Finish the rice.
7. Fry the fish and tofu.

Batter-Fried Cod/Tofu with Kimchi

SERVES 4 TO 6: 2 TO 3 SERVINGS FISH, 2 TO 3 SERVINGS TOFU

Deep-frying is a cold-weather technique that doesn't deserve its bad rap—with your oil at the right temperature, and with the cod or tofu coated in a delicate, crisp tempura batter, the results are hardly junk food! To be sure the oil temperature doesn't drop too much (cold oil will be absorbed by the batter, making the results heavy and greasy), cook in batches, and keep the temperature of the oil above 350 degrees. Cod is an excellent fish to fry, but other thick white-fleshed fish fillets, such as hake, sea bass, or snapper, will be great as well.

Note: You can double either cod or tofu and leave out the other if you prefer.

Tips: To keep the tempura coating light and crisp, avoid overstirring the batter—some lumps are fine, and most will disappear during frying.

Some kimchi is made with dried anchovies, so seek out a vegetarian one from a natural food store if necessary.

> 1 16-ounce jar kimchi
>
> 1 cup water
>
> 4–6 cups vegetable oil, for deep-frying
>
> 1 cup unbleached all-purpose flour
>
> 2 tablespoons arrowroot or cornstarch
>
> Sea salt or kosher salt
>
> 1 cup ice water
>
> 1 pound extra-firm tofu, cut into 8 slabs and pressed
>
> 1 pound skinless cod fillets, cut into 1- to 2-inch chunks

Fry Right

For deep-frying, choose a flavorless, preferably organic, vegetable oil that can be brought to a high temperature without beginning to smoke (that is, an oil with a "high smoke point"), such as grapeseed, peanut, or canola. Or use "pure" olive oil, which is both lighter and more affordable (though less flavorful) than extra-virgin.

Pressing Matters

To rid tofu of excess water so that it will fry (or pan-sear) nicely, forming a crisp crust, cut it into slabs and lay them in one layer on half of a clean kitchen towel. Fold the other half of the towel over the tofu and gently press down several times to extract the excess water. Be careful not to press too firmly, or the tofu may bruise and lose its shape.

4 scallions, white and pale green parts only, thinly sliced, for garnish

Toasted nori strips, for garnish

In a medium saucepan combine the kimchi and water and bring to a simmer over medium heat. Cover and cook gently until the kimchi is tender, 10 to 15 minutes. Keep warm until serving.

Meanwhile, fill a heavy large saucepan with at least 2 inches of oil. Attach a deep-frying thermometer to the side of the pan and heat the oil to 375 degrees. Line a platter with paper towels.

In a medium bowl, combine the flour, arrowroot or cornstarch, and a pinch of salt. Whisk in the ice water.

When the oil is hot, working in batches, dip the tofu in the batter, turning to coat and allowing the excess batter to drip back into the bowl, and carefully lower it into the hot oil. Raise the heat as needed to keep the oil from dropping below 350 degrees, and fry, turning once, until golden, about 2 minutes per side. Transfer to the paper-towel-lined platter and sprinkle with a little salt. Repeat with the cod, again in batches.

Divide the hot kimchi, with some of its liquid, among four to six serving bowls. Place the tofu or fish over the kimchi, top with the sliced scallions and nori strips, and serve.

Gingery Rice with Hiziki, Shredded Omelet, and Shiitakes

Chewy hiziki, savory dried shiitakes, and sesame seeds make this rice deeply flavorful. You'll need to cook the rice and soak the shiitakes and hiziki the night before. If you want, you can prepare the omelet in advance, too, and keep it in the fridge for up to a day.

One- or two-day-old cooked rice is ideal for stir-frying. The slightly dried rice is given new life much as day-old bread is revived in a bread soup or panzanella (bread salad). You can make the dish using long-grain white rice, but I prefer the flavor and texture of short- or medium-grain brown rice or plump white Arborio rice.

OMELET

4 large eggs

Large pinch of sea salt or kosher salt

Pinch of cayenne pepper

1 tablespoon vegetable oil

1 teaspoon toasted sesame oil

RICE

¼ cup vegetable oil

1 tablespoon sesame seeds

1 medium red onion, slivered

1 tablespoon finely chopped peeled fresh ginger

1 medium carrot, peeled and cut into matchsticks

8 dried shiitake mushrooms, soaked for 2 hours in warm water or in refrigerator overnight, drained, and cut into matchsticks

2 tablespoons hiziki (see page 87), soaked in warm water for 20 minutes and drained

3½ cups cooked short-grain brown rice (from 1½ cups raw rice; see Tip, page 224)

1 pound baby bok choy or pak choy, trimmed and coarsely chopped

3 tablespoons soy sauce, preferably naturally brewed

2 tablespoons mirin (see Tip, page 85)

FOR THE OMELET: Heat a 10-inch skillet over medium heat. Meanwhile, in a small bowl, whisk the eggs with the salt and cayenne. Add the vegetable and sesame oils to the pan. When the oil shimmers, pour in the eggs, raise the heat to medium-high, and cook until the eggs begin to set. With a rubber spatula, draw the cooked edges in toward the center, pulling in opposite sides and tilting the pan so that the uncooked egg pours into the cleared edges. Then break up the center of the omelet, letting the uncooked egg seep down. Fold the omelet over into thirds, transfer to a plate, and let cool.

Slice the omelet crosswise into ¼-inch-wide ribbons.

FOR THE RICE: Heat a large skillet or a wok over high heat. Add the oil and sesame seeds and cook, stirring, until the seeds color and begin to pop. Add the onion and ginger and cook, stirring, until the onion starts to color, about 2 minutes. Stir in the carrot, mushrooms, and hiziki and cook, stirring, for 1 minute. Add the rice and stir until well combined. With a wooden spoon or spatula, press the ingredients down into a single layer. Top with the greens and sliced omelet, cover, and cook undisturbed until a crust begins to form on the bottom, about 2 minutes.

Add the soy sauce and mirin to the rice and stir, scraping up the crust from the bottom of the pan and tossing the ingredients together. Serve immediately.

Who's Julienne?

I prefer to say "cut into matchsticks" instead of using "julienne," the French term for this culinary technique, because it is both descriptive and less intimidating. To julienne something like a carrot, first cut it into 2-inch lengths, then slice it thinly lengthwise (about ⅛ inch thick). Stack the slices and cut them lengthwise into ⅛-inch-wide matchsticks.

Winter

MENU 5
SERVES 4 TO 6

Phyllo Pie with Lemon Tofu, Winter Greens, and Mushrooms

Roasted Winter Vegetable Salad with Red Onion Vinaigrette

This layered phyllo pie and warm, comforting root vegetable salad will please everyone. I made many seasonal variations of the casserole at Angelica Kitchen, where vegans and omnivores of all stripes devoured a hundred or more portions a day. The pie and vegetables bake at the same time, and everything comes together in about an hour. Pour a glass of red wine, light a fire in the fireplace or put some candles on the table, and enjoy.

THE PLAN
1. Assemble the pie.
2. Roast the salad vegetables and bake the pie.
3. Make the vinaigrette.
4. Toss the salad.

Phyllo Pie with Lemon Tofu, Winter Greens, and Mushrooms

SERVES 6

As the pie bakes, the layers of phyllo become rich and chewy in the middle and crisp and flaky on top. The lemony tofu in the filling, mashed to the texture of a fresh cheese, is always popular, even with people who don't tend to appreciate tofu in other forms. You can make the pie vegan simply by substituting a vegetable oil such as grapeseed, olive, or canola for butter. I use white or cremini mushrooms here, but feel free to substitute any mushroom you like.

Tips: Organic phyllo is available in the freezer section of well-stocked natural food markets. The 1-pound boxes contain two individually wrapped 8-ounce rolls of dough. For this recipe, you'll end up using less than 8 ounces, but you will need extra in case of breakage. Thaw the phyllo completely in the fridge (overnight) or at room temperature in the package.

If it's more convenient, use drained sun-dried tomatoes packed in oil. Taste the oil, and if it's nice, use some in place of the cooking oil.

TOFU

1 pound extra-firm tofu

Finely grated zest of 1 lemon

⅓ cup fresh lemon juice

¼ cup extra-virgin olive oil

3 tablespoons chopped fresh dill

3 garlic cloves, finely grated or mashed to a paste

Pinch of red pepper flakes

Sea salt or kosher salt

VEGETABLES

Sea salt or kosher salt

1½ pounds collard greens or kale, tough stems removed

2 tablespoons extra-virgin olive oil

1½ cups thinly sliced onions

12 ounces white or cremini mushrooms, trimmed and thinly sliced (about 3 cups)

Freshly ground black pepper

⅓ cup thinly sliced sun-dried tomatoes

8 tablespoons (1 stick) unsalted butter, melted

8 ounces phyllo, thawed

Paprika, for dusting

FOR THE TOFU: Place the tofu in a bowl and mash to a rough puree with a fork, or squeeze it through your fingers. Add the lemon zest and juice, olive oil, dill, garlic, and pepper flakes. Stir well to combine, then season with salt to taste.

FOR THE VEGETABLES: Bring a large pot of water to a boil and add 1 tablespoon salt. Add the greens and boil until tender but still bright green, 3 to 4 minutes. Drain in a colander or sieve, pressing down hard on the greens with the back of a wooden spoon to remove excess water.

When the greens are cool enough to handle, transfer them to a cutting board and coarsely chop.

In a large skillet, heat the olive oil over medium-high heat. Add the onions and cook, stirring, until browned around the edges, 3 to 4 minutes. Add the mushrooms and season with salt and pepper. Increase the heat and cook, stirring, until the mushrooms are caramelized and the pan juices have thickened and glazed the vegetables, about 5 minutes.

Stir in the greens and sun-dried tomatoes, using a wooden spoon to scrape up any browned bits from the bottom of the pan. If there is a lot of liquid in the pan, simmer, stirring, for a few minutes, until it has evaporated. Remove from the heat.

Set a rack in the lower third of the oven and preheat the oven to 400 degrees.

TO ASSEMBLE THE PIE: Brush a 10-inch skillet or a 10-inch deep pie plate or round baking dish with some of the melted butter. Unwrap the phyllo and unfold on a large work surface. To prevent drying, keep the phyllo covered with a damp kitchen towel as you work. Lay 5 sheets of phyllo in the prepared pan, brushing each layer with melted butter and placing each sheet at a slight angle to the one below, to make an even overhang, and letting the edges hang over the sides.

Spread the vegetable mixture evenly over the phyllo. Cover the vegetables with 2 more layers of butter-brushed phyllo. Spread the tofu mixture evenly on top of this layer, then finish with 8 to 10 more sheets of buttered phyllo.

Trim the edges of the phyllo with kitchen shears. Brush the top layer of phyllo generously with melted butter. With the tip of a sharp knife, score the top layers of phyllo (only as far down as the tofu layer) into 6 wedges—take care not to cut all the way through to the bottom of the pan. Dust the top with paprika.

Bake until golden brown and crisp, about 35 minutes. Allow the pie to rest for 5 minutes, then slice through the score marks and serve.

Garlic Gets Smashed

I find that many garlic presses are too coarse, rendering garlic that is more minced than nicely mashed. Luckily, it's easy to mash garlic with a pinch of kosher salt (the texture of the salt helps mash the garlic) in a mortar and pestle, or even on a cutting board with the side of a large knife. To mash garlic on a cutting board, crush the clove with the side of your knife and pull away the peel. Then sprinkle a little salt on the garlic. With the blade facing away from you, press the side of the knife against the garlic, sliding the knife toward you over the garlic. Turn the blade over and slide it the other way. Repeat this, crushing and smearing the garlic on the board, then using the knife blade to gather it back up again, until the garlic is pureed. If you do not want to use salt, you can grate the peeled cloves on a rasp-style grater—you'll wind up with a fine paste (and garlicky fingers for the rest of the day!).

Roasted Winter Vegetable Salad with Red Onion Vinaigrette

SERVES 4 TO 6

This hearty salad is perfect on nights too wintry for chilled leafy greens. The cooked sweet onion and grainy mustard vinaigrette is quickly absorbed by the warm roasted vegetables, infusing them with flavor.

> 1 pound small red potatoes, scrubbed and quartered
> 1 pound carrots, peeled and cut on the diagonal into ½-inch-thick slices
> 2 tablespoons extra-virgin olive oil
> 1 teaspoon sea salt or kosher salt
>
> ### VINAIGRETTE
> 2 tablespoons extra-virgin olive oil
> 2 medium red onions, halved lengthwise and cut into thin half-moons (about 2 cups)
> 1 teaspoon fresh thyme leaves
> Large pinch of sea salt or kosher salt
> 2 tablespoons red wine vinegar
> 1½ tablespoons grainy mustard
> 1 tablespoon honey
> 2 tablespoons finely chopped fresh flat-leaf parsley
> Freshly ground black pepper

Preheat the oven to 400 degrees.

In a large bowl, toss the potatoes and carrots with the oil and salt. Spread the vegetables in a roasting pan or on a rimmed baking sheet and roast until tender, about 30 minutes.

MEANWHILE, FOR THE VINAIGRETTE: In a medium skillet, heat the oil over medium-high heat. Add the onions, thyme, and salt and cook, stirring, until the onions are softened, about 3 minutes. Add the vinegar, mustard, and honey and stir well.

Transfer the roasted vegetables to a large bowl and pour in the onion mixture. Add the parsley, season with pepper, and toss well. Allow the vegetables to absorb the vinaigrette for at least 5 minutes before serving warm, or serve at room temperature.

Winter

MENU 6
SERVES 4

Creamy Root Vegetable Soup with
Honey-Crisped Walnuts

Braised Duck Legs

Sauerkraut with Fried Tempeh/Smoked Whitefish,
Green Apples, and Onions

This unusual Eastern European–leaning menu is full of pleasing contrasts, from the crisp walnuts (and the sumptuous braised duck, if you choose to include it) in the soup to the tart, sweet apples and crunchy sauerkraut served under the fried tempeh and smoked fish.

THE PLAN
1. Make the soup (reheat before serving if necessary).
2. Cook the duck, if using.
3. Meanwhile, crisp the walnuts.
4. Make the sauerkraut dish.

Creamy Root Vegetable Soup
with Honey-Crisped Walnuts

SERVES 4 TO 6

This soup can be made with whatever roots you happen to have on hand. For a heartier meal, I shred the meat from 2 braised duck legs into the soup before serving. If you do braise the duck, you can use the braising liquid (topped up with water to equal 6 cups) in place of the stock here. Honey-crisped walnuts add a sweet crunch.

1 tablespoon extra-virgin olive oil

1 tablespoon unsalted butter

1 pound onions, coarsely chopped (about 4 cups)

4–6 garlic cloves, peeled

2 tablespoons finely chopped peeled fresh ginger

Sea salt or kosher salt

2 pounds assorted root vegetables, such as rutabaga, carrot, parsnip, turnip, celery root, and/or sunchokes, peeled and coarsely chopped (about 8 cups)

2 teaspoons ground fennel, preferably lightly toasted and freshly ground (see page 12)

¼ teaspoon ground turmeric

6 cups chicken, duck, or vegetable stock or water

1 cup heavy cream or crème fraîche

Freshly ground black pepper

Braised Duck Legs (page 293), meat removed and shredded (optional)

Chopped fresh flat-leaf parsley, for garnish

Honey-Crisped Walnuts (page 292)

In a 4- to 5-quart Dutch oven or other heavy pot, heat the oil and butter over medium heat. Add the onions, garlic, ginger, and 1 teaspoon salt and stir well. Cover, reduce the heat to medium-low, and cook gently until the garlic and onions are soft and juicy, 15 to 20 minutes.

Add the root vegetables, fennel, and turmeric, raise the heat to medium-high, and cook, stirring, for 2 to 3 minutes. Pour in the stock or water and bring to a boil. Reduce the heat to low and simmer until the vegetables are completely tender and can be crushed easily against the side of the pot, 30 to 40 minutes.

Add the cream and simmer for 3 to 4 minutes. Using an immersion blender (or, working carefully in batches, a food processor or stand blender), puree the soup until smooth. Season with black pepper and additional salt if necessary. Stir in the shredded duck meat, if using. Reheat before serving if necessary.

Serve garnished with chopped parsley and the walnuts.

Honey-Crisped Walnuts

MAKES ABOUT 1 CUP

Sweet, crunchy roasted walnuts are the perfect accompaniment to everything from breakfast yogurt to salads, cheese platters, and creamy root vegetable soups.

1 teaspoon unsalted butter, softened
1 cup coarsely chopped walnuts
3 tablespoons honey
 Sea salt or kosher salt

Preheat the oven to 350 degrees. Grease a small baking dish or pie plate with the butter.

Place the walnuts in the prepared baking dish and drizzle evenly with the honey. Roast, stirring every 5 minutes, until golden brown, 13 to 15 minutes.

Scrape the walnuts onto a plate, season lightly with salt, and let cool. The walnuts will keep in an airtight container in the freezer for up to 3 months.

Braised Duck Legs

SERVES 4 TO 6

Duck leg meat is dark, and delicious, but it can be tough. Braising is the solution, rendering fork-tender meat that you can shred and add to soups, pasta sauces, salads, sandwiches, or tacos. The braising liquid left in the pot makes a highly flavorful addition to sauces or soups.

> 2 Long Island (Pekin) duck legs, excess fat removed, preferably presalted (see page 40)
> ½ teaspoon sea salt or kosher salt if the duck is not presalted
>   Freshly ground black pepper
> 3 shallots, halved
> 1 small carrot, peeled and coarsely chopped
> 1 small celery stalk, coarsely chopped
> 1 sprig fresh thyme

Preheat the oven to 350 degrees.

Season the duck all over with the salt if the legs weren't presalted and with black pepper.

Heat a small flameproof casserole or a heavy pot that will hold the duck legs in a single snug layer over medium heat until hot. Place the duck skin side down in the casserole and sear until the skin is deep golden brown and crisp, 8 to 10 minutes. Transfer the duck to a plate, and pour off the fat from the pot.

Add the shallots, carrot, celery, and thyme to the pot. Place the duck skin side up on the vegetables. Pour in enough water to come halfway up the sides of the duck legs and bring to a simmer over medium heat.

Cover the pot, transfer to the oven, and roast until the duck is cooked through, 25 to 30 minutes.

Transfer the duck to a plate to cool. Strain the cooking liquid through a sieve set into a bowl, pressing hard on the solids to extract as much liquid as possible. Cool the broth, then transfer to an airtight container and refrigerate for up to 3 days or freeze for up to 3 months. Shred the duck meat before serving.

Sauerkraut with
Fried Tempeh/Smoked Whitefish,
Green Apples, and Onions

I owe the inspiration for this dish to my dear friend Paul Vandewoude, a marvelous chef from Belgium and the proprietor of New York's charming Miette Culinary Studio.

A jar of sauerkraut from a natural food store will be tastier and have a better texture than the pouches of cabbage sold as sauerkraut in most supermarkets. Look for sauerkraut made with only cabbage, salt, and water—no vinegar or preservatives. Avoid the canned stuff. Smoked paprika and smoked sea salt (see page 182) give the tempeh a great smokiness, but just one of these ingredients would do the trick.

Note: This recipe calls for two pans for the two proteins—if you double the fish or tempeh and exclude the other, use just one large pan.

TEMPEH

2 tablespoons extra-virgin olive oil

8 ounces tempeh, sliced crosswise into 8 pieces

½ cup dry white wine

1 teaspoon sweet Spanish smoked paprika

¾ teaspoon smoked sea salt or regular sea salt or kosher salt

SAUERKRAUT

4 tablespoons (½ stick) unsalted butter

3 cups thinly sliced onions

½ cup diced peeled carrot

½ cup diced celery

1 large Granny Smith apple, peeled, cored, and diced

1 teaspoon caraway seeds

1 cup dry white wine

2 cups sauerkraut, rinsed and drained

1 whole smoked whitefish (or 1 pound kippers), sliced crosswise into 3-inch chunks

2 tablespoons chopped fresh flat-leaf parsley or dill

FOR THE TEMPEH: In a medium skillet, heat the oil over medium heat. Add the tempeh and cook for 2 minutes on each side. Add the wine, paprika, and salt, bring to a boil, and simmer until all the wine has been absorbed, 5 to 7 minutes. Remove from the heat.

FOR THE SAUERKRAUT: Divide the butter between two medium saucepans and melt it over medium heat. Add half of the onions, carrot, celery, apple, and caraway seeds to each pan and cook, stirring, until the vegetables are tender, 8 to 10 minutes.

Divide the wine between the pans, bring to a boil, and cook until it has reduced by half, about 5 minutes. Stir half the sauerkraut and ¼ cup water into each pan and simmer for 3 to 4 minutes.

Lay the tempeh over the vegetables in one pan and the fish over the vegetables in the other. Cover the pans and simmer for 5 to 7 minutes. Add half of the parsley or dill to each pan and simmer for 1 more minute, then serve.

Winter

MENU 7
SERVES 4

My Favorite Winter Tomato Soup with Goat Cheese Crostini

Spanish-Style Eggs with Kimchi/Chorizo over Farro

Fennel with Lemon and Fennel Salt

This meal of sunny tomato soup with eggs fried in olive oil and served over farro with mushrooms is rich in bright, bold flavors and satisfying textures. It's balanced by a refreshing "finger salad" of fennel wedges to dip in seasonings and munch on. On their own, either the soup or farro makes a superb lunch dish this time of year.

THE PLAN
1. Make the soup (reheat before serving).
2. Cook the farro.
3. Bake the crostini.
4. Make the fennel salt and prepare the fennel.
5. Fry the eggs.

My Favorite Winter Tomato Soup with Goat Cheese Crostini

SERVES 4 TO 6

Cheese-topped crostini are a simple and delightful way to add heft, flavor, and texture to vegetable soups of all kinds, from the classic French onion topped with Gruyère toast to this thick tomato potage, with its herbed-goat-cheese-topped floats.

SOUP

⅓ cup extra-virgin olive oil

4 cups thinly sliced onions (3–4 medium onions)

Sea salt or kosher salt

1 head garlic, cloves separated and peeled

1 medium carrot, peeled and thinly sliced

Large pinch of red pepper flakes, or to taste

2 tablespoons tomato paste

1 28-ounce can whole plum tomatoes or diced tomatoes in juice

2 cups vegetable or chicken stock or water

2 2-inch strips orange zest (removed with a vegetable peeler; leave the white pith behind)

1 sprig fresh sage

Freshly ground black pepper

CROSTINI

4 ounces fresh goat cheese (about ½ cup)

1 tablespoon extra-virgin olive oil

¼ teaspoon finely chopped fresh thyme

¼ teaspoon finely grated lemon zest

Freshly ground black pepper

½ baguette

1 garlic clove, halved

2 tablespoons chopped fresh chives or flat-leaf parsley, for serving

FOR THE SOUP: In a 3- to 4-quart Dutch oven or other heavy pot, heat the olive oil over medium-high heat. Add the onions and ½ teaspoon salt and cook, stirring, until the onions are softened, 3 to 4 minutes. Add the garlic cloves, carrot, and pepper flakes, lower the heat, cover, and cook until the vegetables are sweet and juicy but not browned, 15 to 20 minutes. Check, stirring occasionally, and add 1 tablespoon water if the vegetables appear dry.

Add the tomato paste and cook, stirring, until the olive oil turns reddish orange, 1 to 2 minutes. Add the tomatoes with their juice, the stock or water, orange zest, and sage and bring to a boil, then reduce the heat and simmer for 15 minutes.

Remove the pot from the heat and discard the orange zest and sage. Puree the soup with an immersion blender (or, working in batches, in a regular blender or a food processor) until smooth. Season with salt and black pepper. Transfer to a saucepan and reheat before serving.

FOR THE CROSTINI: Preheat the oven to 400 degrees.

In a small bowl, use a fork to beat together the goat cheese, olive oil, thyme, lemon zest, and a few grinds of black pepper until smooth.

Slice the baguette on the bias into four to six ⅓-inch-thick slices that are 2 to 3 inches long. Lay the slices in a single layer on a baking sheet and toast in the oven until crisp, 5 to 7 minutes.

Rub the toasts with the garlic halves and spread with the goat cheese mixture.

Pour the soup into four bowls and float a crostini on each. Sprinkle with the chopped chives or parsley and serve immediately.

Spanish-Style Eggs with Kimchi/**Chorizo** over Farro

SERVES 4 TO 6: 2 TO 3 SERVINGS WITH KIMCHI, 2 TO 3 SERVINGS WITH CHORIZO

This is my favorite way to eat eggs, heady with the scent of extra-virgin olive oil, with crispy whites and perfectly cooked yolks. The yolks and olive oil make a rich, flavorful sauce that's great served over the farro. Choose the freshest free-range eggs you can find and use a fragrant, preferably Spanish, olive oil.

Note: Cook half of the eggs in the chorizo pan for extra flavor and color. Serve the eggs made in the chorizo pan with the chorizo, keeping the other servings chorizo-free. Or, if you're doubling either the chorizo or the kimchi to serve all meat eaters or all vegetarians, make the eggs in one large skillet.

CHORIZO

¼ cup extra-virgin olive oil

1 2- to 3-inch piece Spanish-style precooked chorizo, peeled and thinly sliced

8–12 large eggs

¼ cup extra-virgin olive oil

Sea salt or kosher salt and freshly ground black pepper

Farro (page 303)

1–2 cups kimchi

Chopped fresh flat-leaf parsley, for garnish

FOR THE CHORIZO: In a large skillet, heat ¼ cup olive oil over medium heat. Add the chorizo and fry until heated through, turning once, about 1 minute. Use a slotted spoon to transfer the chorizo to a plate, leaving the oil in the pan.

Crack half the eggs into each of two bowls.

Pour the remaining ¼ cup oil into a second large skillet and place both pans over medium-high heat. When the oil shimmers, slide half the eggs into each skillet and immediately use a rubber spatula to push and curl the edges of the eggs onto themselves to separate them. As the eggs fry, tip the pans and use a wide spoon to scoop up the oil and pour it over the eggs. Continue to baste the eggs until the whites are set and the yolks are barely cooked. Season with salt and pepper and take the pans off the heat.

Divide the farro among four to six shallow soup plates. Transfer a portion of fried eggs to each bowl and top with kimchi or chorizo. Drizzle a little of the olive oil from the pans around the farro and sprinkle with parsley.

Farro

Farro (pearled or cleaned spelt berries) cooked with vegetables, mushrooms, and soy sauce is savory, chewy, and satisfying. Pearl barley can be substituted if farro is unavailable.

> 1 tablespoon unsalted butter
>
> 1 small red onion, finely chopped
>
> 1 medium celery stalk, finely diced
>
> 1 small carrot, peeled and finely diced
>
> 4 ounces white, cremini, or shiitake mushrooms, tough stems discarded and thinly sliced (about 1 cup)
>
> 1 cup farro
>
> 3 cups cold water
>
> 2 teaspoons soy sauce, preferably naturally brewed
>
> 1 sprig fresh thyme
>
> ½ teaspoon sea salt or kosher salt

In a heavy 3- to 4-quart saucepan, melt the butter over medium heat. Add the onion, celery, and carrot, raise the heat to high, and cook, stirring occasionally, for 4 minutes. Add the mushrooms and cook until all the vegetables are golden brown and lightly caramelized, about 2 minutes.

Add the farro and cook, stirring, for 1 to 2 minutes. Pour in the water and bring to a boil. Add the soy sauce, thyme, and salt, cover, reduce the heat, and simmer gently until the farro is tender, about 25 minutes. Remove the thyme sprig and serve.

Fennel with Lemon and Fennel Salt

SERVES 4

With its clean taste and crisp texture, fennel offers a reviving contrast to this winter meal. The spiced salt adds another layer of anise flavor. Leftover salt can be stored in a tightly sealed container for up to 2 months; it's great to have on hand to season fish, seafood, beans, or chicken.

Tip: You can toast and grind the fennel seeds and peppercorns together.

- **1 tablespoon coarse sea salt or kosher salt**
- **2 teaspoons fennel seeds, lightly toasted and coarsely ground (see page 12)**
- **¼ teaspoon whole black peppercorns, lightly toasted and coarsely ground**
- **2 large fennel bulbs, trimmed, cored, and cut lengthwise into 10–12 wedges**
- **½ lemon**
- **Extra-virgin olive oil, for drizzling**

In a small bowl, stir together the salt, ground fennel, and pepper.

Arrange the fennel wedges on a platter. Squeeze the lemon half over the fennel and drizzle with olive oil. Sprinkle lightly with fennel salt and serve.

Winter

MENU 8
SERVES 4 TO 6

Short Rib Cholent

Seitan Cholent

Shaved Winter Vegetable Salad
with Apple and Raisins

Cholent is one of my favorite Jewish braises. Usually composed of meat, grains, and beans (though meatless versions exist), it is always cooked for a long time. This is convenient, especially for those who keep kosher, since it can be started the night before the Sabbath and will be ready for lunch on the day when no work is permitted. During the long, slow cooking, the meat and beans become velvety and the flavors meld.

Since most of the ingredients in both the vegetarian and meat versions are the same, it's not much more work to assemble two cholents—one with eggs, beans, grains, dried shiitake mushrooms, and seitan, the other with eggs, beans, grains, brisket, and short ribs (flanken, if you're at a kosher butcher). You'll need two 4- to 5-quart Dutch ovens or other heavy pots in that case. The stews spend 8 hours in the oven, making the recipe a great activity for a weekend day when you're planning to be around the house anyway. I like to serve the cholent with a crunchy, raisin-studded fennel and cabbage salad for contrast.

Note: One of these cholents, served with the salad, will feed 4 to 6 diners. If you're making both versions, you can double the salad to feed 8 to 12, or enjoy the leftovers—they get even better the next day.

THE PLAN

1. The night before you make the cholent, salt the meat for the short rib version and/or soak the shiitakes for the seitan version. Soak the beans.
2. Make the cholent(s).
3. Make the salad.

Short Rib Cholent

SERVES 4 TO 6

The whole wheat (or other grain) is cooked in a cheesecloth bag so it can be served on the side, for a nicer presentation.

Tip: Short ribs are the most luxurious cut of beef for braising because their connective tissue is transformed into succulence by the moist, slow heat.

A layer of fat will rise to the top of this stew, which should be skimmed away. Should you be feeling particularly patient, you can make the stew a day in advance, cool, and refrigerate it, then simply lift off the congealed fat and reheat gently, covered.

1½ pounds bone-in beef chuck or brisket

1 pound beef short ribs, trimmed of excess fat

Sea salt or kosher salt

½ cup dried chickpeas, picked over

½ cup dried kidney beans, picked over

1 tablespoon vegetable oil

1 cup dry red wine

1 tablespoon extra-virgin olive oil

1 pound onions, coarsely chopped

¼ cup (peeled) garlic cloves

2 tablespoons dark brown sugar

1 tablespoon sweet paprika

1 teaspoon sweet Spanish smoked paprika

1 teaspoon cumin seeds

½ teaspoon freshly ground black pepper

1 cup whole wheat, rye, or spelt berries, wrapped loosely in a square of cheesecloth and tied

12 ounces russet (baking) potatoes, peeled and halved, or quartered if large

8 ounces carrots, peeled and cut into chunks

4 large eggs (in the shell)

Chopped fresh flat-leaf parsley, for garnish

The night before you make the cholent, sprinkle the meat and short ribs all over with 2 teaspoons salt. Place on a plate, cover with plastic, and refrigerate. Combine the chickpeas and kidney beans in a large bowl and cover with 3 inches cold water (or use the quick-soak method on page 9). Refrigerate the beans.

The next day, set a rack in the middle of the oven and preheat the oven to 200 degrees.

Wick away any moisture from the surface of the meat with a paper towel. In a large skillet, heat the vegetable oil over medium heat until hot but not smoking. Add the meat and sear in batches, turning occasionally, until well browned, 15 to 20 minutes. Don't rush the browning, or the meat could burn, resulting in a bitter-tasting cholent. Transfer the meat to a platter and pour off the fat from the pan.

Return the pan to medium heat and pour in the wine, scraping up the browned bits from the bottom of the pan. Pour the wine and browned bits into a bowl and reserve.

In a 4- to 5-quart Dutch oven or other heavy pot, heat the olive oil over medium heat. Add the onions and cook, stirring, until translucent, 3 to 4 minutes. Add the garlic cloves, brown sugar, sweet and smoked paprika, cumin seeds, 1 teaspoon salt, and the pepper and cook, stirring, until the spices are fragrant, about 2 minutes. Stir in the reserved wine.

Drain the soaked beans and spread them over the onion mixture. Place the cheesecloth sack of grain on top of the beans. Layer the browned meat, potatoes, and carrots on top, then arrange the whole eggs on top. Slowly pour 4 cups of water down the side of the pot, so as not to disturb the layers. Raise the heat to medium-high and bring to a boil. Skim off and discard the scum that rises to the surface.

Cover the pot, transfer to the oven, and braise until the meat can be easily pierced with a fork, about 8 hours.

Uncover the pot and spoon off and discard as much of the surface fat as you can (or cool, refrigerate, and skim, then reheat to serve). Transfer the eggs to a bowl. Transfer the vegetables and meat to a warm serving platter. Retrieve the cheesecloth sack containing the grain and set aside on a plate until it is cool enough to handle, then cut open the sack and pour the grains onto the serving platter. With a slotted spoon, scoop the beans and onions onto the platter.

Strain the braising liquid into a gravy boat. Peel the eggs, halve them lengthwise, and arrange them around the vegetables and meat. Scatter the cholent with parsley and serve with the braising juices on the side.

Seitan Cholent

Shiitake mushrooms add a meaty chew to the cholent and infuse the braising liquid with a woodsy fragrance. As in the short rib cholent, the whole wheat (or other grain) is cooked in a cheesecloth bag so it can be served on the side.

12 dried shiitake mushrooms

½ cup dried chickpeas, picked over

½ cup dried kidney beans, picked over

⅓ cup extra-virgin olive oil

1 pound onions, cut into 1-inch chunks

2 4-inch pieces kombu

¼ cup (peeled) garlic cloves

2 tablespoons dark brown sugar

1 tablespoon sweet paprika

1 teaspoon sweet Spanish smoked paprika

1 teaspoon cumin seeds

2 teaspoons sea salt or kosher salt

1 cup whole wheat, rye, or spelt berries, wrapped loosely in a square of cheesecloth and tied

1 pound seitan, cut into 1-inch chunks

12 ounces russet (baking) potatoes, peeled and halved, or quartered if large

8 ounces carrots, peeled and cut into chunks

4 large eggs (in the shell)

3 tablespoons soy sauce, preferably naturally brewed

¼ teaspoon freshly ground black pepper

Chopped fresh flat-leaf parsley, for garnish

The night before you make the cholent, place the dried shiitakes in a bowl with 3 cups water and set a small plate on top of the mushrooms to keep them submerged. Refrigerate. Combine the chickpeas and kidney beans in a large bowl, cover with 3 inches of cold water, and refrigerate, or use the quick-soak method (see page 9).

The next day, set a rack in the middle of the oven and preheat the oven to 200 degrees.

Lift out the shiitakes from the soaking liquid and set aside. Carefully pour the soaking liquid into a large measuring cup or bowl, stopping short of any grit that has collected at the bottom of the soaking bowl. Add enough cold water to the mushroom liquid to equal 6 cups.

In a 4- to 5-quart Dutch oven or other heavy pot, heat the olive oil over medium heat. Add the onions and cook, stirring, until translucent, 3 to 4 minutes. Add the kombu, garlic cloves, brown sugar, sweet and smoked paprika, cumin seeds, and 1 teaspoon of the salt and cook, stirring, until the spices are fragrant, about 2 minutes.

Drain and rinse the beans, then spread them over the onion mixture. Place the cheesecloth sack of grains over the beans. Layer the seitan, shiitakes, potatoes, and carrots on top, then arrange the whole eggs on top. Slowly pour the shiitake liquid down the side of the pot, so as not to disturb the layers. Add the soy sauce, pepper, and the remaining 1 teaspoon salt. Raise the heat to medium-high and bring to a boil.

Cover the pot, transfer to the oven, and braise until the beans are very tender but still hold their shape and the juices have thickened to a rich gravy, about 8 hours.

Uncover the pot and transfer the eggs to a bowl. Transfer the vegetables and seitan to a warm serving platter. Retrieve the cheesecloth sack containing the grain and set aside on a plate until cool enough to handle, then cut open the sack and pour the grains onto the platter. With a slotted spoon, scoop the beans, onions, and kombu onto the platter.

Strain the braising liquid into a gravy boat. Peel the eggs, halve them lengthwise, and arrange them around the vegetables and seitan. Scatter the cholent with parsley and serve with the braising juices on the side.

Shaved Winter Vegetable Salad with Apple and Raisins

SERVES 4 TO 6

This is a little like a slaw, with a cheerful mix of fennel, red cabbage, green apple, and raisins. A mandoline or Benriner will speed up all the slicing, but you can certainly do it by hand with a very sharp knife—slice thin, so the sheets of vegetable and fruit combine nicely with each other and the dressing. Garnish with the fennel fronds, or add chopped fresh dill if you're short on fronds.

3 tablespoons plus 1 teaspoon fresh lemon juice

1 tablespoon whole-grain Dijon mustard

1 teaspoon ground fennel, preferably toasted and freshly ground (see page 12)

3 tablespoons plus 1 teaspoon extra-virgin olive oil

Sea salt or kosher salt and freshly ground black pepper

1 large fennel bulb, cored, trimmed, tender fronds reserved, bulb halved lengthwise and sliced paper-thin crosswise

Chopped fresh dill (optional)

½ small head red cabbage, halved, cored, and thinly sliced crosswise (about 3 cups)

1 medium carrot, peeled and sliced paper-thin

1 Granny Smith apple, cored and sliced paper-thin

3 tablespoons raisins or dried currants

In a salad bowl, combine the lemon juice, mustard, and ground fennel. Slowly whisk in the oil, then season with salt and pepper to taste.

Finely chop enough of the fennel fronds to make 2 tablespoons; if necessary, add a little chopped dill. Add the sliced fennel, cabbage, carrot, apple, raisins or currants and chopped fennel fronds and/or dill to the dressing. Toss to combine. Refrigerate for 15 minutes.

Season the salad with additional salt and/or pepper if necessary and serve.

Winter

MENU 9
SERVES 4 TO 6

Pizzoccheri Casserole

Seitan/Chicken Liver Schnitzel
with Red Wine–Shallot Compote and Bitter Greens

This unusual menu is elegant, wine-friendly, and perfect for a dinner party. The liver or seitan is breaded and fried so it is crisp on the outside and soft within, a textural contrast that highlights the savory flavor of both ingredients. The sweet-tart shallot compote and bitter greens round out the dish, balancing the rich schnitzel. *Pizzoccheri* are homemade buckwheat noodles. Here they are baked with vegetables in a warming and comforting casserole topped liberally with cheese.

THE PLAN
1. Make the shallot compote.
2. Make the pizzoccheri.
3. Cook the schnitzel.
4. Make the greens.

Pizzoccheri Casserole

SERVES 4 TO 6

Buckwheat, a traditional food in many cold, mountainous regions, from Japan, China, and Russia to northern Italy and Switzerland, is used in everything from breads to polenta to rustic noodles like these. I first encountered pizzoccheri in Switzerland, where the hefty noodles were served in a brothy soup with cheese, as well as baked in a vegetable casserole like this one.

Buckwheat is good for your heart and liver, and mixing the beautiful gray noodle dough is good for your soul. I roll the pasta out by hand, as the results are supposed to be rustic and imperfect. The dish is all about texture and the way the wine and vegetable mixture cooks into the chewy noodles.

If you are not serving a vegetarian meal, this casserole is a good place to use homemade duck (see page 71) or chicken stock in place of the pasta cooking water.

Tip: Since buckwheat flour gets quite sticky, it's necessary to use at least half white flour in the dough and to let the rolled-out pasta sit and dry briefly before you slice it into noodles.

PASTA

1 cup buckwheat flour

1 cup unbleached all-purpose flour, plus additional for kneading

Large pinch of sea salt or kosher salt

4 large eggs

CASSEROLE

Sea salt or kosher salt

2 sprigs fresh thyme

1 sprig fresh sage

2 tablespoons extra-virgin olive oil

2 tablespoons unsalted butter

1½ cups thinly sliced onions

1 large garlic clove, chopped

Pinch of red pepper flakes

¼ medium head green cabbage, cored and sliced crosswise into ¼-inch-wide strips (2½ cups)

1 cup thinly sliced peeled carrots

1 small potato, cubed

1 cup fruity red wine, such as Côtes du Rhône, Shiraz, or Pinot Noir

8 large collard greens, thick central veins removed, leaves cut crosswise into ¼-inch-wide ribbons (6 cups)

Freshly ground black pepper

12 ounces Gruyère cheese, coarsely grated (about 3 cups)

Chopped fresh flat-leaf parsley, for garnish

FOR THE PASTA: In a large bowl, combine the flours with the salt. Make a well in the center and crack in the eggs. Use a fork to beat the eggs, then gradually incorporate the flour to form a soft dough. Transfer the dough to a lightly floured surface, and wash and dry your hands. Knead the dough until smooth, firm, and elastic, about 15 minutes, adding additional white flour as necessary if it gets too sticky. Wrap the dough in plastic and let rest for 30 minutes. (The dough can be refrigerated for up to 24 hours or frozen, well wrapped, for up to 3 months. Thaw overnight in the fridge and bring to room temperature before proceeding.)

Divide the dough in half and flatten each half into a disk. Using a rolling pin, roll each piece on the floured work surface to about ¹/₁₆ inch thick. Dust the sheets with flour and let rest for 20 minutes, turning them over after 10 minutes, to let the pasta firm and dry a little.

Roll each pasta sheet up into a loose cylinder and slice it into ½-inch-wide noodles. Make loose little nests of a few noodles each and let rest on a kitchen towel until you are ready to boil them.

FOR THE CASSEROLE: Preheat the oven to 375 degrees. Bring a large pot of salted water to a boil.

Use kitchen twine to tie the thyme and sage sprigs together. In a 4- to 5-quart Dutch oven or other heavy pot, heat the olive oil and butter over medium-high heat. Add the onions and herb bundle and cook, stirring occasionally, until the onions are translucent, about 4 minutes. Add the garlic and pepper flakes and cook, stirring, for 1 minute, then stir in the cabbage, carrots, and potato and cook until the vegetables begin to soften, about 3 minutes. Raise the heat to high, pour in the wine, and boil until it has reduced by half, about 3 minutes. Add the collard greens and stir until they wilt.

Meanwhile, boil the noodles until they are nearly cooked through, about 2 minutes. Ladle out 3 cups of the pasta cooking water and reserve, then drain the pasta.

Pour the reserved cooking water into the vegetable mixture and bring to a boil. Take the pot off the heat, add the noodles, and toss to combine. Season generously with salt and pepper, and sprinkle the cheese evenly over the top.

Transfer the pot to the oven and bake, uncovered, until the vegetables are tender and the cheese is bubbling, about 30 minutes.

Remove the casserole from the oven and turn on the broiler. Place the casserole under the broiler and broil until golden brown on top and crispy on the edges, 1 to 2 minutes. Scatter with parsley and serve.

Seitan/Chicken Liver Schnitzel with Red Wine–Shallot Compote and Bitter Greens

SERVES 4 TO 6: 2 TO 3 SERVINGS SEITAN, 2 TO 3 SERVINGS LIVER

At Ici, a cozy restaurant in Fort Greene, Brooklyn, I had a delicious first course of chicken liver breaded and fried like schnitzel. I immediately thought of trying the technique with seitan. The results took me back to Boston in the 1970s, when I was first getting into macrobiotics, and a street fair stand was frying cornmeal-coated seitan "pups"—I loved them! The crispy coating is similar, but the presentation, with a sweet and savory shallot compote and a bitter green salad, couldn't be farther removed from that youthful time of fried macrobiotic food.

Note: If you want to serve only one kind of schnitzel, use 8 ounces of seitan or liver.

Tip: Liver spits as it fries, so a mesh splatter screen is helpful here. Frying the seitan first, then the liver, will allow you to use the same breading and oil for both. Keep the seitan warm in the oven while you cook the liver.

> 1 cup dried bread crumbs (see page 263)
> 1 cup unbleached all-purpose flour
> 1¼ teaspoons sea salt or kosher salt
> ½ teaspoon freshly ground black pepper
> 2 large eggs
>
> 4–6 ounces seitan, cut into six ½-inch-thick slices
> 4–6 ounces chicken livers, rinsed, patted dry, and cut into six ½-inch-thick slices
>
> About 2 cups vegetable oil, for shallow-frying
> Lemon wedges, for serving
> Red Wine–Shallot Compote (page 321)
> Bitter Greens (page 322)

Spread the bread crumbs in a shallow dish or pie plate. In a shallow bowl, combine the flour with 1 teaspoon of the salt and the pepper. In another bowl, beat the eggs with the remaining ¼ teaspoon salt.

With one hand, dredge each piece of seitan in the flour, then in the egg, and transfer to the bowl of bread crumbs. Using your other (dry) hand, scoop some bread crumbs over the seitan, then transfer the seitan to a plate. After all the seitan has been breaded, repeat the procedure with the livers, transferring them to a separate plate. Refrigerate the breaded seitan and liver for 20 minutes to allow the coating to set.

Preheat the oven to 250 degrees.

Fill a large skillet with about ½ inch oil and heat the oil over medium heat until shimmering. Fry the seitan, turning once, until the breading is crisp and golden, about 2 minutes on the first side and 1 minute on the second side. Transfer to a paper-towel-lined plate and keep warm in the oven. Fry the livers until crisp and browned, about 1 minute per side. Transfer to another paper-towel-lined plate. Serve immediately, accompanied by lemon wedges, the shallot compote, and the greens.

Red Wine–Shallot Compote

This compote is so delicious you will hope for leftovers to serve with potato pancakes, steak, or roast chicken, or simply pair with goat cheese on a piece of bread. The compote will keep, tightly sealed, in the refrigerator for up to 2 weeks.

1 pound shallots (about 12 large), halved lengthwise and thinly sliced crosswise

1½ cups fruity low-tannin red wine, such as Shiraz, Rioja, or Pinot Noir

1 cup water

3 tablespoons red wine vinegar

3 tablespoons sugar

2 tablespoons unsalted butter

2 tablespoons balsamic vinegar

1 teaspoon whole black peppercorns

½ teaspoon sea salt or kosher salt

2 whole cloves

1 sprig fresh rosemary

Freshly ground black pepper to taste

In a medium skillet, combine all the ingredients and bring to a boil. Reduce the heat to medium and simmer, stirring occasionally, until the liquid has reduced to a syrupy glaze, about 1 hour.

Discard the cloves and rosemary . Serve the compote warm or at room temperature.

Bitter Greens

The greens in this salad are assertive enough to counter rich or sweet foods. For a dinner party, wash and spin the greens ahead and have them ready in the fridge. Make the dressing in the bowl in advance and let it sit on the counter, then, when you're ready to serve, whisk it again before tossing in the greens. If you like, use a medium head of frisée in place of one bunch of watercress.

1 small garlic clove, halved

3 tablespoons red wine vinegar

2 teaspoons Dijon mustard

6 tablespoons extra-virgin olive oil

Sea salt or kosher salt and freshly ground black pepper

2 large bunches watercress, tough stems discarded, and torn

2 Belgian endive, any damaged outer leaves discarded, sliced on the diagonal ¼ inch thick

Rub the inside of a large salad bowl with the garlic; discard the garlic. Add the vinegar and mustard to the bowl and stir to combine. Whisk in the oil and season with salt and a few grinds of pepper.

Add the greens to the bowl, toss gently to coat, and season with additional salt if necessary. Serve immediately.

Winter

MENU 10
SERVES 4

Chicken/Tempeh in Mole Negro

Creamy Masa Harina

Pickled Vegetable Salad

I serve this Mexican-inspired menu with plenty of creamy cooked masa harina (corn flour) or steamed basmati rice to capture the warm, rich mole sauce. The salad is crunchy and tangy. Pickled vegetables seem particularly healthy at this time of year because they aid digestion and refresh the palate, so I make a lot and keep them in the fridge for snacking or putting in salads. The pickles should be prepared at least 2 days in advance.

THE PLAN
1. Pickle the vegetables.
2. Make the mole sauce.
3. Finish the mole.
4. Cook the masa.
5. Assemble the salad.

Chicken/Tempeh in Mole Negro

SERVES 4: 2 SERVINGS CHICKEN,
2 SERVINGS TEMPEH

This mole is a complex sauce with the sophisticated, bittersweet flavor of toasted chilies and chocolate. Sesame seeds, pumpkin seeds, peanuts, almonds, cinnamon, cumin, and raisins join the fruity flavor of ancho chilies in a dark, thick sauce that hits practically every note on the flavor spectrum. Equally good on chicken and tempeh, mole is a great sauce to keep on hand in the freezer—you might want to make a double batch, since you're gathering all the ingredients.

Note: If you prefer, double the tempeh or chicken and leave out the other.

MOLE

- ¼ cup vegetable oil
- 2 large dried ancho chilies
- 3 cups hot water
- ½ cup finely diced onion
- ¼ cup unsalted dry-roasted peanuts
- ¼ cup blanched whole almonds
- ¼ cup raisins
- 2 tablespoons sesame seeds
- 2 tablespoons pumpkin seeds
- 1 teaspoon cumin seeds
- 2 chipotle chilies in adobo sauce, seeded
  Sea salt or kosher salt
- 1 ounce bittersweet chocolate, broken into pieces or coarsely chopped
- 1 cinnamon stick

CHICKEN

1 3-pound chicken, preferably organic, cut into 8 pieces, skin removed

2 teaspoons sea salt or kosher salt

Freshly ground black pepper

1 tablespoon extra-virgin olive oil

TEMPEH

2 tablespoons extra-virgin olive oil

2 8-ounce packages tempeh, cut into 1-inch squares

1 cup water

½ teaspoon sea salt or kosher salt

Lime wedges, for serving

Chopped cilantro and/or scallions, for garnish

FOR THE MOLE: In a medium skillet, heat the oil over medium heat. Add the ancho chilies and fry, turning with tongs, until they blister (take care not to burn them). Transfer to a plate to cool. Set the skillet of oil aside.

MEANWHILE, SEASON THE CHICKEN: Season the chicken pieces all over with the 2 teaspoons salt and pepper to taste and refrigerate for 1 hour.

When the ancho chilies are cool enough to handle, break them open and discard the seeds. Place the chilies in a bowl and cover with the water. Let soak until soft, 15 to 20 minutes. Drain, reserving the liquid.

Return the skillet to medium heat. Add the onion and cook, stirring, until softened, 2 to 3 minutes. Add the peanuts, almonds, raisins, sesame seeds, pumpkin seeds, and cumin seeds and stir and toast until the nuts and seeds are fragrant and the raisins are puffed, 8 to 10 minutes.

Using a rubber spatula, scrape the contents of the pan into a blender (set the skillet aside). Add the chipotle chilies and 1 teaspoon salt, then add the softened ancho chilies and 1 cup of the reserved liquid. Puree, gradually adding the remaining liquid, until the mixture is smooth.

Pour the puree back into the skillet and bring to a simmer over medium heat. Add the chocolate and stir until melted. Add the cinnamon stick, reduce the heat to low, and simmer gently until the mole thickens, about 20 minutes.

Remove the pan from the heat and discard the cinnamon stick. Season the mole with additional salt to taste, and set aside.

FOR THE CHICKEN: Wick away the moisture from the chicken with paper towels. In a heavy 10-inch skillet or 3-quart casserole, heat the oil over medium heat. Add the chicken and cook, turning occasionally, until lightly browned on all sides, about 15 minutes.

Pour in half the mole and simmer until the chicken is cooked through, about 20 minutes longer.

MEANWHILE, FOR THE TEMPEH: In another heavy 10-inch skillet or 3-quart casserole, heat the oil over medium heat. Add the tempeh and cook, turning frequently, until lightly browned all over, about 10 minutes. Add the water and salt to the pan and bring to a boil. Cover, reduce the heat, and simmer for 8 minutes.

Drain the tempeh and return it to the pan. Pour in the remaining mole, and bring to a simmer. Simmer, covered, for 20 minutes.

Serve the mole garnished with chopped cilantro and/or scallions, with the lime wedges alongside.

Creamy Masa Harina

Masa harina is the corn flour used to make tamales and tortillas. It has a warm, sweet, toasty corn flavor and makes a satisfying mush when cooked like hot cereal.

> 1 cup masa harina
>
> 3 cups cold water
>
> ½ teaspoon sea salt or kosher salt

In a medium saucepan, combine the masa harina with the cold water over medium heat and stir until it comes to a simmer. Add the salt and continue to stir until the mixture is thick and creamy, about 7 minutes. Serve hot.

Pickled Vegetable Salad

MAKES 2 QUARTS

You'll need 2 quarts of crunchy vegetables for this lively pickle. The vegetable types and quantities I have listed are just a suggestion, and the ratios are up to you. The whole chilies give a slight warmth to the pickle—just be sure to remove them before serving.

BRINE

4 cups water

⅔ cup cider vinegar, preferably unpasteurized

3 tablespoons kosher salt

2 tablespoons sugar

1 teaspoon coriander seeds

1 teaspoon cumin seeds

5–6 small dried red chilies or ½ teaspoon red pepper flakes

2 bay leaves

VEGETABLES

1 small onion, thinly sliced

2 medium carrots, peeled and thinly sliced

½ medium cauliflower, cut into florets

1 fennel bulb, trimmed, cored, and sliced

¼ medium head red cabbage, cored and thinly sliced

1 large bunch arugula or 1 head butter lettuce, trimmed or cored and torn, for serving

Extra-virgin olive oil, for serving

Sea salt or kosher salt and freshly ground black pepper

FOR THE BRINE: In a large saucepan, combine all the ingredients and bring to a simmer over medium-high heat. Reduce the heat slightly and simmer for 3 to 4 minutes. Remove from the heat and let cool.

FOR THE VEGETABLES: In a large bowl, toss together all the vegetables. Transfer them to a 2-quart jar and cover with the cooled brine. Cover the jar and refrigerate for at least 2 days (or up to 4 months).

To serve, gloss the arugula or lettuce with a little olive oil, season with salt and pepper, and toss with some of the pickled vegetables.

Index

Aleppo pepper, about, 25
almond flour, preparing, 152
appetizers
    bulgur with roasted chickpeas, red onion, and
        lemon, 36
    cucumber lime raita, 22
    dilled yogurt dip, 29–30
    green olive frittata with ricotta, pine nuts, and
        thyme, 60–61
    Parmesan toasts, 67
    sautéed baby artichokes with garlic and wine,
        34–35
    sesame tahini sauce, 166
    spicy grilled chicken wings with lemon and
        garlic, 147
    stuffed eggs with capers and garlic, 32
    summer vegetable ragout, 155
    tapenade, 31
apple(s)
    chestnut soup, 205–6
    green, fried tempeh/smoked whitefish, and
        onions, sauerkraut with, 294–95
    and raisins, shaved winter vegetable salad with,
        312–13
    shaved, and spring vegetable salad, 43–44
artichoke(s)
    baby, preparing for cooking, 34
    baby, sautéed, with garlic and wine, 34–35
    cut, preventing discoloration of, 34
    potato, and leek gratin, 81–82
arugula salad with mustard vinaigrette, 110
Asiago and spring greens, creamy risotto-style
    brown rice with, 41–42

Asian noodles in broth with vegetables and
    tofu/steak, 85–86
asparagus
    and fiddlehead ferns, sautéed, with garlic, 76
    salad, chilled, with sherry vinaigrette, 56–57
avocado(s)
    chopped salad with sherry vinaigrette, 156
    corn, and red beans, farro with, 139–40
    cucumber, and hiziki salsa, 184

bacon
    cooking, in oven, 249
    corn, red beans, and scallops/avocado, farro
        with, 139–40
    uncured smoked, flavor of, 7
barley mushroom soup, 261
basil and Parmesan, zucchini-rice soup with,
    134–35
bean(s)
    black, enchiladas with smoked tofu/chicken
        and mole verde, 180–83
    canned, rinsing and draining, 8
    chickpeas, roasted, red onion, and lemon, with
        bulgur, 36
    cooked, serving ideas, 212
    dried, soaking and cooking, 9
    dried, yield from, 212
    falafel, 164–65
    green, corn, and tomatoes, quinoa salad with,
        128–29
    green, preparing, for salads, 129
    heirloom varieties, 8

bean(s) *cont.*

navy, fresh pea, and leek soup, 48

pinto, with chipotle and melted garlic, 247–48

red, corn, and scallops/avocado, farro with, 139–40

red, slow-cooked, in white wine with escarole, 272–73

salade Niçoise with many possibilities, 120–22

seitan cholent, 311–12

shell, fresh, preparing, 8

short rib cholent, 308–9

substituting types of, 8

summer, ratatouille, 106–7

white, and cherry tomatoes, gratin of, 54–55

white, with brown butter and tons of herbs, 212–14

beef

Asian noodles in broth with vegetables and tofu/steak, 85–86

grain-fed, about, 6–7

grass-fed, about, 6–7

steak with bread crumb salsa, 108–9

searing, tip for, 108

short rib cholent, 308–9

short ribs, braising, 308

beets

baby, and mustard vinaigrette, mâche and pea shoots with, 94–95

beet greens, goat cheese, and walnuts, penne with, 207–8

bread(s)

crumbs, fresh, preparing, 263

crumb salsa, 108–9

goat cheese crostini, 298–99

naan, 23–24

panzanella, 150

Parmesan toasts, 67

pita, store-bought, warming, 29

pita, whole wheat, 161–62

broccoli, roasted, with Parmesan, 216

Brussels sprouts

preparing for cooking, 230

roasted, with fennel seeds and balsamic, 230

bulgur with roasted chickpeas, red onion, and lemon, 36

burdock

autumn stew with miso and duck/tofu, 218–21

buying, 256

carrots, and leeks, teriyaki-style, 256–57

preparing for cooking, 256

butter

brown, serving ideas, 214

browning, method for, 214

heating, for ghee, 21

cabbage. *See also* kimchi; sauerkraut

gratin of winter vegetables, 262–63

napa, salad with sweet peppers and sesame vinaigrette, 222–23

pickled vegetable salad, 329–30

pizzoccheri casserole, 316–18

shaved winter vegetable salad with apple and raisins, 312–13

cannelloni with ricotta, Parmesan, and mint, 152–54

caper vinaigrette, 120–21

carrot(s)

with black olives and mint, 239

burdock, and leeks, teriyaki-style, 256–57

creamy root vegetable soup with honey-crisped walnuts, 290–91

to julienne, with knife, 281

to julienne, with mandoline, 79

pea shoot, radish, and smoked trout/tofu salad, 79–80

pickled vegetable salad, 329–30

roasted spring, with cumin and lime, 25

roasted winter vegetable salad with red onion vinaigrette, 287

-yogurt chutney, 177

cauliflower

millet "polenta" with crispy shallots, 274–75

pickled vegetable salad, 329–30

ceviche, seafood/tofu, with quick-pickled red onion, 132–33

chard

and feta cheese, fregola risotto-style with, 90–93

mole verde, 180–82

charmoula lamb/tempeh kebabs, 100–101

cheese. *See also* feta cheese; goat cheese
    baked fish/ricotta dumplings over French
        lentils, 190–92
    black bean enchiladas with smoked
        tofu/chicken and mole verde, 180–83
    cannelloni with ricotta, Parmesan, and mint,
        152–54
    creamy risotto-style brown rice with spring
        greens and Asiago, 41–42
    gratin of winter vegetables, 262–63
    green olive frittata with ricotta, pine nuts, and
        thyme, 60–61
    hard, grating, 134
    lasagna with fall vegetables, Gruyère, and sage
        béchamel, 226–29
    organic, buying, 10
    Parmesan toasts, 67
    pizzoccheri casserole, 316–18
    roasted broccoli with Parmesan, 216
    salade Niçoise with many possibilities,
        120–22
    smoked salmon/sun-dried-tomato croque
        monsieur, 50–51
    zucchini-rice soup with basil and Parmesan,
        134–35
chestnut(s)
    apple soup, 205–6
    to score, 205
    soaking before roasting, 205
chicken
    crispy pressed, with garlic and mint, 38–40
    feet, for chicken stock, 6
    "free-range," about, 5–6
    heritage breeds, 6
    liver schnitzel with red wine–shallot compote
        and bitter greens, 319–20
    in mole negro, 324–27
    organic, about, 5
    poussin with quinoa, dried fruit, and pumpkin
        seeds, 244–46
    roast, lemon-thyme, 197–98
    seasoning, before cooking, 40
    smoked, black bean enchiladas with, and mole
        verde, 180–83
    wings, spicy grilled, with lemon and garlic,
        147

chickpeas
    falafel, 164–65
    roasted, red onion, and lemon, bulgur with, 36
chili peppers
    hot sauce (zhoug), 165
    mole negro, 324–27
    mole verde, 180–82
    pinto beans with chipotle and melted garlic,
        247–48
Chinese chives, about, 72
chives, about, 72
chive sour cream, 185
chocolate, in mole negro, 324–27
cholent, seitan, 311–12
cholent, short rib, 308–9
chopped salad with sherry vinaigrette, 156
chorizo, Spanish-style eggs with, over farro, 300–302
chutney, carrot-yogurt, 177
cod/tofu, batter-fried, with kimchi, 278–79
compote, red wine–shallot, 321
condiments
    carrot-yogurt chutney, 177
    cucumber lime raita, 22
    harissa, 112–13
    hot sauce (zhoug), 165
    mellow curry powder, 146
    pickled red onions, 122
    quick-pickled red onion, 132–33
    red wine–shallot compote, 321
    spiced red onion marmalade, 72–73
corn
    chopped salad with sherry vinaigrette, 156
    fresh, polenta with sautéed cherry tomatoes,
        114–15
    green beans, and tomatoes, quinoa salad with,
        128–29
    red beans, and scallops/avocado, farro with,
        139–40
corn grits. *See* polenta
couscous
    with dried fruit and pine nuts, 103
    spicy lentils with pumpkin and greens over,
        240–41
crème fraîche, spiced, 189
croque monsieur, smoked salmon/sun-dried-
    tomato, 50–51

crostini, goat cheese, 298–99
cucumber(s)
    avocado, and hiziki salsa, 184
    chopped salad with sherry vinaigrette, 156
    gazpacho with crumbled feta cheese, 138
    lime raita, 22
    panzanella, 150
    red onion, and tomato salad, 167
    seafood/tofu ceviche with quick-pickled red
        onion, 132–33
    to seed, 22
curried red lentil and peach soup, chilled,
    144–45
curry, lentil and rhubarb, with potatoes and peas,
    20–21
curry powder, mellow, 146

daikon radish
    julienning, tip for, 79
    pea shoot, radish, and smoked trout/tofu salad,
        79–80
dairy products. *See also* cheese; yogurt
    buying, 10
dal, golden split pea, 175–76
dilled yogurt dip, 29–30
dill vinaigrette, spring greens in, 52
dips and spreads
    cucumber lime raita, 22
    dilled yogurt dip, 29–30
    mayonnaise, 33
    sesame tahini sauce, 166
    summer vegetable ragout, 155
    tapenade, 31
duck
    breasts, pan-seared rosemary, 254–55
    legs, braised, 293
    and miso, autumn stew with, 218–21
    preparing cracklings from, 71
    rendering fat from, 71
    roast, with spiced red onion marmalade, 70–71
    seasoning, before cooking, 40
    stock, 71
    whole, cutting up, 71
dumplings, ricotta, /baked fish over French lentils,
    190–92

eggplant(s)
    baked baby, stuffed with rice, feta, and
        rosemary, 148–49
    buying, 148
    summer bean ratatouille, 106–7
eggs
    fresh corn polenta with sautéed cherry
        tomatoes, 114–15
    gingery rice with hiziki, shredded omelet, and
        shiitakes, 280–81
    goat cheese frittata with spiced red onion
        marmalade, 74
    green olive frittata with ricotta, pine nuts, and
        thyme, 60–61
    to hard-cook, 56
    local, buying, 10–11
    raw, salmonella risk from, 33
    salade Niçoise with many possibilities,
        120–22
    Spanish-style, with kimchi/chorizo over farro,
        300–302
    stuffed, with capers and garlic, 32
enchiladas, black bean, with smoked tofu/chicken
    and mole verde, 180–83
escarole
    sautéed, with red pepper and garlic, 193
    slow-cooked lamb shanks in white wine with,
        270–71
    slow-cooked red beans in white wine with,
        272–73

falafel, 164–65
fall season
    menus, 168–69
    seasonal foods, 14
farro, 303
    about, 139
    with corn, red beans, and scallops/avocado,
        139–40
    Spanish-style eggs with kimchi/chorizo over,
        300–302
fennel
    with lemon and fennel salt, 305
    pickled vegetable salad, 329–30
    seeds, crushing, 230

shaved, salad with olives/marinated sardines, 265–66

shaved spring vegetable and apple salad, 43–44

shaved winter vegetable salad with apple and raisins, 312–13

feta cheese
and chard, fregola risotto-style with, 90–93
crumbled, gazpacho with, 138
Greek, rinsing salt from, 90
rice, and rosemary, baked baby eggplants stuffed with, 148–49

fiddlehead ferns and asparagus, sautéed, with garlic, 76

fish. *See also* shellfish
baked, over French lentils, 190–92
batter-fried cod with kimchi, 278–79
endangered species, avoiding, 7
farmed, about, 7
gratin of cherry tomatoes and sardines, 54–55
pea shoot, radish, and smoked trout salad, 79–80
preserved, buying, 8
salade Niçoise with many possibilities, 120–22
sardines, buying, 265
sardines, serving ideas, 265
sauerkraut with smoked whitefish, green apples, and onions, 294–95
seafood ceviche with quick-pickled red onion, 132–33
shaved fennel salad with marinated sardines, 265–66
smoked salmon croque monsieur, 50–51
striped bass with lemon, white wine, and butter sauce, 127
substituting types of, 7
testing for doneness, 192
whole, buying, 8
wild, about, 7

fregola risotto-style with chard and feta cheese, 90–93

frittatas
goat cheese, with spiced red onion marmalade, 74

green olive, with ricotta, pine nuts, and thyme, 60–61

fruit. *See also specific fruits*
dried, and pine nuts, couscous with, 103
dried, quinoa, and pumpkin seeds, stuffed dumpling squash/poussin with, 244–46

garlic
mashing, 286
and mint, crispy pressed chicken/tofu with, 38–40

garlic chives, about, 72

gazpacho with crumbled feta cheese, 138

ghee, about, 21

gingery rice with hiziki, shredded omelet, and shiitakes, 280–81

goat cheese
beets, beet greens, and walnuts, penne with, 207–8
and chives, spicy roasted pepper soup with, 159–60
crostini, 298–99
frittata with spiced red onion marmalade, 74

grains. *See also* rice
barley mushroom soup, 261
bulgur with roasted chickpeas, red onion, and lemon, 36
farro, 303
farro, about, 139
farro, Spanish-style eggs with kimchi/chorizo over, 300–302
farro with corn, red beans, and scallops/avocado, 139–40
masa harina, creamy, 328
millet cauliflower "polenta" with crispy shallots, 274–75
millet pilaf, toasted, 201
polenta, fresh corn, with sautéed cherry tomatoes, 114–15
polenta, leftover, serving ideas, 215
polenta, soft, 215
quinoa, stuffed dumpling squash/poussin with, dried fruit, and pumpkin seeds, 244–46
quinoa salad with green beans, corn, and tomatoes, 128–29

gratin(s)
    artichoke, potato, and leek, 81–82
    of cherry tomatoes and white beans/sardines, 54–55
    of winter vegetables, 262–63
green beans
    corn, and tomatoes, quinoa salad with, 128–29
    preparing, for salads, 129
    salade Niçoise with many possibilities, 120–22
greens
    arugula salad with mustard vinaigrette, 110
    beet, goat cheese, beets, and walnuts, penne with, 207–8
    bitter, 322
    bitter, seitan/chicken liver schnitzel with red wine–shallot compote and, 319–20
    chard, fregola risotto-style with, and feta cheese, 90–93
    chopped salad with sherry vinaigrette, 156
    escarole, sautéed, with red pepper and garlic, 193
    escarole, slow-cooked lamb shanks in white wine with, 270–71
    escarole, slow-cooked red beans in white wine with, 272–73
    giant lamb/seitan turnovers, 172–74
    kale, buying, 240
    kale, trimming, 203
    kale with cremini mushrooms, 203
    lasagna with fall vegetables, Gruyère, and sage béchamel, 226–29
    mâche and pea shoots with baby beets and mustard vinaigrette, 94–95
    mole verde, 180–82
    mustard, with shallots and vinegar, 249
    and pumpkin, spicy lentils with, over couscous, 240–41
    radishes with their, butter-braised, 64–65
    salade Niçoise with many possibilities, 120–22
    spinach, garlicky, and sesame oil, with soba, 259
    spinning dry, 110
    spring, and Asiago, creamy risotto-style brown rice with, 41–42
    spring, in dill vinaigrette, 52
    winter, lemon tofu, and mushrooms, phyllo pie with, 284–86
grits, corn. *See* polenta

harissa, 112–13
hazelnuts, toasting, 11
herbs. *See also* basil; mint
    rice with, 75
hiziki
    about, 87
    avocado, and cucumber salsa, 184
    salad with sweet sesame vinaigrette, 87–88
    seafood/tofu ceviche with quick-pickled red onion, 132–33
    shredded omelet, and shiitakes, gingery rice with, 280–81
honey-crisped walnuts, 292
hot sauce (zhoug), 165

kale
    buying, 240
    with cremini mushrooms, 203
    phyllo pie with lemon tofu, winter greens, and mushrooms, 284–86
    spicy lentils with pumpkin and greens over couscous, 240–41
    trimming leaves from stems, 203
kimchi
    batter-fried cod/tofu with, 278–79
    Spanish-style eggs with, over farro, 300–302
    vegetarian, buying, 278

lamb
    chops, baby, pan-seared, with lemon and green olives, 62–63
    croquettes, spiced, 163
    grain-fed, about, 6–7
    grass-fed, about, 6–7
    kebabs, charmoula, 100–101
    shanks, slow-cooked, in white wine with escarole, 270–71

steaks, pan-seared, with thyme, lemon, and
mustard, 238
turnovers, giant, 172–74
lasagna with fall vegetables, Gruyère, and sage
béchamel, 226–29
leek(s)
artichoke, and potato gratin, 81–82
navy bean, and fresh pea soup, 48
slicing, 49
washing and drying, 49
legumes. *See also* bean(s); lentil(s)
golden split pea dal, 175–76
lemon-thyme roast chicken, 197–98
lemon-thyme tofu, 199
lentil(s)
French, about, 20
French, baked fish/ricotta dumplings over,
190–92
French, presoaking, 20
red, and peach soup, chilled curried, 144–45
and rhubarb curry with potatoes and peas,
20–21
spicy, with pumpkin and greens over couscous,
240–41
liver
chicken, schnitzel with red wine–shallot
compote and bitter greens, 319–20
cooking, tip for, 319

mâche and pea shoots with baby beets and mustard
vinaigrette, 94–95
marmalade, spiced red onion, 72–73
masa harina, creamy, 328
mayonnaise, 33
meat. *See also* beef; lamb; pork
grain-fed, about, 6–7
grass-fed, about, 6–7
searing, tip for, 108
melon soup, chilled, 118
milk, buying, 10
millet
cauliflower "polenta" with crispy shallots,
274–75
toasted, pilaf, 201

mint
and black olives, carrots with, 239
and garlic, crispy pressed chicken/tofu with,
38–40
oil, grilled zucchini with, 116
ricotta, and Parmesan, cannelloni with,
152–54
mirin, about, 85
miso
cooking with, 221
and duck/tofu, autumn stew with, 218–21
uses for, 221
varieties of, 221
mole negro, 324–27
mole verde, 180–82
mushroom(s)
barley soup, 261
crimini, kale with, 203
farro, 303
lasagna with fall vegetables, Gruyère, and sage
béchamel, 226–29
lemon tofu, and winter greens, phyllo pie with,
284–86
portobello, with bread crumb salsa, 108–9
mustard greens with shallots and vinegar, 249

naan bread, 23–24
napa cabbage salad with sweet peppers and sesame
vinaigrette, 222–23
noodles
Asian, in broth with vegetables and tofu/steak,
85–86
pizzoccheri casserole, 316–18
soba with garlicky spinach and sesame oil,
259
nori, about, 255
nuts. *See also* walnuts
almond flour, preparing, 152
buying and storing, 11
chestnut apple soup, 205–6
chestnuts, scoring and soaking, 205
mole negro, 324–27
shelled, toasting, 11
whole unshelled, roasting, 208

olive(s)
> black, and mint, carrots with, 239
> green, and lemon, pan-seared baby lamb chops with, 62–63
> green, frittata with ricotta, pine nuts, and thyme, 60–61
> shaved fennel salad with, 265–66
> salade Niçoise with many possibilities, 120–22
> tapenade, 31

onion(s)
> red, marmalade, spiced, 72–73
> red, pickled, 122
> red, quick-pickled, 132–33
> red, vinaigrette, roasted winter vegetable salad with, 287
> spring, about, 72
> varieties of, 72

panzanella, 150
Parmesan
> and basil, zucchini-rice soup with, 134–35
> ricotta, and mint, cannelloni, 152–54
> roasted broccoli with, 216
> toasts, 67

pasta. *See also* couscous
> Asian noodles in broth with vegetables and tofu/steak, 85–86
> cannelloni with ricotta, Parmesan, and mint, 152–54
> fregola risotto-style with chard and feta cheese, 90–93
> lasagna with fall vegetables, Gruyère, and sage béchamel, 226–29
> penne with beets, beet greens, goat cheese, and walnuts, 207–8
> pizzoccheri casserole, 316–18
> soba with garlicky spinach and sesame oil, 259

pea, split, dal, golden, 175–76
pea(s)
> fresh, navy bean, and leek soup, 48
> frozen, buying, 174
> and potatoes, lentil and rhubarb curry with, 20–21
> snow, removing string from, 86
> sugar snap, removing string from, 86

peach and red lentil soup, chilled curried, 144–45
pea shoot(s)
> and mâche with baby beets and mustard vinaigrette, 94–95
> radish, and smoked trout/tofu salad, 79–80

pepper(s). *See also* chili peppers
> gazpacho with crumbled feta cheese, 138
> peeling, 131
> roasted, soup, spicy, with goat cheese and chives, 159–60
> roasting, 160
> summer vegetable ragout, 155
> sweet, and sesame vinaigrette, napa cabbage salad with, 222–23

phyllo
> frozen, thawing, 284
> giant lamb/seitan turnovers, 172–74
> organic, buying, 284
> pie with lemon tofu, winter greens, and mushrooms, 284–86

pickled red onion, quick, 132–33
pickled red onions, 122
pickled vegetable salad, 329–30
pie, phyllo, with lemon tofu, winter greens, and mushrooms, 284–86
pilaf, toasted millet, 201
pita bread, whole wheat, 161–62
pizzoccheri casserole, 316–18
polenta
> fresh corn, with sautéed cherry tomatoes, 114–15
> leftover, serving ideas, 215
> soft, 215

"polenta," millet cauliflower, with crispy shallots, 274–75
pork. *See also* bacon
> Spanish-style eggs with chorizo over farro, 300–302

potato(es)
> artichoke, and leek gratin, 81–82
> gratin of winter vegetables, 262–63
> and peas, lentil and rhubarb curry with, 20–21
> roasted winter vegetable salad with red onion vinaigrette, 287

salade Niçoise with many possibilities,
    120–22
poultry. *See also* chicken; duck
    "free-range," about, 5–6
    heritage breeds, 6
    organic, about, 5
    seasoning, before cooking, 40
poussin/dumpling squash, stuffed, with quinoa,
    dried fruit, and pumpkin seeds, 244–46
pumpkin and greens, spicy lentils with, over
    couscous, 240–41
pumpkin seeds
    dried fruit, and quinoa, stuffed dumpling
        squash/poussin with, 244–46
    mole verde, 180–82
    toasted, 202

quinoa
    dried fruit, and pumpkin seeds, stuffed
        dumpling squash/poussin with, 244–46
    salad with green beans, corn, and tomatoes,
        128–29

radish(es)
    butter-braised, with their greens, 64–65
    health benefits from, 29
    pea shoot, and smoked trout/tofu salad, 79–80
    shaved spring vegetable and apple salad, 43–44
    slicing, tip for, 79
raita, cucumber lime, 22
ratatouille, summer bean, 106–7
red wine–shallot compote, 321
rhubarb and lentil curry with potatoes and peas,
    20–21
rice
    brown, cooking directions, 41
    brown, creamy risotto-style, with spring greens
        and Asiago, 41–42
    brown, quick-soaking, 224
    feta, and rosemary, baked baby eggplants
        stuffed with, 148–49
    gingery, with hiziki, shredded omelet, and
        shiitakes, 280–81
    with herbs, 75

leftover, preparing croquettes from, 41
    sweet brown, 224
    varieties of, 42
    -zucchini soup with basil and Parmesan,
        134–35
ricotta
    dumplings/baked fish over French lentils,
        190–92
    Parmesan, and mint, cannelloni, 152–54
    pine nuts, and thyme, green olive frittata with,
        60–61
    risotto-style, fregola, with chard and feta cheese,
        90–93
    risotto-style brown rice, creamy, with spring greens
        and Asiago, 41–42
rutabaga
    creamy root vegetable soup with honey-crisped
        walnuts, 290–91
    gratin of winter vegetables, 262–63

salads
    arugula, with mustard vinaigrette, 110
    bitter greens, 322
    chilled asparagus, with sherry vinaigrette,
        56–57
    chopped, with sherry vinaigrette, 156
    cucumber, red onion, and tomato, 167
    cucumber lime raita, 22
    fennel, shaved, with olives/marinated sardines,
        265–66
    fennel with lemon and fennel salt, 305
    hiziki, with sweet sesame vinaigrette, 87–88
    mâche and pea shoots with baby beets and
        mustard vinaigrette, 94–95
    napa cabbage, with sweet peppers and sesame
        vinaigrette, 222–23
    panzanella, 150
    pea shoot, radish, and smoked trout/tofu,
        79–80
    pickled vegetable, 329–30
    quinoa, with green beans, corn, and tomatoes,
        128–29
    salade Niçoise with many possibilities, 120–22
    spring greens in dill vinaigrette, 52
    spring vegetable and apple, shaved, 43–44

salads *cont.*

    winter vegetable, roasted, with red onion vinaigrette, 287

    winter vegetable, shaved, with apple and raisins, 312–13

salmon, smoked, /sun-dried-tomato croque monsieur, 50–51

salsa, avocado, cucumber, and hiziki, 184

sandwiches

    smoked salmon/sun-dried-tomato croque monsieur, 50–51

sardines

    buying, 265

    and cherry tomatoes, gratin of, 54–55

    marinated, shaved fennel salad with, 265–66

    serving ideas, 265

sauces

    hot, (zhoug), 165

    mole negro, 324–27

    mole verde, 180–82

    sesame tahini, 166

sauerkraut

    buying, 294

    with fried tempeh/smoked whitefish, green apples, and onions, 294–95

    navy bean, fresh pea, and leek soup, 48

sausages. *See* chorizo

scallions, about, 72

scallops

    buying, 140

    corn, and red beans, farro with, 139–40

    seafood/tofu ceviche with quick-pickled red onion, 132–33

    searing, 140

seaweed. *See also* hiziki

    health benefits from, 184

    nori, about, 255

    serving ideas, 184

    varieties of, 184

seeds. *See also* pumpkin seeds

    storing, 11

    toasting, 11

seitan

    about, 10

    cholent, 311–12

    pan-seared, with thyme, lemon, and mustard, 234–35

    schnitzel with red wine–shallot compote and bitter greens, 319–20

    turnovers, giant, 172–74

sesame tahini sauce, 166

shallot–red wine compote, 321

shallots, crispy, millet cauliflower "polenta" with, 274–75

shellfish

    buying, 7

    farro with corn, red beans, and scallops, 139–40

    grilled shrimp in harissa, 112–13

    scallops, buying, 140

    scallops, searing, 140

    seafood ceviche with quick-pickled red onion, 132–33

    shrimp, grilling, tip for, 112

    shrimp with brown butter and tons of herbs, 212–14

shrimp

    with brown butter and tons of herbs, 212–14

    grilled, in harissa, 112–13

    grilling, tip for, 112

soba with garlicky spinach and sesame oil, 259

soups

    Asian noodles in broth with vegetables and tofu/steak, 85–86

    barley mushroom, 261

    chestnut apple, 205–6

    chilling, tip for, 144

    creamy root vegetable, with honey-crisped walnuts, 290–91

    curried red lentil and peach, chilled, 144–45

    gazpacho with crumbled feta cheese, 138

    melon, chilled, 118

    navy bean, fresh pea, and leek, 48

    roasted pepper, spicy, with goat cheese and chives, 159–60

    roasted squash potage with spiced crème fraîche, 188–89

    tomato, my favorite winter, with goat cheese crostini, 298–99

    zucchini-rice, with basil and Parmesan, 134–35

sour cream, chive, 185
spices
    Aleppo pepper, about, 25
    preground, buying, 12
    whole, buying, 12
    whole, grinding, 12
    whole, toasting, 12
spinach
    garlicky, and sesame oil, soba with, 259
    giant lamb/seitan turnovers, 172–74
    lasagna with fall vegetables, Gruyère, and sage
        béchamel, 226–29
split pea dal, golden, 175–76
spring season
    menus, 16–17
    seasonal foods, 13
squash
    autumn stew with miso and duck/tofu,
        218–21
    dumpling, stuffed, with quinoa, dried fruit, and
        pumpkin seeds, 244–46
    grilled zucchini with mint oil, 116
    lasagna with fall vegetables, Gruyère, and sage
        béchamel, 226–29
    roasted, potage with spiced crème fraîche,
        188–89
    spicy lentils with pumpkin and greens over
        couscous, 240–41
    summer bean ratatouille, 106–7
    summer vegetable simmer, 102–3
    winter, spicy roasted, 200
    zucchini-rice soup with basil and Parmesan,
        134–35
stew. See cholent
stock
    duck, 71
    vegetable, preparing, 188
striped bass with lemon, white wine, and butter
    sauce, 127
summer season
    menus, 96–97
    seasonal foods, 13–14
sunchokes
    about, 43
    creamy root vegetable soup with honey-crisped
        walnuts, 290–91

shaved spring vegetable and apple salad,
    43–44

tahini sauce, sesame, 166
tapenade, 31
tempeh
    about, 9–10
    charmoula, 100–101
    cooking, note about, 100
    fried, green apples, and onions, sauerkraut
        with, 294–95
    in mole negro, 324–27
teriyaki-style burdock, carrots, and leeks, 256–57
tofu
    about, 8–9
    batter-fried, with kimchi, 278–79
    ceviche with quick-pickled red onion,
        132–33
    crispy pressed, with garlic and mint, 38–40
    lemon, winter greens, and mushrooms, phyllo
        pie with, 284–86
    with lemon, soy, white wine, and butter sauce,
        126
    lemon-thyme, 199
    and miso, autumn stew with, 218–21
    pan-seared rosemary, 254–55
    pea shoot, and radish salad, 79–80
    pressing excess water from, 279
    smoked, about, 182
    smoked, black bean enchiladas with, and mole
        verde, 180–83
    and vegetables, Asian noodles in broth with,
        85–86
tomatillos
    mole verde, 180–82
tomato(es)
    cherry, and white beans/sardines, gratin of,
        54–55
    cherry, sautéed, fresh corn polenta with,
        114–15
    chopped salad with sherry vinaigrette, 156
    cucumber, and red onion salad, 167
    gazpacho with crumbled feta cheese, 138
    green beans, and corn, quinoa salad with,
        128–29

tomato(es) *cont.*
    panzanella, 150
    peeling, 102
    seeding, 102
    soup, my favorite winter, with goat cheese
        crostini, 298–99
    summer bean ratatouille, 106–7
    summer vegetable ragout, 155
    summer vegetable simmer, 102–3
    sun-dried, croque monsieur, 50–51
tortillas
    black bean enchiladas with smoked
        tofu/chicken and mole verde, 180–83
trout, smoked, /tofu, pea shoot, and radish salad,
    79–80
tuna
    salade Niçoise with many possibilities, 120–22
turkey
    "free-range," about, 5–6
    heritage breeds, 6
    organic, about, 5
turnovers, giant lamb/seitan, 172–74

vegetable(s). *See also specific vegetables*
    cutting, best knives for, 106
    fall, Gruyère, and sage béchamel, lasagna with,
        226–29
    how to julienne, 281
    root, slicing thinly, 262
    root, soup, creamy, with honey-crisped walnuts,
        290–91
    spring, shaved, and apple salad, 43–44
    stock, preparing, 188
    summer, ragout, 155
    summer, simmer, 102–3
    and tofu/steak, Asian noodles in broth with,
        85–86

winter, gratin of, 262–63
winter, roasted, salad with red onion
    vinaigrette, 287
winter, shaved, salad with apple and raisins,
    312–13
vinaigrettes, 80. *See also specific salad recipes*
    caper, 120–21
    mustard, 94–95
    red onion, 287
    sesame, 222–23

walnuts
    beets, beet greens, and goat cheese, penne with,
        207–8
    honey-crisped, 292
    toasting, 11
wheat gluten. *See* seitan
whitefish, smoked/fried tempeh, green apples, and
    onions, sauerkraut with, 294–95
winter season
    menus, 250–51
    seasonal foods, 14

yogurt
    -carrot chutney, 177
    cucumber lime raita, 22
    dip, dilled, 29–30
    draining whey from, 22

zhoug (hot sauce), 165
zucchini
    grilled, with mint oil, 116
    -rice soup with basil and Parmesan, 134–35
    summer bean ratatouille, 106–7
    summer vegetable simmer, 102–3